OLD SERPENT NILE

The alien and mysterious Nile, that gigantic serpent that winds so fabulously, so ungraspably, back through history.

Rose Macaulay, *Pleasure of Ruins*

I do not know much about gods; but I think that the river
Is a strong brown god – sullen, untamed and intractable . . .

Keeping his seasons and rages, destroyer, reminder
Of what men choose to forget.

T. S. Eliot, *The Dry Salvages*

OLD SERPENT NILE

A JOURNEY TO THE SOURCE

STANLEY STEWART

JOHN MURRAY

© Stanley Stewart 1991

First published in 1991 by
John Murray (Publishers) Ltd
50 Albemarle Street, London W1X 4BD

The moral right of the author has been asserted

British Library Cataloguing in Publication Data
Stewart, Stanley
  Old Serpent Nile
  1. Africa. Nile River region. Description & travel
  I. Title
  916.204

  ISBN 0-7195-4864-0

Typeset and printed in Great Britain by
Butler & Tanner Ltd, Frome and London

Contents

Illustrations

For Melinda

πάντα χωρεῖ, ὀυδὲν μένει ...

δὶς ἐς τὸν ἀυτὸν ποταμὸν οὐκ ἂν εμβαίης

Acknowledgements

Every traveller accumulates debts of gratitude he can never hope to repay. The hospitality and generosity of the people we travelled amongst was humbling. My frustration at being unable to thank them in a way which does justice to their kindness is tempered by the knowledge that they did not look for gratitude. Egyptians, Sudanese and Ugandans, too numerous to mention, made the journey a pleasure and this book possible. A few are recorded in its pages; many are not. To them all, I owe a very great deal.

Particular thanks are due to Philip and Michele Hawkes who did so much to make our stay in Cairo a pleasure. I would also like to thank Naguib Amin, Joe Cornish, Ehsan Malik, Dr George Bebawi, Steve Jackson and Mary Conlon. As always I am greatly indebted to my parents whose support and encouragement for this book, as for so much else, has been unstinting.

Others have contributed to the telling of the story. Rebecca Waters, at a crucial stage, proved a sympathetic and perceptive critic. Dr Sucheta Martin has offered much sound advice and help. I am indebted to Jock Murray for his enthusiasm for the book and for such a warm welcome to Albemarle Street. Grant McIntyre and Gail Pirkis have both made great contributions to whatever brevity and clarity the book can claim. All their efforts have produced a better book. Its faults remain my own.

I am grateful for the permission of Weidenfeld & Nicolson to quote from *Pleasure of Ruins* by Rose Macaulay and of Faber & Faber to quote lines from 'The Dry Salvages' from *Four Quartets* by T. S. Eliot.

Finally I must thank Melinda Letts who accompanied me up the Nile. I could not have wished for a better companion. She brought to the journey far more than is conveyed in the pages of this book. Her fluency in Arabic made much of it possible, and her presence made all of it a delight.

PROLOGUE

This story of the Nile began some years ago in the Piazza Navona in Rome. It was late on a winter's evening, and I was making my way home through streets as cold as stone.

The piazza was deserted. I passed the crumpled face of the Church of S. Agnese. In the middle of the piazza stands Bernini's Fontana dei Quattro Fiumi, a splendid fountain whose water jets depict four great rivers. The evening had been rowdy, and I paused by the fountain to savour the calm of the place. The sound of the water pouring into the marble basins seemed for a moment to be the only sound in Rome.

The rivers – the Plate, the Danube, the Ganges and the Nile – are represented by four human figures. The figures have a heavy muscularity, sagging into middle age, men with broad thighs and thick beards.

The figure of the Nile, seated on a shelf of rock from which poured a curtain of clear water, caught my attention. Its head was completely enveloped in a long cloth. Only the beard protruded. The left hand clutched a corner of this veil as if to lift it. This was the moment suspended: the moment of promise, the veil about to be thrown aside.

Roman wags said that Bernini had veiled the figure so that it would not be obliged to look at the Church of S. Agnese opposite, the work of Borromini, Bernini's great rival. But the veil referred to the fact that the sources of the Nile were unknown, its headwaters still a mystery to Europeans of the seventeenth century. It was a mystery they were not to solve for another two hundred years.

A pale moon was clearing the rooftops at the far end of the piazza.

Somewhere a dog barked, and a scooter whined on the Via del Corso.

I was entranced by the veiled figure, this seductive image of concealment and expectation. It was then that I was taken with the idea of travelling the length of the Nile, from its mouth to its source, from the moment of promise to the moment of revelation. The figure sat balanced between the two with the sweet clear water pouring down beneath it, and I dreamt of boats and currents, of narrow riverbanks and wide savanna, and of the long uncoiling river leading into the heart of a continent.

BOOK I
EGYPT

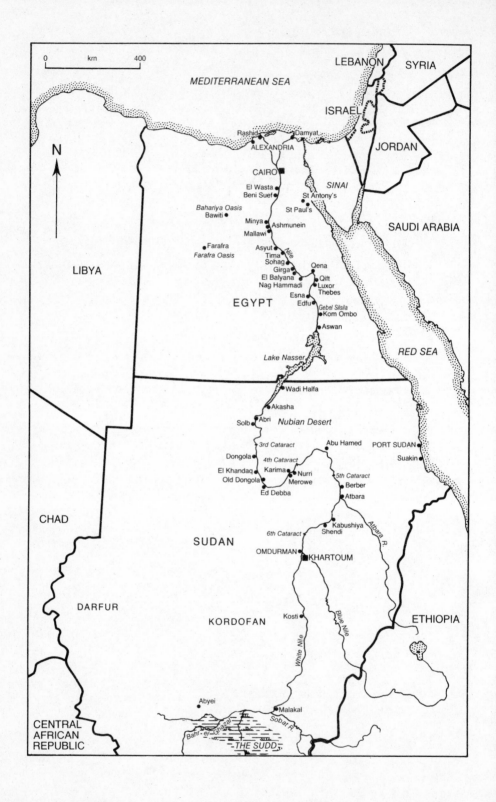

1

From the windows of the train, the world appeared to be emerging still from the waters of the Deluge. Everywhere one looked there was water, and the narrow tongues of land seemed newly born and tenuous.

The railway line to Rashid, where the Nile disgorges into the sea, ran along a low ridge between the Mediterranean and the marshy expanse of Lake Edku. The train was a shabby affair of two antique carriages which creaked and pitched like tethered ships. Bars of sunlight broke through the slatted windows and swept back and forth across the floor, and the smell of the sea came up the carriage bearing memories of childhood outings.

We passed the village of Edku secure on a mound above the watery plains. Against the sky were the ruins of windmills.

Beyond dunes of palm trees, the sea was grey. Far out on the horizon a ship glinted in the sun. Across the lake, a remnant of an earlier mouth of the river, fishermen poled boats past great banks of reeds. The low flat boats were barely visible, and the distant figures appeared to be walking on water with tall poles and long smooth strides.

2

In Rashid the cobbled streets were too narrow for cars, and the town was crowded with donkeys and carts.

We went looking for the river. The houses of eighteenth-century merchants, with *mashribiya* windows and columns pillaged from a more ancient town, leant over the streets. Outside a corner tea-house long-eared donkeys gazed mournfully through the windows at their owners chatting over breakfasts of tea and beans and tobacco. We passed a mosque with a deep forest of columns where men in white gallibayas sat reading in the gloom.

The Nile appeared quite suddenly at the end of a street, blue and shining between the tall houses.

We came out on the waterfront into a gust of wind. It was roughening the surface of the river and turning a row of feluccas moored along the bank. On the far bank were thick reeds, a line of palm trees leaning in the wind, and a dust road. The sea was just out of sight, a mile or two downstream.

A man was unfurling a sail on one of the feluccas, and we ran along the bank and asked him if he would take us across the river. He waved us aboard. With the hem of his gallibaya caught between his teeth to keep it dry, the boatman waded into the river, pushed the bow out, then climbed aboard and swung the tiller over. The sail filled and the boat lifted in the water as the wind took it. In a moment we were in mid-stream, caught up in the arms of the river.

The boatman laughed and shook his head when we said we didn't know where we were going.

'Anywhere,' we called back to him from the bow. 'Anywhere on the far bank.'

He stood in the stern balancing himself against a stay, guiding the tiller with his bare foot. We slanted across the river, the wind carrying us against the current, and coasted up the far bank. We passed a sheikh's tomb, a small white-domed shrine almost buried in the reeds.

'Sheikh Ibrahim,' the boatman called to us. He made the gesture of someone sleeping, tilting his head and laying it on his hands, and smiling peacefully. Then he looked up and appealed to the tomb with a traditional boatman's chant: 'It is not our will that we sail past, O Father. But the wind blows and the boat goes, and we have no power to stay.'

3

The Nile has two mouths, one at Rashid and the other some 90 miles to the east at Damyat; just below Cairo the river bifurcates for its last run to the sea. In this matter of mouths, the Nile can be said to be modest. The river is not more than 300 yards wide at either mouth. The mouth of the Amazon, the Nile's only serious rival, is over 150 miles across. The Nile has little need of such display.

It is a giant amongst rivers, the longest and mightiest in the world. From Rashid to the river's headwaters in the heart of the continent is over 4,000 miles. For almost half that length, through northern Sudan and all of Egypt, it is joined by no tributary, flowing as it does through pure desert. For millennia the people along its banks have depended entirely on its bounty. The twentieth century has done little to reduce its importance. For over fifty million people, the Nile remains life itself.

Melinda and I lay on the hot bank, watching the swallows dive. Their migrations were the journey on which we were embarking, following the course of the Nile, through Egypt and Sudan and on into Uganda.

I had not known Melinda when I first entertained the idea of travelling the length of the Nile. But now, going to the Mountains of the Moon without her would have been heart-breaking, and I was overjoyed when she decided to join me. With typical diligence she undertook an intensive Arabic course, and arrived in Egypt chatting to boatmen like a veteran.

The river slid by at our feet, broad and tangible and full of promise. The north wind gave the day a restless feeling, and the journey stretched before us like an early map whose faint features were pleasingly unreliable.

4

In the garden of a blue house, a few yards from the rivermouth, we met a holy man with a cherub's face and a patchy beard. He shook our hands, holding them for a moment and laughing softly. He was much given to questions and hilarity. He enquired about where we were from, why we had come here, and where we were going, and laughed uproariously at all our answers. It was a soft infectious laughter, as if we were sharing private jokes.

He sat with his back against a palm tree. He spent most of his time in this one spot for he was a cripple. He raised the skirts of his gallibaya to show us his legs. They were short and deformed and looked as if they were made of rubber. He lifted one of the plump feet and let it drop again to show us how lifeless it was. He laughed at this too. He rocked his head and his shoulders shook. Then suddenly, without introduction or explanation, he began to recite verses of the Koran in a sing-song chant. His voice was strong and thrilling. He sat with his eyes closed, lifting his head to sing each verse and dropping it again in the silences between the passages. Gone was the comic character. His voice filled the garden.

He stopped as abruptly as he had begun.

'*Wallah*,' he said, taking our hands and laughing. He was his old self again. 'A blessing for your journey.'

'Tell me,' he continued. 'Have you no rivers in your own country?'

'Only little ones,' I replied.

'Yes, of course. Inglistan is a very little country, isn't it? And yet always making such big noises. But listen, you must come and see me after your journey. Tell me what the other end of the river is like. You will find me here.' He patted the ground.

'I don't think we will be going home this way.'

'In that case, a letter will do. I want to know a number of things. Religion, of course. Are the people worshipping Allah? Food. How many wives the men take. Do they have policemen? Are they friends with the Libyans? Oh, and the question of nakedness.'

'Nakedness?'

'The women going about in the streets showing their nakedness to everyone who passes. I have heard much about this.'

We promised to write, and he waved farewell from his place beneath the tree. We could hear him laughing as we closed the garden door.

In the main square in Rashid we caught a taxi back to Alexandria. The driver drove like a madman. On the dark road unlit lorries loomed up like demons.

5

It is said that Alexander himself paced out the plan for his Egyptian city before hurrying off to conquer the rest of the world. He returned to Alexandria some eight years later, in his coffin. His tomb is reputed to lie beneath a mosque in what is now the Sharia Nebi Danyal. Excavation has proved impossible but there is a story that hints at great finds. In 1850 a dragoman from the Russian consulate claimed, marvellously, to have seen the body of Alexander through a hole in a wooden door in the cellars of the mosque. It sat, he reported, 'in a sort of glass cage with a diadem on its head and half bowed on a sort of elevation or throne. A quantity of books or papyrus were scattered round'. Sadly, the man was a notorious liar.

Ancient Alexandria was the prototype of the Hellenistic city, open, enquiring, cosmopolitan. The great public buildings were stuccoed with gypsum to make them dazzle in the bright sea-light. The Canopic Way, lined with marbled colonnades, ran from one end of the city to the other, from the Gate of the Sun to the Gate of the Moon. It was the city of the Ptolemies, of Callimachus and Euclid and Eratosthenes, and of Antony and Cleopatra.

Even then Alexandria had been a city of expatriates, maintaining a precarious balance between two worlds, the world of the Mediterranean and the world of the Nile. It was a Hellenistic city in Egypt, and an Egyptian city in the classical world. Both worlds mistrusted it as alien; its inhabitants belonged to no one. Their loyalties were personal and their tastes cosmopolitan.

The decline of the Hellenistic world left Alexandria isolated, and it did not again become a great cosmopolitan city until the nineteenth century when its resurrection was built on the profits of cotton. Greeks and Levantines, French and Italians all made the city their home. But this later Alexandria had little of the conviction of its

Hellenistic predecessor. It was a subtle, sophisticated, languorous place, a city of intrigue and profane ambition. It had about it an air of doom. For a long time that was a great part of its charm.

European Alexandria lingers on in the Italianate architecture, the long lines of balconies along the seafront, in the old shop signs in French and Arabic, in the Greek cafés like Trianon's and Pastroudis with their air of idleness and neglect, and in old-fashioned pensions like the Hôtel Normandie.

6

The Hôtel Normandie was on the fifth floor of one of the tall buildings overlooking the east harbour. Sand had drifted into the hallway on the ground floor where a one-eyed watchman, who remembered the names of all the English officers who had stayed there during the war, lived beneath the stairs. The lift, an ancient grilled affair, was a silent relic for which spare parts could no longer be found.

The lobby of the hotel was a large room crowded with dark bureaux and wicker settees with dusty velvet cushions. There were chandeliers but the burnt-out bulbs had not been replaced. Ranged round the lobby were the rooms of the hotel. They were light and spacious with tall double doors and small balconies overlooking the harbour. Hanging by the entranceway was a framed photograph which showed an expatriate gathering in the lobby in 1950, a happy smiling group. Standing in their midst, beaming out at the camera, her arms linked with two guests, was the plump figure of Madame Melasse, the former proprietress.

Two years after the photograph had been taken Nasser came to power in a nationalist revolution which signalled the end for the European community in Alexandria, as it did for European domi- nation of Egyptian affairs. Expatriates, who between the wars num- bered 80,000 in a city of half a million, began to depart. It was a painful process. Most had made their lives in Alexandria; many families had lived there for generations. The Suez crisis, which

10

prompted the expulsion of all French and British citizens, hastened the end.

Madame Melasse was one of the handful of Europeans who remained. She had nowhere else to go. As her friends left the city one by one, she carried on at the Hôtel Normandie in spite of the declining trade. Her evening soirées, like the one in the photograph, became a thing of the past. Standards slipped but there were none of the old crowd now to witness the decay.

The Madame lived to the age of 90. When she died, some time in the 1970s, the hotel was left to Abdulrahim, a Nubian from Aswan who had come to work for the Madame as a young boy before the Second World War. The hotel had become his home, and it was fitting in the new Egypt that he should own it.

Abdu was now a considerable patriarch who moved about the lounge in the evenings in a splendid white gallibaya which did much to hide his enormous paunch. He spoke four languages, as well as his native Arabic, the languages of old Alexandria: Greek, French, Italian and English. His large family lived on the floor above and scampered between hotel and home by climbing through a window and up a fire escape. Abdu retained a great loyalty to his former mistress and spoke of her with reverence. The photograph confirmed that he had changed almost nothing in the hotel. The heavy furniture of the lobby was still arranged exactly as it had been in 1950.

The only expatriate survivor from the old days was Sophie, a Pole whose family had lost all their property when the Communists came to power after the Second World War. She had lived in Cairo since childhood. Her friends were all White Russians. She had been coming to Alexandria, to the Hôtel Normandie, for a few weeks every spring for almost forty years.

Sophie was a small frail woman who moved about the lounge as silently as a cat, greeting everyone in whispered French. She remembered Abdu as the little Nubian boy sent out to fetch the morning editions of the European newspapers. Her friends were all gone now, even the White Russians.

'Egypt is no good,' she sighed. 'If you have somewhere else to go, you will go.'

11

She remembered Madame Melasse well. In the last years she was one of the few people to visit her in her room.

'She became *un petit fou*, you understand. Always she was wanting the window open. And asking about boats. Could we see any boats arriving in the harbour? She was waiting for a boat, you understand. She thought someone was coming to fetch her in a boat to take her away. No one ever knew where it was she hoped to go. She had been such a fine woman. Everyone had liked her.'

7

One morning in the Sharia Salah Salem we came upon a shop of curios and antiques. Inside it was dark and cavernous. At a desk by the window sat a round-shouldered man. He did not look up when we came in. He was counting money. The desk lamp was on, and his hands moving over the piles of money were bathed in yellow light.

The shop was crowded with relics of old European Alexandria, the things left behind by people abandoning a way of life. There was a stuffed and mounted gazelle's head with one of its glass eyes missing. There was an ornate sofa with velvet brocade cushions which raised clouds of dust when we sat on them. There was an oak hallstand with a fogged mirror, a pile of faded carpets and tapestries, oriental vases, a complete leather-bound edition of Balzac, and glass cases of silver and china. At the back of the shop we found an old mannequin with a bob hair-do and a 1920s low-waisted dress.

Beside the mannequin was a wind-up gramophone in a dark cabinet. As we examined it the man from behind the desk appeared soundlessly at our side. He was a heavy man in a baggy suit. He had a grey face and there was something wrong with his eyes. He wore spectacles and behind the thick lenses his eyes were cloudy and shifted continually from side to side so you were never sure where he was looking.

'His Master's Voice,' he said, stroking the dark wood of the cabinet. 'English company.'

We nodded. The eyes shifted back and forth like a metronome.

He took a 78 from the shelf in the cabinet, wiped it with a fat hand, and laid it on the turntable. He wound the crank and lifted the heavy needle on to the record. It crackled like a ship's radio, and then, as if from a very great distance, we heard a band strike up. It was an old dance melody of the thirties. The music sounded so faint and far-off it seemed to come from somewhere streets away, a voice from a vanished Alexandria:

> 'Will you love me for ever and ever,
> So that nothing will sever this love?'

The manager sank into the dust of the brocaded sofa.

'The gramophone belonged to a Hungarian count,' he said.

We must have looked suspicious.

'I acquired it from him myself, along with a few other incidentals. He was very proud of the gramophone. He used it, he said, when he was courting the daughters of wealthy cotton magnates. The rich are so hungry for titles. The one thing they cannot buy. At least not without selling their offspring.'

'Was the count successful?' I asked.

'Rather too successful, I understand. He married twice.'

'Not so unusual.'

'The problem was he omitted to divorce the first wife. Her father had proved less generous than expected.'

'How did he hope to get away with it?'

'Oh, I think he was accustomed to getting away with a great deal. They lived in Rome, the first wife and her family. I presume he believed they would never hear of the second marriage. But bad news has a way of travelling.'

'What happened?'

'The father of the first wife was friendly with the Interior Minister. Problems arose about his papers and he was deported.'

'What happened to him?' Melinda asked.

'Went to America. Ran a garage in Pittsburgh. The second wife, I understand, ran off with a baseball player.'

13

8

We took a bus south through the Delta to Cairo. The road was crowded with ancient American cars. Men in flapping gallibayas hung from the running boards like gangsters. As we passed them on the road we glimpsed great crowds of people in the wide back seats, a jumble of merry faces at the windows. The more crowded the car the merrier the faces seemed to be.

The Delta was a confusion of water and lush fields beneath a huge pale sky. Its labyrinth of canals was clogged with water hyacinths, and small bands of moorhens pushed their way through the shiny leaves. Willow trees along the banks trailed their branches in the current. Irrigation ditches like thin strips of sky ran away through the flat fields where figures bent to work with short hoes.

At midday we crossed the Nile at Kafr el-Zaiyat. A felucca, piled high with newly baked water jugs the colour of wet earth, ran upstream before the north wind. On the far bank children played on an old boat, rotting at the river's edge, jumping from the stern into the water, their brown bodies glistening like fish. Women came down to the river in groups to wash clothes and pots. They stood in the water up to their knees, their bright skirts floating about them. Then they lifted the wide metal pans of washing on to their heads and set off back to their villages, erect along white lanes, their clothes a bright flash of colour in the green landscape.

In ancient times there was none of this cultivated order about the Delta: it was a wilderness of undrained marshes, just the kind of primeval watery wastes from which the ancient Egyptians believed the world first emerged. In those days it was the haunt of crocodiles and hippopotami, both symbols of evil in the iconography of ancient Egypt.

Today neither inhabits the Delta, nor for that matter any of the Egyptian Nile. Now one must go a long way upriver to find them, far into Sudan and Uganda.

9

The Nile passes through Cairo like a stranger. In all its long journey from the heart of Africa, it has seen nothing like this: the tall modern buildings sprouting suddenly along its banks, the incessant flow of traffic across bridges, the noise, the confusion. The river is like the *fellahin* newly arrived from the countryside, appalled, hoping to pass through the city unnoticed. Like everything in Egypt, Cairo is the creation of the Nile but the river and the city seem estranged.

Cairo's problem is the problem of Egypt epitomized: a huge and rapidly growing population in a confined space. Its population has doubled in the past ten years and will double again in the next ten; its growth is due as much to the constant influx of newcomers from the Nile villages as to Egypt's birth-rate. The shortage of housing is so acute that the vast Cairene cemeteries, known as the City of the Dead, host a population of squatters thought to number over a million. They eke out an existence in cardboard and tin shacks amongst the graves.

There is a Dickensian quality about Cairo: the dense narrow lanes, the rubbish and stench of the streets, the jostling crowds, the animals, the dramatic disparity between rich and poor, the spectacle of young children hard at work, the host of people scraping a living from the most menial of tasks – porters, scavengers, match-sellers, bootblacks, water-carriers.

But like the flyovers which effortlessly criss-cross the city above the congested streets, there is another Cairo removed from the distress of the slums. It is a Cairo of wealthy suburbs and western consumer affluence. The lifestyle of its inhabitants is not markedly different in style or expectation from the middle classes of Los Angeles or Lyons. Though they inhabit the same city as the great mass of the Cairene poor, theirs is another world entirely. Their conspicuous consumption of all that is beyond the reach of most Egyptians and their eager embrace of foreign influences is a breeding ground for political unrest and religious fundamentalism which, increasingly in Egypt, are two sides of the same coin.

10

We spent two months in Cairo, living in the western suburb of Shafeyeen in an apartment rented from a French teacher who was away on home leave in Normandy. The apartment was prone to nocturnal visitations, for the teacher had neglected to inform her many lovers of her absence. We came to recognize the furtive knocking of these late callers, and tried to alleviate their disappointment by inviting them in for tea and sympathy.

They proved a pleasant and varied lot: a secret policeman, an Under-Secretary, a garage mechanic from Damyat, and an alcoholic expatriate. One evening the Under-Secretary and the expatriate managed to call within minutes of each other and we found ourselves playing host to them both. They got on exceptionally well over a bottle of whisky which the expatriate had brought as a gift.

The streets around the apartment building were invariably submerged, like many parts of Cairo, beneath an overflow of sewage. These lakes of black fetid water were tidal, reaching their high point in the early evening before subsiding again through the night. Only the fact that the streets were also under construction made them passable; one made one's way cautiously from one mound of earth to another.

The building's elderly *bowwab* or watchman lived with his family in a shed in the yard. When the tides were in, the black water ran through the yard and invaded his home. From our balcony we could see pots floating through the doorway and the family wading in and out in their bare feet. His wife, an enormous woman in black, wailed and wrung out the ends of her skirt.

Eventually it became too much, and one afternoon we looked down to see the *bowwab* moving out. Men were piling his furniture on to a cart in the street. It took three of them to hoist his wife up. She sat wedged between a bureau and a wet mattress. The cart trundled off through the greasy water. In the bureau mirror we could see the wife's doleful reflection bouncing against a background of blue sky. Neighbours said they were going back to the country.

11

We spent days exploring the old quarters of the city. The bus for the centre of Cairo took us down to the Nile and then along the Corniche to the 6th of October bridge. The river shone in the early light. Along the banks the acacia trees were heavy with red and purple blossoms. We passed a small park where a row of conscript soldiers slept beneath the trees. They were, in their way, an incentive to early departure for if we passed a little later than usual we would find them at their morning defecation, squatting in a row along a low wall.

The bus terminated in the chaos of Midan el-Tahrir, Liberation Square. The bus station was a nightmare of greasy pavements, surging crowds and hot engines. Only the fit and the young braved the terrific congestion of Cairo's buses, which careered through the city with men hanging from their doors and windows like barnacles.

Behind the bus station, through the glass doors of a luxury hotel, you could see the feluccas passing on the river. In the other direction is nineteenth-century European Cairo with its straight avenues and tall Parisian façades, reminiscent of Haussmann. Huge painted posters overhang the streets depicting the garish colossi of the latest films: threatening moustachioed young men and sultry women in tight dresses. Beneath them cars sit bumper to bumper in a haze of exhaust fumes.

Beyond the Ezbekia Gardens and as far as the Moqqatam Hills lies the medieval city, dense, ruinous and vital. In its narrow streets are to be found the great architectural masterpieces of Fatamid and Mamaluke Cairo.

The Sharia al-Mu'izz was the High Street of medieval Cairo. Now it is filled with the cacophony of coppersmiths. Domes and minarets rise above the street, the *madrasahs* and mausoleums of Qalaun, of al-Nasir, his son, and of the Sultan Barquq. Built in the thirteenth and fourteenth century, they are contemporaneous with many of the great Gothic cathedrals of Europe. Their virtues, evident even in decay, tend towards intimacy. Away from the noisy public confessional of the street, the quiet courtyards, the stuccoed passageways and the domed tomb chambers offer the solace of fine detail, birdsong and a watery half-light.

Nearby, in the courtyard of the *madrasah* of al-Salih Ayyub, we found two boys kicking a football through the dust. Ruins, which had once sheltered all the intricate legal debates of medieval Cairo, loomed over their game. A Corinthian column, plundered by the Muslim builders from a Greek ruin, supported the torn awning of a tea-house. A line of washing, big white drawers and a pink headscarf, hung from a Mamaluke window.

In the southern quarter of the city is the Mosque of Ibn Tulun, the finest monument of Islamic Cairo. We found the courtyard a wide sea of light. At midday we climbed the minaret and looked out over the rooftops of Cairo, stretching like a vast uneven plain from the Moqqatam Hills to the tall modern buildings along the river.

The terrible teeming streets appeared only as dark clefts between the buildings. The rooftops looked like some devastated land, arid and littered with debris. Here and there a few people moved about amongst the chicken coops and the junk: a girl chasing a goose into a pen, a boy flying a kite. Bright lines of washing flapped in the wind.

Away to the south-west, on the far bank of the river, standing up on the desert bluffs, we could see the Pyramids of Giza, shimmering through the haze above the city.

12

In the early morning at Giza, before the tourist buses and the touts, you can almost have the pyramids to yourself. Walking up from the main road we passed the camel drivers squatting round their early morning fires. Their animals, richly caparisoned for the tourists, were munching at green piles of clover and swatting their tails against the early flies. It seemed, fleetingly, like an encampment of Bedouin on the edge of the desert.

The morning was full of sounds. The voices of camel riders half a mile away were uncannily clear. The pyramids acted as great sounding boards in the thin air of the desert. Disembodied whispers, laughter, voices fell from their slopes like stones.

At a distance the effect of the pyramids is aesthetic; close up, simply astonishment, for nothing can prepare you for their scale. Attempts to illustrate their size tend to stupefy rather than enlighten. Napoleon calculated that the stone from the three Giza pyramids would build a wall, three metres high, round the whole of France.

Their size is only matched by the scale of human suffering which they represent. The pyramids were already 2,000 years old when Herodotus visited them in the middle of the fifth century BC, but he found the Egyptians still told tales of misery about their construction, the horrors suffered by the populace. The Egyptians could hardly bring themselves to mention the names of Cheops and Chephren, he reports, and preferred to call the pyramids after Philitis, a shepherd who tended his flocks in the area.

Their long history as tourist attractions reveals the sad decline in standards of graffiti. Early practitioners were poetic. A Roman woman inscribed a simple lament on the casing stones: 'I saw the pyramids without you; sadly I shed tears here.' On one of the Sphinx's toes there is quite a passable poem in ancient Greek:

> '... they are perished also,
> Those walls of Thebes which the Muses built;
> But the wall that belongs to me has no fear of war,
> It knows not either the ravages of war or the sobbing.
> It rejoices always in feasts and banquets
> And to choruses of young people united from all parts.
> We hear the flutes, not the trumpets of war,
> And the blood that waters the earth is of sacrificial bulls,
> Not from the slashed throats of men ...'

Later visitors tended to forgo such poetic forays. Flaubert denounced the great number of 'imbeciles' whose names littered antiquities. He climbed to the top of the Great Pyramid only to find inscribed in black letters 'a certain Buffard, 79 Rue Saint-Martin, wallpaper manufacturer.'

13

We became friends with the Under-Secretary who, always hopeful of the French teacher's early return, paid a number of late-night visits to the flat. He gave us his telephone number at the Ministry, and one afternoon when we rang him there he invited us to dinner.

Hasan lived in an exclusive suburb to the west of the city. His apartment was decorated like a hunting lodge. There were racks of rifles of various sizes and vintages, a stand of archery bows, a wall display of arrows, a mounted cross-bow, and a glass case with a pair of eighteenth-century pistols. Between the weapons were the mounted heads of the victims, mainly gazelle and ibex which he hunted in the eastern desert.

We sat on a sofa beneath the doleful gaze of these trophies while Hasan plied us with drinks and an array of Egyptian delicacies which he brought simmering from the kitchen.

He himself ate nothing but stood beaming in the middle of the room, his whisky glass clutched in his hand. He had a wonderful smile which took hold of his whole face. He was a small man with the posture of a pigeon, chest and buttocks protruding. His arms hung at his sides slightly apart from his body. When he turned or moved, they swung about stiffly like things that did not belong to him. He had been blown up by a landmine in the '73 war and he was held together, he told us, with metal pins.

He was dismissive of our plan to travel the length of the Nile. 'The desert,' Hasan sighed. 'You must go to the desert. In the desert nothing changes. Not like the river valley. And in the desert you are alone. That is a great thing in Egypt. To be in an empty place.'

He showed us his collection of guns, taking them down from their racks and handing them out to us as if we were about to set off on some dangerous mission. We stood about the living-room heavily armed.

Then he seized on the idea of demonstrating his cross-bow. He set up a pile of cushions on the sofa and propped two telephone directories against them. He waved us across the room to stand behind him. There was a delay while he struggled to load it.

'I never use it for hunting,' he said as he wrestled with the mechanism.

He knelt and sighted, swaying slightly. The loading had made him break out in a terrible sweat and perspiration ran down his forehead into his eyes. He stopped to wipe it away, then sighted again.

The bow went off with a terrible noise, like bones breaking. The arrow had gone through the directories, through the pillows and the back of the sofa, and into the wall behind. The tip was barbed and we couldn't get it out. The sofa, pinned to the wall, had been killed with a single shot.

'Very powerful bow,' Hasan muttered, pulling in vain at the shaft.

He slumped in a chair, still smiling. He was pouring with sweat. We sat on the sofa with the arrow shaft between us at eye-level. He topped up our glasses and filled his own.

'I am a very good Muslim,' he laughed. 'The Koran tells me never to drink a drop of wine.' He gulped his whisky. 'I never do.'

He sat in the chair for a moment, breathing heavily. Then he was seized with a new idea.

'Let us go for a drive. And see Cairo.'

Hasan hunched over the wheel of his car with a great effort of concentration, swinging it this way and that to avoid the atrocious pot-holes. We bounced against the roof as the car banged in and out of each one.

We became alarmed as he turned the car towards El Gala bridge and the city. Rush-hour in Cairo lasts all night. The streets were still teeming. Chatting gaily to us over his shoulder, he sped between clanging trams and wayward donkey carts and crowds of children chasing footballs.

Finally we drove up into the Moqqatam Hills whose wide boulevards were mercifully empty. It was a delightful place, wooded and spacious, with views over the whole city. The hectic streets were reduced to strings of lights.

Without warning Hasan bumped over a kerb and drove across a stretch of grass towards a precipitous drop. For an awful moment I thought he was going to drive over the edge, but he stopped abruptly and we all got out.

We could see the Kasr el-Nil bridge, the lights of the cars streaming over it and the dark width of the river.

'My father left me land here,' Hasan said. He seemed more sober out from behind the wheel.

'Where?' I asked.

'Here. This land. We are standing on it. My father left it to me. There were many children and this is what he left me.'

'What are you going to do with it?' I asked.

'I sold it. Almost twenty years ago, just after the '67 war. We were young, we lived for the moment. We didn't know if we would be alive next month, next year. I sold it and used the money for a good time.'

He was turning about to look at the view and the slope of grass back up to the road. His arms swung round.

'It is my great regret. My father loved this place. It was his legacy to me. Now it is too late. What can I do? I cannot afford to buy it back at today's prices.' He gestured towards the road. 'They are making plans. They are going to build houses next year. This will be someone else's garden where we are standing. What did Hannibal say? The gods do not give you two chances.'

14

We spent several days in the Egyptian Museum, a large sandstone building between the river and Midan el-Tahrir. The rooms were tall and dusty, and I had the feeling of rooting through an attic chest, the effects of a dead person, and coming to know them, through the old letters, the scraps of journals, the keepsakes, with a disturbing intimacy.

The world of ancient Egypt is one of order and optimism. The Egyptians portrayed themselves, striding forward, as confident civilized beings, in harmony with the gods and with their fellow men and women. There is an effortless quality to their endeavours. Crops are harvested almost without sweat, boats set off on journeys with full sails, celebrations are carried off with style and decorum. No nightmares cloud this vision. The streets of Cairo, the squalor of its slums, the pain and ineptitude of life, find no echo here. It is a strangely innocent world, without a single moment of distress. Ancient Egypt has been called the infancy of the soul, but coupled with that innocence is the terrible knowledge of death. More than anything else, the Egyptians feared personal obliteration.

The museum contained rooms full of the most delicate domestic articles, not just tomb artefacts but things people had handled and loved. There were vases of schist and porphyry and alabaster, hand mirrors of polished brass, paste jars shaped like flowers and hairpins shaped like hands, necklaces of turquoise, garnet and lapis lazuli. One imagined the fine-featured Egyptian women at their toilet, carefully choosing their jewellery for the eyes of friends or lovers. Four of the most beautiful bracelets had been found on the skeletal arm of a female mummy.

At the far end of one room was a wooden false door of the kind which enabled the spirit to leave its tomb at will. The wood was riven with deep cracks and smelled, after all these millennia, as old wood always smells, of libraries.

Many of the life-size figures, with their polished skin and fine long limbs, have a terrific sensuality. Mykerinus, who built the third pyramid at Giza, is seen with the beautiful goddess Hathor, the goddess of dance, music and love. Her breasts show through her tunic. Her arm is round his waist. The light touch of her hand is electrifying.

Everywhere there were boats, endless models of boats like discarded toys. They sail the Nile unworried by rogue currents or ill winds. Beneath the awnings little toy people chat and listen to the music of harpists. A pilot points the way ahead as if to will the journey was sufficient to make it happen. Many of the boats carry sarcophagi for it was the wish of all Egyptians to journey after death to Abydos, the abode of Osiris, the god of the Underworld and of Resurrection. The miniature boats were placed in their tombs like promises.

Everywhere too was the figure of Anubis, the dog-headed god, the major-domo of the Underworld. He seemed a sinister character with his long snout and bony body, alert, watchful, suspicious. His daughters, the serpents, the goddesses of freshness, waited nearby.

The coffins of the dead seemed innumerable, one inside another like Russian dolls, like layers of meaning, with only the thin desiccated mummy at their heart.

Carved on the lid of the sarcophagus of Psusennes I is the pharaoh's effigy, his arms folded contentedly across his chest. A kneeling figure, the goddess of the North Wind, cradles his head. She will carry his boat 'home' to Abydos, to Osiris and eternal life. On the underside of the lid is carved the goddess Nut, the goddess of the Sky. The heavenly bodies are her children; they enter her mouth and emerge again from her womb in their endless cycles. Thus she too is connected with resurrection.

Beneath the coffin lid, the goddess lies above the wrapped body of the pharaoh. She is barefoot and her arms are extended above her head. She is clothed in a simple shift which reveals the outline of her thighs, the slight curve of her abdomen, her small round breasts. Her body is adorned with the stars of the night sky, and round her limbs boats sail the Nile.

Coming out from the museum one evening into the Cairene twilight, we strolled along the Corniche. The lights of the Gezira stretched across the darkening river. Beyond the 6th of October bridge we found ourselves amongst an agitated crowd. A body had been spotted in the Nile. From the bank we could see it floating through the reflected lights like a submerged log. Two men swam out to guide it towards a moored boat.

It was bloated and heavy, and the men gathered on the deck of the boat to receive it had great difficulty lifting it out of the water. As they hauled it aboard, it spewed water over them like a broken vessel.

15

There is an idea, anciently held, that rivers, like gods, require sacrifices. In Greece, the Arcadian boys of Phigalia cut their hair and threw the locks into the river which ran through the wooded glen below the city. It was a way of feeding its fertility.

In Egypt, where the Nile is life itself, more extreme customs once prevailed. Every year when the Nile began to rise at Cairo, a young virgin was dressed in bright apparel and thrown into the river. She was the *arooseh*, the bride of the Nile, and her sacrifice was meant to ensure a plentiful inundation. When the Muslims arrived in Egypt in the seventh century, they put a stop to this particular barbarity. The custom continued, however, with inanimate stand-ins. Edward Lane, writing in the mid-nineteenth century, described the celebrations which still greeted the rising Nile each summer. The climax of the festivities was the Yom Wefa el-Bahr, the Day of the Breaking of the River, when a small earthen dam built across the main canal at Cairo, dry in the low season, was breached by the rising waters.

People spent the previous night in boats sailing up and down the river, watching the fireworks. Boats full of musicians and dancing girls passed amongst them. At dawn, amidst much clamour, a channel was cut through the dam and the Nile surged into the dry canal. Beyond the dam, in the middle of the canal, was a pillar of earth which the river now swept away in its swirling waters. The earthen pillar was still called the *arooseh*, the bride of the Nile, and its drowning by the rising waters was greeted with great cheers and tumult by the watching crowds.

16

There are two parts to Egypt, the desert and the river, what the ancient Egyptians called the Red Land and the Black Land. Though virtually nothing grows in the desert, the dry sands will preserve all that is left in them intact. The river valley is a place of decomposition and transformation.

Egypt is 98 per cent desert. Rainfall, except along the Mediterranean coast, is minimal. Without the Nile, the whole country would be a barren wasteland.

It was not always so. Millennia ago the Sahara was a green rain-fed savanna, not unlike the plains of East Africa today. Its many rivers can still be seen from the air, etched like fossils across the desert's blank expanses. In the hills of Fezzan in southern Libya and at Tassili-n-Ajjer in Algeria are galleries of madder-coloured animals engraved on the rocks: rhinoceros and giraffes, elephants and hippopotami, buffalo and antelope, all of which once grazed the lush pastures of the Sahara. The best of the human figures are lithe and graceful with slender necks and delicate hands. They were nomads who hunted the plentiful game and tended herds of cattle and sheep. Throughout these long millennia of rain the Nile valley was a trough of dense and inhospitable swamp, a place of terror for the nomads of the sunny uplands.

The dramatic desiccation of North Africa is a perplexing phenomenon. Pluvial and arid periods had always alternated but at some point the latter must have come to dominate in a prolonged drought. The failure of the rains led to overgrazing and deforestation. In time the landscape was stripped, the soil blew away, and the barrenness reinforced the drought. This sad cycle of drought, deforestation and desertification continues to this day as the Sahara grows year by year.

With the withering of their grasslands, the nomads of the Sahara were forced to descend into the narrow jungle of the Nile valley, there to take up the toil of agriculture. The golden age of pastoralism was finished. Henceforth life in Egypt was forever tied to the banks of the river.

To understand the river, one must see the desert.

17

On our way to the oasis of Bahriyah in the western desert I had a misadventure with my hat. It was an old-fashioned straw hat of the kind worn by alcoholic husbands in Somerset Maugham stories. I had purchased it in a back street in Alexandria, and had become, in a short time, unreasonably attached to it.

We had taken a taxi to the Sharia el-Azhar from where the buses depart. While we were unloading our bags and paying the driver, a bus behind us began honking its horn impatiently. We ignored it.

But when the taxi drove off and the bus continued to honk, I looked round. The driver of the bus was pointing frantically at the now disappearing taxi. In its back window sat my hat.

I set off in pursuit. The taxi driver, unaware of his cargo, twisted expertly through the traffic, and I fell further and further behind. But just as I was on the point of giving up, the honking bus swerved past me. The driver was bent over the wheel, while his passengers leant out of their windows waving and shouting to attract the attention of the taxi driver. With its horn blaring and its lights flashing, the bus had left its route to take up the chase.

Beyond the Ezbekia Gardens heavy traffic slowed both vehicles. The bus driver threw the door open and a stream of passengers leapt down to give chase on foot, finally catching the taxi at a red light. By the time I arrived, breathless, my hat was being borne in triumph through the traffic to be presented to me.

18

I met Salah in a dingy toilet at the back of the greasy yard where the oasis bus was preparing to leave. He was a short crumpled man, with a swollen nose and an anxious unshaven face. He grinned at me in the gloom, and introduced himself as if I might recognize the name.

'You have the tickets?' he asked.

I nodded.

'Good, good. Crazy people, no tickets, big problem.'

He wandered off, smoothing his unruly hair with his palm.

In the yard, under the gaze of the assembled passengers, an old man in his underwear, his head wrapped in a towel, was hosing down the inside of our bus. The water sluiced out through the open door carrying all before it: cigarette packets, banana skins, the shells of nuts, an old shoe. It was an ancient bus with a broken windscreen and a variety of rusting bruises. When the old man was finished we trooped aboard and settled ourselves on to the wet seats.

The oasis of Bahriyah is over 200 miles from Cairo. In the old days the journey took nine or ten days by camel. Now it is eight hours by bus along a narrow asphalt road. Not far from Cairo the road was joined by a single-track railway line which carries mined iron ore from the oasis and a line of telegraph poles. In the great expanse of desert these three, the road, the railway, the telegraph poles, were inseparable.

19

At midday we stopped at a rest-house, a square concrete building by the roadside, the only structure we had seen since leaving Cairo, four hours before.

'Tea, tea,' Salah said to us as he passed our seats on the way to the door of the bus.

At the tables the passengers unfolded elaborate picnics. A young bridal couple at the next table, returning from their honeymoon in Cairo, peeled hard-boiled eggs and ate in silence. The man wore an old grey suit with a white shirt and no tie. He had a depressed face with long lines of worry. The bride wore a heavy black dress beautifully embroidered on its bodice with red and yellow silk. Across its breast were rows of copper discs like coins. She had a small mouth and large eyes, darkly outlined with kohl. Her hands, struggling with the egg-shells, were the hands of a child. She looked no older than 14.

Salah, smoking a strange-looking cigarette with the driver, waved to us from across the room.

'Who is he?' Melinda asked.

'I don't know,' I said. 'I met him in the toilet at the bus station.'

Back in the bus, hot winds blew through the windows. We slept fitfully, waking always to the flickering telegraph poles and the same glaring emptiness stretching away to distant horizons beneath a vast sky. In the west, it ran thus the width of the continent – 3,000 miles to the Atlantic Ocean.

Later in the afternoon the desert became stony. Small hills appeared, then beyond them higher ridges with dark outcrops of rock. Finally we crossed a low pass and descended into the wide depression of the oasis where straggling clumps of trees and patchy cultivation marked the first springs. We dropped people at outlying villages. The railway veered off towards the mine.

The bridal couple got down at a tiny village of low mud houses. The only sign of life was a goat chewing on a rag at the corner of a house. From the road we could see them walking, small dark figures in the white desert, the young bride trailing a few paces behind her husband, with the wind beating her dress.

20

In Bawiti, the main village of the oasis, Salah got down from the bus and waved us after him.

'Come. Come. No problem.'

We found ourselves in a wide desert street, lined unevenly with flat adobe buildings, the same dun colour as the street and the surrounding desert. Salah was half-way up a rising side street, dragging an outsize suitcase behind him. He called back to us.

'Come. Come. Hotel. No problem.'

At the top of the hill, past a cemetery and a low wall, were two white-washed buildings on either side of a yard. Over the door of one, in large bleached letters, was 'Casino Alpenblick' while over the door of the other was 'Hotel Salah'.

The 'Casino' was a primitive tea-house with an earthen floor and a roof of reed matting. Low adobe platforms round the walls served as benches for one or two rickety tables. It was dark; the two windows were shuttered against the afternoon heat. By the door was a large earthenware pot of water with a metal drinking cup set on its lid.

Salah stood grinning in the gloom.

'Welcome to Bawiti,' he said, stretching his arms to encompass all the charms of the room. 'Tea, tea. You like.'

He went behind a counter and put a kettle on a gas ring.

'Bus too long. Too much problem. Crazy people.'

'Bawiti?' he asked. 'One day, two days?'

'We'll stay three or four days, I think. Then we'll go on to Farafra.'

'Okay. No problem. Welcome Hotel Salah.' He beamed a big smile full of silver teeth. His anxieties seemed to have been left behind in Cairo.

The hotel, across the yard, had six rooms off a wide central hallway. The floors were bare adobe and the walls had been painted pale blue. In each room a naked bulb hung from a flex above the metal cots. Electricity in Bahriyah was erratic, and the bulbs proved more decorative than practical. A rusty barrel in the yard served as washroom. Round it a prolific jungle of weeds had grown up in the otherwise bare yard.

Under a pillow on our bed I found a cache of fat neatly rolled marijuana joints. I showed them to Salah.

'No problem. No problem,' he said, stuffing them into his pockets. 'Music, dancing, crazy people.'

21

Bawiti was a village of crooked streets and blank-walled houses which faced inward on to courtyards. Mud channels carried the precious spring water through the streets to walled gardens and orchards. There were a couple of shops. They sold tinned fish and beans, packets of stale biscuits and dates. In a side street a vegetable seller, squatting in the shade of a wall, offered fresh produce. On a cloth before him was a mound of soft tomatoes, and another of spoiling melons.

Tacked to the wall in the Casino Alpenblick was a long misspelt menu. It ranged from omelettes and vegetables to kebabs and beer, none of which was available.

When asked about the dishes on the menu, Salah shrugged. 'Maybe yes. Maybe no. Maybe tomorrow.'

Tomorrow never came, and we made do with bread, onions, and a form of processed cheese called *La vache qui rit*, the Laughing Cow.

On the packet was a toothy cow, laughing. When you ate the cheese, you understood the joke.

Salah led a roguish and uncertain existence. He had the air, not of the proprietor of the hotel, but of a long-term guest who no longer bothered to pay his bills. Despite Melinda's proficiency in Arabic, he preferred to keep others in ignorance of our conversations by speaking to us in English. In this he achieved a remarkable fluency without the benefit of grammar or vocabulary.

Every afternoon Salah drove us in his jeep to a spring in the desert where he sat in the shade of the palm trees eating watermelon and smoking hashish while we swam. The jeep was called SuSu and her name was painted with Salah's, rather romantically, on both doors in intertwining calligraphy. She was an ancient and temperamental Russian jeep of a sort seen now only in old war films. She had her faults – she needed to be push-started and she had lost gears the way old people lose teeth – but it was difficult not to love her. As she jolted gamely through the desert, her torn canvas top unravelled in the wind like a loose turban.

On the way home every day SuSu broke down. The first day a tyre burst with such a loud crack I thought someone was shooting at us. There was no spare. Another time the carburettor became clogged with sand, and a third time she simply ran out of fuel. There was no fuel gauge.

'Crazy Salah, crazy SuSu,' Salah sighed.

We sat in the shade of a wall while a boy went for help. A stream of riders passed on reliable donkeys, making their way home to Bawiti from the outlying springs. The desert was the colour of almonds. In the distance were pink mountains deeply furrowed with shadow.

The hashish had made Salah reflective. He mused on the problems of the world.

'One crazy, two crazy, no problem,' he announced. 'Many crazy, big problem.'

In the evenings musicians from the village gathered in the 'Casino'. They brought skin drums stretched over round frames, and *narghils*, a long double-shafted wind instrument. They sat cross-legged on the adobe platforms round the walls of the room, and drank hot tea with loud sucking noises.

They were shy, quiet men with old-fashioned country manners. Each new arrival went around the room greeting individually every-one present before finding a place to sit. The greetings were warm and elaborate, like those of old friends who had not met for years.

They sat for some time talking and drinking tea before the music began. A man with a pointed head rolled joints of hashish. Salah brought in a plate of watermelon pieces. The men were too polite to accept them without being pressed a second and third time. When they finally took them, they inclined their heads with a dignified gratitude.

The music began casually, almost as part of the conversation, a falling line of notes and a soft wooden rhythm near the edge of the drum. Then the voices fell away and the music took hold of the room. It was a wailing plaintive sound given a febrile edge by the African rhythms of the drumming.

The *narghil* is a remarkable instrument, rather like an oboe. One of its shafts provides a bass drone and the other the melody. Like the bagpipes, the drone requires sustained wind. To provide this, players develop a technique of circular breathing which involves making their cheeks and throats into wind chambers, from which they can continue to exhale, while inhaling through the nose. The effect is like a frog swelling its neck.

Buoyed up on the crescendo of the drum and the wailing *narghil*, the men sang. Their voices hovered between joy and anguish, as if there was little to distinguish between the two. One old man, sitting on the edge of his seat and leaning forward on his stick, sang to thrilling effect. He shouted out the lyrics in a coarse powerful voice, and the musicians smiled and redoubled their efforts to keep pace with him.

When he ran out of verses, the old man got up to dance. He danced with his stick, planting it firmly on the ground and shuffling round and round it, hunching his shoulders and swaying in the gaslight like a man possessed.

The only other dancer was Salah, who brought a louche air to the proceedings. As the music grew frenzied, he took to the floor. With one hand behind his head and the other at his waist, he swivelled and ground his hips in a parody of the belly dance. He went on and on, faster and faster, until he collapsed into his seat, his face bathed with sweat.

'Crazy Salah,' he laughed. 'Crazy music.'

The most beautiful song of the evening was a long lament, a Bedouin song about a desert journey from Siwa on the Libyan borders to the Nile. The singer was bringing camels to market. But he did not spend a single night in the river valley, preferring to return to his camp in the desert. The people of the valley, he sang, were rogues and thieves. The river was a blue serpent.

23

A hundred miles beyond Bahriyah lies the further oasis of Farafra, to which few people ventured. It was the smallest and the most remote of the four western oases. Compared to Farafra, Bahriyah was a metropolis.

We got a lift with three lorries transporting water pipes. The lorries appeared one morning in the main street in Bawiti. When we walked down to investigate, we found the drivers asleep in the road beneath their cabs.

When they emerged from their slumbers at about five o'clock in the afternoon, they repaired to the tea-house in the main street, calling for tea and *seishas*, or water-pipes. They were rough uncouth men with the air of outcasts, unshaven and unwashed. They smelt of sweat and tobacco and oil, and they picked their teeth with twigs torn from a bush. They bantered and argued with each other, laughed raucously, became angry and fell into sulks, changing moods as quickly and as unpredictably as children. A group of shy

Bawiti men, seated at another table in their immaculate gallibayas, eyed them with alarm.

The journey to Farafra was not an easy one. Squashed between the driver and the mechanic on top of the engine housing in the first truck, we found ourselves in the role of unwitting umpires, keeping the two men from each other's throats. They quarrelled fiercely, spitting at each other across our laps.

The road ran on into the desert alone, no longer accompanied by the railway line or the telegraph poles. Sand drifted over the asphalt like curling wisps of smoke. The desert was scattered with hills, like smooth dark whales riding in a flat sea. After a time a magnificent escarpment of red and pink stone closed on the road from the east. Similar escarpments appeared in the west, their faces in shadow. Slopes of sand had drifted up against their flanks, moulding themselves into the deep crevices.

Night fell. Beyond the scope of the headlights, the narrow road and the gravel verges, all was blackness.

Farafra, when it appeared, was a distant cluster of lights floating like a single constellation in a great black sky.

24

The village of Farafra was like a bare room, swept clean. There was none of the decay or rubble of the crowded villages along the Nile. In the treeless streets between high blank walls one saw no cars and only a few people. There were no shops, and no tea-houses or eating-houses. We had, it seemed, ventured beyond the realm of commercial activity. But where commerce ended traditional hospitality blossomed.

We met a small boy, and asked the way to one of the springs. He looked at us solemnly for a moment then, without a word, took us home for lunch. Farafra still enjoyed the strict rites of Arab desert etiquette in which hospitality was considered both a duty and an honour. The whole village saw themselves as our hosts. We had only to go for a walk through the empty streets and someone would appear in a doorway to invite us for dinner.

On the edge of the mound was a broad open area, set apart from the houses, overlooking the desert. It was the doorstep of the village, where people paused to chat. There was little to see: the expanse of sand, occasionally a rider making his way homeward on his donkey. But at night the sky was dense with stars, and the men stretched out on the sand to gaze heavenward. It is said that Farafrans know the night sky better than most people know the rooms of their own home.

25

The gardens formed another part of Farafra, quite separate from the houses. They were threaded with narrow winding lanes and the lanes were bounded with crumbling walls and lattices of dry palm fronds. Irrigation ditches, cracked like parchment, ran through the lanes. Sometimes one found them frothing with water from the spring. Everywhere there was the smell of wet earth and dry dung. Insects droned in the hot stillness.

The garden doors, splintered with age, were so low it seemed that only children were meant to enter. They were opened with huge and ancient keys, and led one into a secret world of liquid green shadows. Silent birds stirred in the foliage. Pruning seemed unknown here. The olive trees were like thick bushes. The grass grew wild, and the heavy bunches of grapes were almost hidden amongst the vine leaves. Deeper into the gardens, beyond the scaly shafts of the palm trees, were groves of orange and lemon, pomegranate and apricot trees. Clouds of spiders' webs hung from their leaves.

Perhaps because I always went there in the heat of the afternoon, I rarely saw anyone in the gardens. After the shadeless streets and the barren desert, they were a green and enchanted world, an echo of the lushness of the river valley, enclosed and protected behind their ramshackle walls. They felt sweetly immune to distress. I sat in the still shadows and listened to the water bubbling in a ditch beyond the wall. From somewhere came the sound of a woodman's axe, like the final moments of Chekhov's *The Cherry Orchard*.

The next day we got a ride back to Bahriyah in the back of a pick-up truck. At the hotel, Salah greeted us as if we had returned from the dead, pumping our hands and laughing, 'Crazy English, crazy English.' The following morning we caught the bus back to Cairo.

26

Some malicious twist in the labyrinth of Sudanese bureaucracy required us to obtain our Sudanese visas, not at the embassy in London, in the tranquillity of St James's, but in Cairo.

The first challenge of the embassy in Cairo was one of access. Martial law had recently been declared in Sudan which meant that all Sudanese nationals abroad required a visa to return home. Egypt is host to thousands of Sudanese students and workers, and most of them appeared to be assembled outside the gates of the embassy when I found it one morning in a leafy street not far from the Nile. Behind the grilled window of the visa section were three weary-looking men, their heads buried in ledgers. The surging crowds pressed against the grille and clamoured for attention.

I retreated. I could be days working my way to the front of that crowd. I would have to find a way of bypassing it.

I donned a tie and went to call on the manager of the Sudan Air office in the guise of an Important Person. I told him I was writing a book about Sudan, and managed to make some tenuous link between this and benefit to his airline. He was busy, and to get rid of me he wrote me a letter of introduction to Ahmed Ahmedi, the vice-consul at the embassy.

The letter proved a great success. The following day it gained me entrance to the main gate of the embassy. Ahmed Ahmedi was at the airport and for a time no one knew what to do with me. I was transferred from one office to another before being shown into an office whose occupant was asleep in an armchair by the window.

I woke him gently, and handed him my letter. He sat slumped in his chair with the letter propped against his belly and drifted off to sleep again. Fearful of waking him a second time I waited. After a time he awoke again and asked me what I wanted.

'A visa,' I said.

He considered this in silence, gazing at the letter with a glazed expression. His eyelids were drooping.

Eventually he whispered, 'Where to?'

'To Sudan.'

I showed him our itinerary and he read the names aloud slowly and haltingly as if they were the names of some distant land whose pronunciation he was unsure of. Then he asked for our passports, made some notes at the bottom of the itinerary and handed the passports back.

'No problem,' he said. 'Come back in three weeks.'

He closed his eyes. As I shut the door quietly behind me, I saw our itinerary flutter to the floor.

I returned to the embassy a month later. My now dog-eared letter gained me admission again through the main gates and into the office of a Mr Saleb, a shabby fellow in slippers and an undershirt.

'Mr Ahmed Ahmedi is at the airport,' he announced.

I began to feel that this was a euphemism for 'fall from grace'. I imagined Mr Ahmedi in some upstairs room, sweating in the glare of a lamp, being questioned by security men under orders from Khartoum. When I explained about the sleeping man and his promise of a visa, Mr Saleb looked at me as if I was talking gibberish.

'We have no sleeping man here,' he said with a note of pity.

There followed an interlude of musical offices. It went like this. I was shown into an empty office where I sat waiting for a minimum of ten minutes. A man entered who I had not seen before. 'Please follow me,' he said. I followed him along corridors to another empty office. 'Wait here, please,' the man said, then disappeared. I waited another ten minutes and then the ritual was repeated, a different man, another office.

Eventually I came to rest again in Mr Saleb's office. Here a new character entered the drama, an elderly Englishman kitted out in an English safari costume of the pre-war years: baggy khaki shorts, long stockings, a khaki shirt with big pockets and epaulettes, and a broad-brimmed hat. He had pale eyes, grazed bony knees and very pink skin.

We exchanged news. He had been waiting for his visa for three months.

After a time Mr Saleb reappeared. He seemed startled to see me as if applicants, once embarked on musical offices, rarely returned.

'I will see Mr Ahmed Ahmedi about your case,' he said impatiently. 'Unfortunately he is at the airport today. Come back in two or three days.'

With this he dismissed me. At the door the pink Englishman gripped my arm.

'Wait,' he whispered. 'Have they looked in the book?'

'What book?'

'The book, the book. They must check for your name in the book.'

He looked over my shoulder at Mr Saleb who was talking to a colleague in the corner.

'Wait outside the office,' he hissed. 'He is taking me to see the book. When we come out follow us.'

Something about the place, the ritual of musical offices or the mystery of the sleeping man, encouraged a conspiratorial approach. The acquisition of a visa was clearly a matter of guile.

A few minutes later Mr Saleb emerged. He swept along the corridor and up a flight of stairs with the Englishman at his heels. I followed at a distance. We passed through the embassy and emerged in a yard beside the office of the visa section. Before we knew what was happening a guard had ushered us outside the gate and into the milling crowd in the street. Mr Saleb had gone into the visa office. We could see him behind the grille over the heads of the crowd.

The Englishman knew the form. For all his apparent frailty, he dove into the crowd and fought his way towards the grille like a rugby forward. When he reached the front, Mr Saleb handed him a huge ledger over the top of the grille. I reached his side as he finished scanning the list of names on the last page.

He was despondent. 'It's no good,' he said. 'One's name is never in the book.'

I peered over his shoulder at the spidery script. The last name on the last page was my own.

'That's my name,' I said pointing.

'That is your name? Here, this name?' He was overwhelmed. 'Your name is in the book. This is wonderful.'

He handed the book to me. 'Hang on to it,' he said. 'Whatever you do do not let them take the book back without admitting that your name is in it.' He leaned towards me and whispered. 'The book is everything. When you know your name is in the book, they are powerless. They must act.' With that, he disappeared.

In the office beyond the grille, Mr Saleb was calling for the book. The surging crowd had carried me some rows back from the front. I held the book aloft.

'My name,' I shouted, 'my name is in the book.'

He could not hear me above the din of the crowd. He climbed on to the counter and, reaching over the grille, grabbed the book. I hung on, and we stood thus, on tiptoe, joined over the heads of the crowd by the famous book.

'My name,' I shouted again, 'my name is in the book.'

The clerks at the counter looked up from their ledgers. Mr Saleb stopped tugging.

'Your name is in the book?' He looked at me with disbelief.

I nodded frantically. In the excitement I seemed to have lost my voice.

Mr Saleb's face broke into a huge grin. 'Congratulations,' he shouted. 'Welcome in the Sudan. You have a visa. Ten pounds please.'

27

We set off upriver one hot morning in July, on the train south from Cairo. The taxi driver who left us at the station, enchanted by the idea that we were setting off for the source of the Nile, refused to accept any fare. This remarkable event, as unlikely as a Papal Bull encouraging polyandry, we took for a good omen.

The fields of maize and sugar-cane along the track were bedraggled and white with dust. Beyond them, a brown light seeped through the columned groves of palm trees. Chaff blew across the beaten earth between the trees, powdering it with yellow. In the patches of shade, men and dogs and heavy-headed cattle slept through the midday heat. At the edge of the villages were huge pigeon towers like crumbling castles full of birds and turrets. Out of sight beyond the trees and the flat fields lay the river, marked by the tall slanting masts of moored feluccas. Now and then it came into view, wide and smoothly blue, with low reedy islands breaking its shining surface.

Just before El Wasta we passed the Pyramid of Meidum, which rose above the cultivation on the edge of the desert. Built about 2600 BC, it was the first true pyramid. We had visited it from Cairo.

On the black walls of the tomb chamber were scraps of graffiti written in the eighteenth dynasty, a thousand years after the pyramid was built. It had already been looted. One passage was penned by the scribe Aa-Kheper-Rē-senb. He chose to ignore the ultimate horror of the looted tomb and inscribed his lines as if all was well: 'Aa-Kheper-Rē-senb came to see the beautiful temple of King Seneferu. He found it as though heaven were within it and the sun rising in it. Then he said: "May heaven rain with fresh myrrh, may it drip with incense upon the roof of the temple of King Seneferu." '

The air of the tomb chamber had tasted of lime.

28

At El Wasta we changed trains. It was a small town of dust lanes and wide shade trees. The river passed at its feet, pulling at the reeds along the bank. Tall egrets picked their way daintily through the shallows, and away upstream feluccas were adrift on their own reflections.

At the railway station families were encamped between walls of baggage. The smell of onions and kerosene drifted across the platform where women were cooking supper. The women here did not wear the outer black street dress common in Cairo but bright knee-length dresses and baggy harem pantaloons. The dresses were open-necked and the women were continually drawing out long thin breasts to feed one of the multitude of infants crawling amongst the baggage.

A train hooted and a moment later flashed past with a shriek. Beyond the flies and the squatting figures of the platform was a sudden streak of metal, a glimpse of shiny carriages, venetian blinds, heads asleep against the windows. It was the express train to Aswan, its first-class carriages full of tourists.

Our train was late. The sun was settling into the tree-tops up the line when it finally curved into view. Silhouetted against the red sky were rows of people on the roofs of the carriages. The train was overflowing. The passengers inside, already hopelessly crowded, had locked all the doors. They looked out through the grimy windows and shook their heads. The crowds on the platform shrieked at them and banged on the glass, then ran to the end of the carriages to climb on to the roof.

Roofs presented us with a problem: Melinda was adamant that we were not travelling on them. She was happy to go any-where, under any conditions, with the sole exception of the roofs of trains.

We ran the length of the train looking for an unlocked door. I had finally resolved to stage a roof *coup*, to climb on to one of the forbidden roofs in the probably vain hope that the prospect of being left behind might change Melinda's views, when suddenly a metal door opened and arms reached down to pull us up. We were deposited on a rough floor as the train jerked and started.

It was the guard's van. Rows of mustachioed men looked down at us from their perches on metal shelves along the walls. A guard tipped a heavy safe on to its side and offered it to us as a seat. He squatted opposite us in the open doorway and lit a cigarette.

'It is forbidden for anyone to travel in the guard's van,' he said. He shrugged and pointed to his guard's uniform. 'I am the guard but what can I do on such a train? There are too many people. They have locked all the doors. I cannot even collect tickets. The passengers are revolting.'

41

'We can see the difficulties,' Melinda said. 'There are crowds of people on the roofs.'

'It is forbidden for anyone to travel on the roof,' the guard said. He had the air of a man overwhelmed by cruel fate. 'What can I do? They are like flies.'

'It must be very dangerous on the roof,' Melinda said. I felt that she had read my mind, that she knew I had contemplated transgressing the roof taboo. I avoided her eye.

'They are regularly falling off,' the guard said glumly. I looked guiltily out of the open door. Melinda coughed meaningfully.

The guard blew smoke out through the doorway. '*Maleesh*,' he said. 'Never mind. There is nothing to do.'

The setting sun flickered through the trunks of the palm trees along the track, disappearing into haze before it reached the horizon. Lakes of blue mist appeared in the palm groves. In the failing light the men on the shelves of the unlit van became indistinguishable.

To cheer himself up, the guard asked about us and what had brought us to Egypt. He was surprised to see foreigners on a local train from El Wasta. But our answers only deepened his depression.

'I am not a guard at all.' He plucked at his uniform as if meaning to tear it off. 'I am poet. But a poet in Egypt is a sad man. The nation does not listen. Do you write poetry?' he asked me.

'Not that I allow anyone to read,' I said.

'I understand. It is too painful. I am a follower of Lorca myself. I am very much in love with this man.'

There seemed no end to his grief. He squatted in the doorway with the darkening landscape passing behind him, and quoted Lorca:

> Cordoba. Remote and lonesome.
> Ay! The road is dark and long.
> Ay! My horse is tired yet brave.
> Death is waiting for me there
> Before I get to Cordoba.

At Beni Suef we got down into a dusty twilight. The streets were full of people going home. A few cars honked their way through the crowds and cyclists rang their bells. A line of dark barouches waited outside the station, the horses' heads buried in their nose bags. Billowing smoke drifted across the street from the grilled fish and kebab stalls.

We found a room in a hotel on the far side of the canal. The room reeked of the cheap perfume worn by the blowzy woman who was vacating it as we arrived.

The night was busy. The amplified muezzins of the town's mosques spent much of it chanting at full volume. Beneath the window dogs howled and fought. Somewhere in the hotel a woman wailed and broke china. When our exhaustion overcame even this, the trains awoke us. They hurtled past, just across the street, with their whistles blaring. The sound was so terrific the trains seemed to pass across the end of the bed, and we drew up our feet instinctively.

They sounded, Melinda said sleepily over breakfast, like Judgement Day.

29

In the lobby of the hotel we met a Coptic priest. He wore dusty black robes, a black square hat and a white beard. He spoke English with a Texan drawl he had acquired at the University of Austin. A large wooden cross hung from a chain round his neck. His wife, an American, was a tall exhausted-looking woman. Strain had settled round her eyes like old make-up.

'You have heard of course of the famous monasteries of St Antony's and St Paul's in the eastern desert,' the priest said.

We had.

'Permit me to invite you. I am leading a pilgrimage to the monasteries and would be most pleased if you joined us.'

It seemed too good to pass up. 'When is the pilgrimage?' I asked.

He consulted his watch. 'In about twenty minutes.'

30

Christianity came early to Egypt. According to tradition it was brought by the apostle Mark who is said to have written his gospel on the banks of the Nile. The old religion of ancient Egypt had ossified, and the country was ripe for conversion. But the old religion had elements which prepared its adherents for the symbolism of the new: the death and resurrection of Osiris, the representations of the mother goddess Isis with her son Horus on her lap, the symbol of life in the form of a cross, the Egyptian *ankh*.

When the Arab armies of Amr ibn el-As arrived in Egypt in the seventh century, Egyptian Christians welcomed them as deliverers from Byzantine tyranny. The Arabs gave the Christians the name Copt which was a corruption of the ancient Egyptian word for 'Egyptian'. But the Arabs and their own new religion proved even more persuasive than Christianity. Much of the population quickly embraced Islam, and the Copts were reduced to a minority. Today they number about one in five of the Egyptian population.

Their reputation amongst Europeans has not always been high. In the mid-nineteenth century, Edward Lane found them 'of sullen temper, extremely avaricious, and abominable dissemblers'.

31

Within half an hour a crowd of pilgrims had gathered outside the hotel. When the priest emerged they gathered round him, kissing his hand and greeting him, '*Abuna, Abuna*. Our Father, Our Father.'

We crossed the river on felucca ferries to where a long modern bus waited on the east bank. The road into the desert was empty. Outside the windows the landscape shimmered.

In the air-conditioned cocoon of the bus, the Copts prayed and sang songs of praise. Our Father went up and down the aisle with a microphone, leading the singing in a tuneless baritone which boomed from a loudspeaker at the front of the bus. The microphone and the evangelical enthusiasm seemed at odds with the orthodox robes and the white beard. Our Father bestrode the aisle like a cross between the late Archbishop Makarios and Billy Graham.

Our Father's mother, an old woman with a luminous face, sat across the aisle from us. She seemed to have come on the retreat more out of maternal loyalty than religious devotion. She saw us as allies and babbled to us in a mixture of French and Arabic throughout the hymns, then sighed loudly and looked out of the window as the prayers droned on.

'*La monasterie,*' she whispered across the aisle, '*ce n'est pas belle.*'

Beyond the window the desert looked like the tough dry hide of some prehistoric beast.

32

Monasticism began in the deserts of Egypt. Its earliest inspiration was a young man born in a village on the banks of the Nile about 250 AD.

At the age of 18, Antony heard the passage of scripture that was to change his life: 'If thou wilt be perfect, go and sell that thou hast, and give it to the poor' (Matt. 19: 21). Perfection is a powerful incentive. Antony gave away his money and his land, and began an ascetic life of prayer, fasting and manual labour. His neighbours, caustically, nicknamed him God's Friend.

But Antony felt his life was still too indulgent and he longed for more complete mortification. He left his village and went to live in a deserted tomb; an obliging friend locked him inside and brought him bread from time to time. Then at the age of 35 he moved to the ruined fortress of Pispir on the east bank of the Nile. His growing band of admirers, who gathered outside, were accustomed to hearing a great tumult from inside the walls, like riotous crowds fighting. It was Antony and the Devil in yet another engagement of their continual war. According to Antony the Devil came to tempt and torture him in a variety of fantastical forms from lascivious women to wild beasts. He wrestled manfully with them all.

The Temptations of St Antony were later to prove a rich theme for European painters.

The flight to the desert which Antony had begun became a flood during the fourth and fifth centuries. Men and women in their tens of thousands left the Nile to join monastic desert communities. It was claimed that the population of these desert ascetics was equal to that of the Nile towns, but religious fervour can hardly be trusted to have a head for figures.

Not long after Antony's death, Athanasius, the patriarch of Alexandria, wrote his biography. With this as its inspirational text, monasticism spread through the Middle East and into Europe. By the middle of the sixth century novices were reading the Life of Antony in remote monasteries in Ireland, and claiming visions modelled on Antony's own temptations.

It was not a phenomenon universally admired:

> There is perhaps no phase in the moral history of mankind of a deeper or more painful interest than this ascetic epidemic. A hideous, distorted, emaciated maniac without knowledge, without patriotism, without natural affection, spending his life in a long routine of useless and atrocious self-torture, and quailing before the ghastly phantoms of his delirious brain had become the ideal of the nations which had known the writings of Plato and Cicero, and the lives of Socrates and Cato.

So wrote Lecky. One has to sympathize. Where was all the self-assurance, the sophisticated enlightenment of the classical world, of which Egypt had been a part since the time of Alexander? And where were the values of ancient Egypt, whose celebration of the physical world runs like a sensual current through the Cairo Museum? Antony was said to blush when he had to eat.

It was this conflict between the physical and the spiritual which formed such a break with the past, that and the idea of the Devil. The Egyptian and the classical worlds knew demons, forces of darkness, but they were bit players compared to Antony's Devil. To the desert ascetic the smell of battle hung over his religious observance.

One cannot help but feel that Antony marks the loss of an irretrievable innocence. In Alexandria armies of monks sacked the Serapeum, the great temple to Osiris, and destroyed the library which had made it one of the world's chief centres of learning. Fundamentalism could brook no rivals; fear and intolerance were ascendant.

33

The Red Sea came into view in the late afternoon, an intense blue that washed along the flat desert shore in a long line of white. On the far shore lay Sinai. Somewhere amongst the ocherous jumble of mountains to the south Moses had received the Ten Commandments.

After a time we turned inland on a rough track which climbed through ravines into the desert hills. When finally we came in sight of the monastery, the pilgrims broke into song, a slow deep melody which matched the laboured progress of the coach up the last half mile of track to the monastery gates.

The monastery of St Paul's stood on a slight rise. It was walled like a fortress, and the only entrance was through a massive pair of wooden gates. Above the wall we could see a few palm trees, a double row of adobe domes and a square keep. The outer wall was pierced high up with the small black windows of the monks' cells. Beneath each window were long encrusted brown stains, stretching to the ground, where the monks over the centuries had emptied their latrine buckets.

Inside the walls the monastery was like an enclosed Nile village whose inhabitants had fled its ruinous lanes. The monks, bearded and serious, passed in their black robes and cowls like cats on padded feet.

A plump monk named Bertie showed Melinda and me round the monastery while the pilgrims ate noisily in a fly-ridden refectory. He was a plodding lugubrious fellow, and we were delighted with his Wodehousian name.

The monastery had been founded in the fourth century, not long after the death of St Paul the Egyptian who, like his contemporary Antony, had been a desert ascetic. There were four churches within

47

its walls. The oldest was built around the cave in which St Paul is said to have lived.

It was a subterranean structure. Bertie led us down a sloping alleyway to a heavy door where we left our shoes. Inside, after the bright desert light, we found ourselves blind in the darkness. The dark church felt cool and velvety. We heard Bertie fumbling with something, then a match struck. He lit candles and handed them to us.

We were standing in a small domed sanctuary. The walls were black with age. Bertie held his candle up to show us frescos of four saints beneath the dome, and then more robed figures around the walls, four archangels and the angel of the fiery furnace. The paint was peeling off the stone, and in places it was difficult to pick out what was left. The faces in the candlelight were distraught, fearful, deranged. Their faith had brought them neither peace nor confidence. To one side of the central sanctuary was a curtain. Bertie kissed it, then drew it aside. Behind was the small cave in which Paul had lived. His remains lay in a coffin beneath a red cloth embroidered with crosses. It seemed hardly large enough for a child.

In the monastery garden the mood lightened. Bertie worked in the garden and he pointed out the rows of vegetables with pride. Beyond the olive trees, beneath the west wall, was the monastery spring, the same spring which had sustained Paul. Jerome speaks of it in his biography of the saint. The view from his cave was of dripping water and a palm tree.

It was the merest trickle, four cubic metres a day according to Bertie, precious little for a monastery of thirty monks and related workers and visitors. Bertie seemed almost giddy in its presence, and talked with animation about the storage pools and irrigation channels.

I thought of the Nile, abundant, seductive and charismatic.

34

In the old days visitors to St Antony's were pulled up in a basket through a trap-door which overhung the entrance. When we reached it the next day, we were disappointed to find that in our more prosaic age they simply open the gates.

Behind the monastery rises Mount Kalalah. High on its flanks was the last retreat of St Antony, a cave in the cliff-face where he went to escape his followers, who gathered below on the site of the first monastery. It is a place of special pilgrimage, and after a hearty lunch our party of pilgrims set off *en masse* to visit it.

It was an arduous climb of over a thousand feet, and we were labouring under a midday sun. Remarkably no one but ourselves brought flasks of water. As the slopes grew steeper people clung to us like limpets in the hope of a drink. Our supplies were quickly depleted.

The climb coincided with a major sporting event in Cairo: a football game between the great rival teams of Zamalek and al-Ahly. All Egypt hung on the result. The game was being broadcast live and the young men of the party, Zamalek supporters, all carried radios. At crucial moments, they froze in mid-stride and stared anxiously at the ground, their radios pressed to their ears.

Two hours' climbing brought us to the narrow ledge from which one entered Antony's cave through a cleft in the cliff-face. The view was one of beautiful desolation. The flanks of the mountainside fell away beneath us, cut by ravines of white boulders. The monastery was hidden by a fold in the lower slopes. Beyond was the Wadi el-Araba, powdered with fine grey gravel. It ran like an empty thoroughfare between the Nile and the Red Sea. On the far side of the wadi were the pale heights of the Gebel el-Galala.

Our Father was the last person to gain the ledge. His robes were wet with perspiration and he was gasping for breath. His face, which had gone green, had collapsed. He drained the last of our water-bottle.

'*Hamdilallah,*' he said hoarsely. Thanks be to God. God, I thought unkindly, had nothing to do with the simple foresight of bringing a water-bottle on a desert outing.

As his eyes began to focus, Our Father took in the vast emptiness before him. Along the ledge a group of young men stood anxiously, their ears cocked to their radios. Zamalek were having trouble clearing the ball.

When he had recovered, Our Father squeezed through the cleft into the cave. The pilgrims went in after him in groups of five or six at a time. The narrow fissure stretched some twenty-five feet into the cliff before opening up into the tiny cave. It was a claustrophobic's nightmare. The chanting of the pilgrims leaked out through the cleft like birdsong.

When it was our turn to go in, we found Our Father looking sinister in the candlelight. There was a gawdy shrine, and for a moment I felt we had entered the den of a fortune-teller. Had he smiled I would have expected gold teeth. Instead he told us sombrely of the deprivations of St Antony. He seemed to speak with some feeling after his climb. But I was weary of this endless masochism. Antony seemed a neurotic, peevish, self-obsessed character, full of self-loathing and delusions. There was nothing in the tradition which implied a man with the humility and charity to sit down and wash the feet of a common prostitute.

That night Melinda was woken by someone tugging at her sheet. Our Father's wife stood at the end of her bunk.

'Cover yourself,' she hissed. 'You will be disturbing the monks.'

Melinda's sheet had risen up to reveal her calf. The monks' cells, just visible through the windows of the women's dormitories, lay 500 yards away, far enough for them to have required a telescope and searchlights if disturbance had been on their minds.

35

The Palace Hotel in Minya was a place of faded but fantastic decoration. A double stairway led up from a dusty hallway past walls of hieroglyphics and adolescent gods, set between huge mirrors advertising an Italian cognac popular in the 1920s. The stairway brought one to a first-floor lobby, a vast room of chandeliers and mahogany panelling and bentwood chairs with velvet cushions.

Stained-glass skylights above an upper gallery framed an enormous ceiling painting of the Egyptian countryside. The rooms had not been ignored. Tall lotus blossoms grew up over their doors, and their ceilings were covered with stars.

At one end of the lobby was a high reception desk. Behind it stood an old-fashioned switchboard and numbered pigeon-holes for the guests' post. Wires hung unconnected out of the back of the switchboard and the pigeon-holes had grown cobwebs. Minya was once an important stage on the journey up the Nile but aeroplanes, express trains and tourist cruise ships have left it a provincial backwater.

The Palace Hotel was run by a trio of brothers: a burly one-eyed masseur, a half-witted fellow with a pointed head, and a hugely obese young man who joked from his chair in the lobby, from which he rarely stirred, that he was expecting twins. The only member of staff with any authority was Muhammad, a boy of 9 or 10, who hurried about the place all day in his pyjamas, seeing to the guests' needs. We soon became fast friends, and the brothers joked that we should take him with us on our journey. Muhammad smiled his delightful smile, and nodded eagerly.

Minya was a genteel tree-lined town of old colonial villas built by Italians for Greek and Egyptian cotton magnates. Behind the high iron railings and the gardens of palm trees, the villas had fallen into quiet decay. The cotton magnates had gone elsewhere and their villas had been taken over as government offices and army posts.

From the square in front of the hotel, an avenue led down to the Corniche where people strolled arm in arm along the Nile. Stallholders sold soft drinks and grilled corn cobs and sweet potatoes. Across the river were orchards where the evening sun hung sheets of coloured gossamer between the trees.

We had come to Minya by train, but hoped to leave by boat. At the far end of the Corniche was the boatyard where felucca ferries came and went delivering people and goods from outlying villages. It was there that we met Ramses.

He was a small wizened man, not much above five feet. The skin of his face and neck was like dark ancient leather, creased and hard and glossy with wear. He had a narrow prunish face with thin yellow eyes and three yellow teeth. He wore a patched gallibaya and the soles of his feet were split with deep cracks like dried mud. His real name was Ahmad Osman but he looked exactly like the mummy of Ramses the Great in the Cairo Museum.

Ramses had sat next to us at the boatyard tea-house, and we had asked him about boats to Beni Hasan, a group of tombs some fifteen miles upstream. There are few passenger-boat services up and down the Egyptian Nile – railways and roads are quicker – but we hoped to find a felucca to hire for the day.

Without a word Ramses led us to a boat moored at the end of the dock, a small felucca with a heavily patched sail. It looked as old as he did. The cracked gunwales showed the faintest traces of paint, and the tiller was a tree branch. We climbed in on to plank benches, and in a moment we were off. We had to assume we were off to Beni Hasan, for Ramses had yet to speak a word to us.

We slanted across to the far bank and ran before the wind, well out of the main current. About a mile upstream Ramses drew the boat into a side pool, scampered into the shallows and lashed the boat to a tree. Then he disappeared into a banana grove.

A trio of geese paddled past. An old boat lay half-submerged against the bank with reeds pushing up through the holes in its hull. Willows with their feet in the water cast green shadows over the pool. A few yards along the bank a group of women were washing enormous pots, scouring them with handfuls of gravel. They were young and sturdy and beautiful. One came shyly along the bank. She wore brass anklets, and her feet were wet from the river.

'Itfadel,' she said, motioning towards a house through the trees. It was the traditional invitation of hospitality. The house looked like a house in a fairy tale. The young woman had a frank and innocent gaze.

We thanked her and explained that we were going upriver. She inclined her head and returned to her friends.

After a time a small boy emerged from the banana grove carrying a kerosene stove, a teapot, a glass, a home-made *seisha* and a bag of bread. Ramses reappeared with another boy of about 15. All three climbed aboard and we pushed off.

The older boy, who took charge of the boat, was a handsome fellow with a lovely turban of purple and white cotton and remarkably soft hands.

'Beni Hasan?' we asked. We had begun to worry that Ramses was a deaf mute.

Ramses was already puffing at his *seisha*, but the older boy nodded.

'*Inshallah*,' he said. 'It will take about five hours.'

'Are these your grandsons?' Melinda asked Ramses.

He looked at her for a long moment, puffing on his *seisha*, then spoke for the first time.

'My sons,' he said.

We suddenly saw the wizened old man in a new light. I realized with a start that the beautiful young woman who had spoken to us on the bank was his wife. Perhaps they were all his wives.

'How old are you?' Melinda asked.

'Seventy-five.' He blew smoke rings over the water. 'I am not ready for grandchildren.'

Bits of coloured rag, sewn to the leech edge of the sail, beat in the wind.

'*Helwa*,' the boy said. '*Helwa hawa*.' A sweet wind.

Egypt is blessed by its wind. It blows year round from the north while the current of the river flows from the south. This happy combination has facilitated travel up and down the Nile since long before the days of the Pharaohs.

37

There are three elements to the Nile valley: the blue river, the green of the cultivated banks and the dun colour of the desert ridges which enclose them both.

The different characters of the two Nile banks reflect the contrast between the two deserts. The eastern desert, rocky and mountainous, closes in aggressively upon the river with high bluffs restricting the fields to a tenuous strip. In places the cultivation is crowded out altogether and stretches of gravel come boldly down to the river's edge. The western desert offers few natural restrictions. The cultivation stretches inland for miles. The desert, if visible at all, appears as a low and distant range of sand hills.

In the mud banks which rise ten feet or so above the water's edge, you can see the strata of silt deposits brought down each year by the river in the days before the High Dam.

Children swam from the banks, and women washed clothes and pots. When they drew water, they climbed the banks on beaten paths, swaying like camels, with the full jugs on their heads. Back from the riverbanks, men in gallibayas glided through orchards of apricot trees. Villages floated up on either bank, with trees crowding round the low jumble of houses. Below them were moored feluccas with their long thin yards curving back and up from the masts in the same immaculate line.

Ramses's son called to people he knew on the banks, hailing them with long drawn-out greetings. After a time we were beyond his own district, and he greeted only the other boatmen, asking them about currents and winds. Their voices echoed back and forth across the water like the calls of water birds.

38

The tombs of Beni Hasan lay in an escarpment on the eastern bank. We followed a raised path from the river through stands of reeds and then through fields of sugar-cane thickly planted between palm trees. The desert appeared abruptly, and we stepped on to sand as one would step across a threshold, in a single stride.

It was half a mile to the bottom of the cliff. A path led up to a level terrace from which one entered the tombs. A watchman came forward to meet us, a splendid fellow in white pantaloons and a white silk waistcoat. At his hip he wore a pistol in an ancient leather holster. He lived in one of the tombs.

There are thirty-nine tombs at Beni Hasan, of which twelve are decorated. They are the tombs of provincial governors, dating roughly from 2000 to 1800 BC, a relatively quiet and prosperous period during the Middle Kingdom.

The guard opened the iron gates with antique keys, and we stepped into the dark chambers. There, when our eyes had adjusted to the gloom, we found the world of the river that we had just left. Painted on the walls were scenes of everyday life. Fellahin bending over their sickles cut swathes through fields of wheat. Women carried water jars. Families picked grapes, trod them and poured the new wine into storage jars. Fishermen pulled Nile perch from the current. A canoe nudged a bank of reeds where herons and ibises perched and swallows swooped overhead. A funeral barge passed upriver towards Abydos, its sails set full to the north wind. Elsewhere another crew struggled against the current, pulling hard on their oars on a windless day.

The paintings lack the finesse of the best Egyptian work, but they have vitality and conviction. The moments they portray are the life of the next world, for the Egyptians saw paradise as an idealized version of their own lives along the banks of the Nile.

It is a remarkably innocent view, this notion of carrying all the beloved moments of this world beyond the grave where one would find the river and the green banks and the boats sailing on the north wind as always.

I was reminded of Camus' comment: 'What does eternity matter to me? To lose the touch of flowers and women's hands is the supreme separation.' Then I thought of St Antony, so horrified by the world that he fled to the desert, and of the faces of the saints at St Paul's staring down from the dome, haunted by demons.

The guard invited us for tea. He lived in the last tomb, a bare chamber with a mat, a kettle, a kerosene stove and a radio which didn't work. He was in a great tradition of Egyptian tomb dwellers. Monks had lived at Beni Hasan for centuries, and their religious graffiti can be seen everywhere. We wondered if the musicians and bare-breasted dancers amongst the tomb paintings brought them comfort or torment.

We drank the tea squatting in the shade, gazing down over the desert and the river valley. We could see our boat moored beyond the reeds and our boatmen asleep beneath a tree. The river was in splendid panoramic form, curving gently away upstream and down, followed by the high ridge of the eastern desert. A large sodden island of reeds lay out in mid-stream like a moored barge. Two feluccas glided over the surface of the water like birds.

On the walls of the guard's tomb was the graffiti symbol of a boat, a stark line drawing of a felucca. We had seen it in the other tombs as well, sometimes carved on top of the paintings. The boats were a recurring metaphor, for the river, for journeys, for rites of passage, carved across the static innocence of the tomb paintings. The guard, an aristocratic character of impeccable manners, believed they were symbols of escape, of flight. He thought they had been carved by people living in the tombs, perhaps the monks, who dreamed fine dreams of other places, who longed for new horizons.

The idea reflected his own frustrated desires, tied as he was to his duties at Beni Hasan. I asked him where he would like to go.

'Mecca,' he said immediately. 'And then Paris.'

40

We sailed home through the late afternoon. The light lengthened through the palm groves and the villages glowed between the trees. The bluffs of the eastern bank were cast in gold light and blue shadows. The blue of the river deepened to dark sapphire. Sound, like light, grew longer and clearer, lingering across the surface of the water: the boy hailing the other boatmen, voices from the villages on the banks, children splashing at the river's edge, calling to one another.

The sun went down, seeping into the darkened fields of the western bank. For a moment the river was washed with pink and then with a beautiful grey. Then the light failed. With twilight a calm descended on the river. The wind died and we lay out in midstream drifting with the current. A few lights came on in the villages. After a time a full yellow moon rose above the ridge of the eastern desert. It whitened as it climbed the sky, casting a long path of broken moonlight across the river.

Ramses slept curled on the bow deck with his turban as a pillow and the youngest boy slept beside his brother at the tiller in the stern. The river was glassy and inviting. From the banks we could hear dogs barking. The night thickened about us, and we drifted home to Minya through the moonlight.

41

In the night, in the Palace Hotel, I became feverish. But towards dawn the fever broke, and after a breakfast of tea and warm bread I felt better. We decided to go on to Mallawi by train.

Sadat's assassin came from Mallawi. It seemed the kind of place in which people grew embittered. It was a shoddy disreputable town which stank of open sewers and rotting vegetables. The buildings were mean and in the streets, littered with rubbish, people jostled against us. Big old American cars pushed their way through the crowds with deranged faces pressed against their windows.

The only hotel overlooked the canal and rows of defecating men. The room was hot and stuffy and swarming with flies. A radio whined somewhere.

My fever had returned and I took to my bed. Fully dressed, I shivered violently beneath a pile of blankets. Huge trucks passed up and down the road outside the hotel, their horns blaring.

Through the window I could see the rooftops of a grand old rococo building, an oriental fantasy of domes and cupolas. Melinda went to investigate and found it ruinous. A small child emerged from a ditch by the entrance and threw a spoon at her.

In the morning we took a shared taxi back to Minya.

I lay in the refuge of our old room in the Palace Hotel. A doctor with a soothing voice and an old-fashioned black bag pronounced, absurdly, that I had a cold. For its cure he prescribed antibiotics.

The three brothers crept in on tiptoe to leave jugs of iced lemon juice by my bedside. The masseur promised to drive the fever out with his special massage. I pleaded with Melinda to take him away. Muhammad appeared regularly, whispering to me in Arabic. He took limes from his pyjama pockets and left them on the blankets. A family came to call, bringing claustrophobia as some people bring fresh air. A Copt who ran the soft drink stall across the square brought three kilos of grapes and prayers. Most of the grapes eventually rotted in the bottom of the wardrobe. The prayers fared better. On the third day I was well again.

42

One morning we set off to find the primal mound where the world began.

An early train from Minya left us at Roda, a country station where old taxis and barouches waited at a crossroads for fares. There were no roads direct from the station to where the world began, but the carriage drivers, squatting over their breakfasts, directed us to an abandoned railway line which cut across country.

The railway line ran through tall fields of durra. The early morning was cool and birds still chattered in the long grasses along the line. In the distance pale trees were wrapped in the morning mists. We passed a huge pigeon tower with pigeons strutting the dung-spattered ramparts. Rising from the blue fields like a medieval castle, it gave the morning a fantastical air.

At this hour the old railway line was a busy thoroughfare. Men riding past on donkeys called elaborate greetings to us. Children grazed water buffalo along the thick grass of the embankment, beating the huge animals into line with tiny sticks. Two old women passed and smiled at us, wrinkling their blue-tattooed cheeks. Two tall young men in finely cut gallibayas and white scarves asked rather formally if they might walk with us, then lapsed into shy silence. At their turning they bowed and shook our hands in farewell.

A man on a donkey directed us to where the world began, pointing up a lane between two walls of durra. We emerged on a dry stretch of open ground. A hundred yards away lay the village of Ashmunein. Camels and oxen nudged each other in front of the painted houses. All about us were the mounds and ruins of Hermopolis.

The visible remains were disappointingly recent, primarily Graeco-Roman. There were various mounds among them. Identifying the one on which the world began proved tricky. Indeed it must be admitted that there are at least two other sites in Egypt which lay claim to this distinction. One is in the Delta; the other is in Heliopolis, now a suburb of Cairo, but not even a cynic could believe the world began in the suburbs.

Having come this far, we had a vested interest in Ashmunein, and we resolutely climbed the largest of its mounds. At the beginning of time it was said to have arisen from the primeval waters, the waters of Chaos. On this mound Thoth, the god of wisdom, engendered four divine couples, the male and female aspects of the four elements of the primeval waters: Eternity, Mystery, Night and Darkness. They in turn created the egg from which the sun was hatched. In the egg with the sun was a goose, and when it emerged it flew honking away: the first sound of this world.

Later, wandering further through the ruins, we noted that the process of creation seemed to have gone into reverse. The water-table at Hermopolis had risen to overtake many of the remains. We found the column bases of the temple of Thoth almost buried in reeds in a black pond where a bloated rat floated belly-up.

The tombs of Tuna el-Gebel, the ancient necropolis of Hermopolis a few miles to the west, appeared to be drowning in desert. The tombs imitated houses with blind windows and mock stone panelling. Sand drifts smothered the front steps, climbed walls almost to the gables, and in one place blocked off a whole street. Against the angular and decaying walls of the tombs, the drifts of sand had a sensuous grace, immaculate and virginal. The wind had rippled their surface like a sea-bed.

We had come to see the tomb of Isidora. She was, apparently, still in residence. We climbed a short flight of steps to the front door. Inside were two bare rooms. In the second room lay Isidora herself, mummified but unwrapped, in a long glass case. She was a slight, delicate figure. There was no trace of breasts, and her hip bones jutted out like a young girl's. Her skin, like leathery bark, was stretched tightly over the skeleton, and in places where it had cracked and parted you could see the bones inside like old wood. She had long slim fingers and very long thumbs. One leg lay slightly askew, broken either when she drowned or by mishandling in death. In the middle of her chest was a gaping hole where the viscera had been removed.

She looked as if she needed a pillow; her head was thrown back awkwardly. Looking closely you could see traces of fine reddish curls at her temples. Only the mouth gave the face its expression. The lips were drawn back over a row of small pointed teeth in a ghastly grimace, a shriek of pain or terror. The preservation of Isidora was the preservation of this death howl. It filled the room, a silent banshee wail.

Isidora had drowned in the Nile in the second century AD. A particular sanctity was attached to victims of the river, as if they embodied some terrible truth. To die in the waters of the Nile, the giver of life, was a paradox which compelled the ancients.

We found it difficult to leave. The room felt horribly lonely. There were no paintings of musicians or dancing girls or peasants treading grapes here. Night, Darkness, Mystery and Eternity seemed to be her only companions.

A fat unshaven man sat opposite us on the train eating guavas. They were very ripe and the juice had squirted on to his shirt-front like bloodstains. It was a white shirt, buttoned at the neck without a tie. The man had large hands covered with dark hairs, and a delicate mouth between fat cheeks. He fumbled in his bag and drew out two guavas.

'*Itfadel*,' he said, handing them to us.

Outside the windows were fields of silver cabbages and tall sunflowers, their heads drooping, exhausted in the heat. The palm groves were full of brick kilns and trails of black smoke snaked between the trees.

'Asyut,' the fat man said, biting into another guava. Juice rolled down his chin. 'I hope you are not going to Asyut.'

He knew we were. He had been eating guavas, and listening, when we had discussed our destination with the conductor.

'We are,' I said.

'Asyut is not good,' the fat man said. 'It is a bad place.'

He crunched another guava. He looked as if he had been shot in the chest.

'My wife is from Asyut,' he said. 'She has gone back there to her family. I told her, "Go to Asyut. Go to hell." ' He laughed, showing us a mouthful of guava.

'Have you any children?' I asked.

'No children. My wife does not give me children. She is cursed. I should not have married her. Now I send her back to Asyut.'

He picked guava pips from his teeth.

'Are you married?' he asked.

'Yes,' we said. It was what we said for convenience; there was no concept in Egypt of unmarried couples.

'Have you children?' he asked.

'No.'

He took this news quietly. I had half expected him to begin raving about cursed women and sending Melinda to Asyut. Perhaps he didn't bother because we were going there anyway.

We passed a small shrine, a humble domed square of white-washed adobe, the tomb of a saint, adorned with rags. It was a common sight in Egypt. The rags were bits of clothing of childless women who came to the shrine to pray for fertility. A woman's position in Egyptian society depended upon her children, particularly her sons. Without children, she had no status.

The rags hung limply on wires round the muddy walls. I imagined the fat man's wife, a fat woman, making her way alone through the palm trees, tearing a strip from her dress and tying it to the shrine.

'How old is your wife?' Melinda asked.

'Sixteen,' the man said. 'It is too bad not to have children. Every man must have children. When he is old they will care for him. When he is dead they will remember him. This is how it should be. They are his blood.'

He got off at the next village and waddled away up a street with his bag of guavas. It was a village of narrow lanes and tilting walls. The lanes were crowded with children and donkeys and geese. Women in black squatted in doorways sifting through pans of dry rice, picking out the stones. From the train we looked down over the clutter of the rooftops, things broken, things abandoned, things stored and forgotten: broken waterjugs, wheel-less bicycles, rolls of rush matting. Everything was brown except for one glorious sunstruck line of washing.

45

The square outside the train station at Asyut was a maelstrom of crowds and buses and shouting taxi drivers. We fled down a long avenue towards the river.

On the Corniche we asked a traffic policeman in a white booth where we might find a hotel. As we were turning to follow his directions, he drew up his cuff and showed us the blue tattooed cross that all Copts have on the inside of their wrists.

'Do *you* love our Lord?' he asked.

In the lobby of the Lotus Hotel a luminous picture of the Virgin Mary, like a Hollywood starlet, filled an entire wall. A sober Copt showed us to a room overlooking the street. The walls were bright green and the mattresses of the cots were littered with dead flies.

After Cairo and Alexandria, Asyut is the largest town in Egypt. There is a barrage and bridge across the river, the first bridge since Helwan just south of Cairo. It has a university and technical colleges, and its large student population has helped to give it a reputation as a trouble-spot. Muslim fundamentalist groups are very active in Asyut, and the Coptic population is large. There have been frequent clashes between Coptic and Muslim students and between fundamentalist groups and the authorities. Troops guarded the crumbling mansions, now government buildings, along the Nile.

For us Asyut had a more innocent significance. It was a place where many of the Nile barges broke their journey.

The barges were moored along the river's edge beneath the Corniche. There was no dock, only a gravel embankment into which the bargemen had driven mooring stakes. At close range, after the feluccas, they seemed vast. They were iron-hulled and their cargoes were in open holds beneath tarpaulins. The engine rooms lay astern and in the bows, beneath awnings, were wheels as tall as a man. The barges were the new lords of the Nile, and we were determined to hitch a lift on one.

The bargemen greeted us as formally as if we were visiting them in their own homes, which I suppose we were. At each barge they ran down boarding planks for us, sat us on a long bench by the wheel and set about producing tea. They were gracious and hospitable. Some were waiting for spare parts from Cairo, some were waiting on instructions from their owners, some were going downriver. None was able to help.

46

In the evening we went to eat in one of the eating houses near the station. We were walking up the road from the hotel when a young man padded up behind us and greeted us in English.

'Hey man,' he said. 'Excuse me for bothering you.'

He had a thin face and pockmarked skin. His hair was plastered forward over his scalp to hide the fact that he was already balding.

'I just wanted to offer you any help if I can. To find the way, or to give you any advices. Where are you from?'

'From England,' I said. We did not like the look of him and kept walking. He matched his stride to ours.

'I am a member of the Friends of the Tourist Organization,' he said. 'It is our duty to help foreigners. We have been watching you, and would like to help you.'

At this point a second young man appeared. He had obviously been waiting to see how the first got on.

'This is my chief in the Organization,' the first one said. The chief smiled and introduced himself. He had the bloated appearance of someone who had gained weight too quickly. A long curving moustache framed his large mouth.

'We hope we are not bothering you,' the chief said. 'But we know it is difficult for foreigners in Egypt to deal with all the many problems. We like to help them. It is our duty. We give them advices about the way to go, the correct prices, many things. We can help you to meet Egyptian people and learn about Egyptian customs.'

'That is very kind of you,' I said. 'But we have been in Egypt for three months. We have learnt to manage.'

'But we would like to help you here in our own city.'

'Thank you. But we can manage.'

'Do you not like talking to Egyptians?' the chief asked. He managed a note of injury.

'Yes of course we do. But we are very busy this evening. We want to post some letters, and then we must go to eat.'

'You have letters,' the chief said. I realized I had made a mistake. 'Please. Allow us to show you where to post them.'

They led us up a series of side streets to a post office near the station. Then they accompanied us to an eating house.

The chief did virtually all the talking. We hoped our lack of response would eventually put him off. His side-kick, the thin man, was edgy and sat forward on his seat. He laughed loudly at things that weren't funny and littered his English with expletives to appear more at home in the language. The chief, smug, supercilious and opinionated, was undaunted by our indifference.

64

The English, he said, were a strange people. They liked to pretend that they were fair-minded and polite, but he himself had found that they were not polite. They did not like to talk to Egyptian people. The sun, he thought, had set on them now for sure.

He was dismissive of Melinda's Arabic, and insisted on speaking to us in English which he declared a simple language, like the language of a child. Our problem was that we had not learned enough. Egyptian Customs, he declared, this is what we must learn. We needed someone like himself, a Friend of the Tourists, who could take us through Egyptian Customs step by step.

After paying the bill, we pointedly shook their hands and said goodbye.

'You are going to your hotel?' the chief asked.

'Yes,' I said. 'Good-night.'

'We will walk with you. We live near the hotel.'

We walked on quickly.

'You are interested in boats?' he asked, quickening his pace to keep up.

'Not particularly.'

'But we saw you today talking with the boatmen on their boats.'

'That's right. We want to travel on one of the barges.'

The chief clung to my side. 'I think perhaps I can help you. My uncle owns a company with many barges. I will speak to him and try to arrange this for you. The boatmen cannot help you. They are bad men. Many are thieves. You must not trust them.'

'They seemed very pleasant.'

'They are bad men.'

At our hotel we bade them good-night again. The chief wanted to know when he could bring us news of his uncle's barges. We told him to look for us in the evening. We hated to give them any encouragement but something might come of his uncle, if he existed.

Upstairs from our window we could see the two men at a soft drinks stall across the road. They were drinking bottles of Coke and trying not to appear as if they were watching the hotel.

We spent the following day on the far bank of the river in a paradise of guava orchards and banana groves. In the afternoon we had tea in a house full of the most beautiful women. They had dark eyes and gold teeth and were all young and slim and muscular and small-breasted. They wore bright scarves and pantaloons and silver anklets. They spoke with almost incomprehensible country accents. They had never heard of England, but thought it must be somewhere near Cairo.

Back in Asyut the Friends of the Tourists were waiting for us outside our hotel. Melinda pleaded a headache and went inside, and I took them across the road to the soft drinks stall to hear the report of the uncle, and then get rid of them.

They seemed disappointed to hear that we had had such a pleasant day on the far bank.

'Why didn't you tell us?' the chief said. 'We could have come with you. Shown you the way. Made the people there give you some hospitality. They are very ignorant, the people in the country-side, and do not know good manners.'

I tried to enquire about the uncle and the boats. He drew on his Coke, savouring the fact that he had something I wanted.

'It is a very difficult matter,' he said. 'Let us go and take some food and I can explain it to you step by step.'

I feigned lack of interest and made to go.

The explanation suddenly became simpler. His uncle, he said, was very displeased that the bargemen had been talking with us. They were not allowed to take passengers on the river. For this they would require the written permission of the owners, and a police permit.

I thanked him for his help, assured him that we would begin to go through the proper channels tomorrow, and said good-night.

While we had been on the opposite bank a new barge had come upriver from the direction of Minya and had moored near the end of the Corniche. Later in the evening, with our two Friends still waiting opposite the hotel, we slipped out by a back door and made our way down to the river. I had no intention of going through the proper channels; it could take weeks. Egyptian bureaucracy is slow and it is common practice to circumvent officialdom whenever possible. But we were concerned now to keep our barge arrangements secret from the Friends of the Tourists, for they could easily thwart us, if they chose to, by denouncing our plans to the authorities.

At the end of the Corniche, opposite where the newly arrived barge was moored, was a police post and an army barracks. We cut down to the riverbank before we reached them and walked along the water's edge out of sight of the buildings above. We hailed the nearest bargemen and they ran a plank down for us. There were five barges moored abreast here, and we climbed over the first four, greeting the startled crews as we went.

On the last barge we found a group of men gathered around a bench beneath a canopy in the bow. Seated cross-legged on the bench at the centre of the group was a large man smoking a home-made *seisha*. He returned our greeting in a loud authoritative voice.

'Are you going upriver?' we asked.

He nodded, puffing on his *seisha*. 'To Luxor.' He pronounced it in the way of Upper Egypt, dropping the 'L'.

'May we travel with you?'

'Of course,' he said, without hesitation.

'When do you leave?'

'Tomorrow morning at five o'clock.'

'Okay,' we said. 'We will be here.'

He nodded again, still puffing away. He asked no questions of us. No one else had spoken.

We hesitated for a moment then took our leave. As we were stepping on to the adjoining barge, the man on the bench called out to us.

'*Hawaga*,' he said. Foreigner.

We looked back.

'*Ahlan w'a sahlan*,' he said. Welcome.

'*Ahlan beek*,' we said, returning the formulaic greeting. This pleased him, that we knew the proper response. He took his pipe out of his mouth, smiled and waved. 'Tomorrow,' he said.

48

In the morning we were woken by the muezzin at four o'clock. We packed in the dark and crept downstairs. Opening the outside door we stepped into the sharp night air. In the pooled streetlights the street was empty. Across the way a man was huddled asleep against the soft drinks stall.

'Turn right,' I whispered.

Melinda looked at me. I took her arm and we turned towards the station away from the river. We had only gone a few steps when a voice called out from across the street.

'Hey, hello. My friends. Where are you going?' Footsteps ran after us. The thin man came panting up to us.

'Where are you going?' he asked. He was confused, befuddled by sleep and the sudden departure of his charges.

'To the train,' I said 'We have decided to go to Luxor by train.' My heart was pounding. I had thought I was being paranoid about their obsessive interest in us, but now, finding one of them waiting outside our hotel at half past four in the morning, I was alarmed.

'Could you help us?' I asked. 'Our bags are heavy. Would you go up to the station and get a taxi for us? Then we could have some tea together before we catch the train.'

He stood for a moment chewing his lip. He didn't know what to do. He was still half asleep.

'Okay,' he said at last. 'I will be right back.'

When he was out of sight we picked up our bags and turned into a side street. Keeping to back lanes we made our way down to the river.

We passed the police sentry who grunted a sleepy greeting. Further on, opposite where the barge was moored, we passed soldiers hunched behind sandbags at the army post. We walked on until we reached an unlit stretch of the Corniche, then climbed over a low wall and down the short slope to the river's edge where we were out of sight of the sentries. Then we doubled back to the barges.

The boarding plank had been taken up for the night. Above us on the wall of the Corniche two men were wrapped in a blanket.

'Hello mister,' they called sleepily.

We had to get on to the barge before these two characters

unwittingly alerted the army sentries across the road, or before the Friends of the Tourists turned up looking for us. The barges, at the end of their mooring ropes, lay some fifteen feet from the shore.

I rolled up my trousers and carried the bags out to the first barge. Behind me I could hear the men calling again, 'Hey, mister. Hello mister.' The water was deeper than I had thought. It swirled up above my waist. The bottom was large slippery boulders. I threw our bags up on to the deck of the first barge, about ten feet above me. Melinda waded out after me and we climbed up one of the mooring ropes on to the deck.

The men on the wall seemed to have lost interest, and burrowed into their blanket again. We made our way across the first four barges. On the fifth we settled down to wait on deck. We could see the army post now and the shuffling sentries and a few jeeps passing in and out of the gate. But the barges were in darkness and they could not see us. A dog whined somewhere in a hold. Thankfully it was tied up.

We sat for about an hour waiting for the bargemen to wake. It was dark and we were cold and wet. We changed into dry trousers and extracted sweaters from the bottom of our bags.

A crescent moon hovered above the trees of the far bank and there was a scattering of cold stars. Dark clumps of water hyacinths floated downstream like tiny islands cut adrift. Moonlight glinted between them. In the dark stillness only the surface of the river moved.

49

In the pre-dawn, the river was the colour of ink. A straggling formation of geese flew upriver, low over the water, squawking faintly. In the town, roosters began to crow.

We could see the bargemen now, asleep about the boat, huddled in blankets. One was on the bench at the front, another atop the tarpaulin over the hold. They awoke all at once, as if an alarm had gone off. Greeting us sleepily, they began immediately to cast off.

The engine started and a moment later we were pulling away from the other barges in a wash of white water. Asyut slipped astern.

The big man, whom we had spoken to the previous evening, sat on the bench in the bow, sucking deeply on his *seisha*. He patted the cushions beside him to indicate that we should join him. He introduced himself as Muhammad, the *reis*, the captain. The pilot, Milhaez, was at the wheel immediately behind the bench. A third man, Romany, the mechanic who looked after the engine, squatted in the bow, sleepily making tea. These three were the barge's crew.

The riverbanks were wreathed in mist. The banana groves and the guava orchards of the east bank were blue and gloomy. There was no one about. Three white ibises flew along the bank, their long yellow legs almost trailing their own blurred reflections.

Gradually the river lightened and the banks began to awake. A man carried a bunch of fishing poles down an empty village street, a dog barking at his heels. Another man in another village was setting off for the fields, his hoe over his shoulder. Now and then people appeared on the banks to wash, squatting on their haunches, leaning forward to scoop up handfuls of water. The river was a lilac grey colour but the water splashing over their upturned faces and running off their arms was silver. Caryatid figures passed through the fields with tall water jugs on their heads.

Finally the sun appeared, rising beyond a stand of palm trees. Their curving silhouettes slid across its red face as we passed upstream.

With the sun, the bargemen came to life. Milhaez, at the wheel, began to sing. He had a good strong voice and he whistled the instrumental parts, shaking his head in time. In his baggy white shorts and bright yellow waistcoat, he looked like a street entertainer.

Romany washed the tea glasses in a bucket of water lifted from the river. He had a gentle startled face, and the skin round his eyes was dark and bruised-looking. He wagged his head to the music and his turban slipped over one eye.

Beside us on the bench the captain, Muhammad, puffed fiercely on his *seisha*. When it expired he handed it to Romany to prepare another.

70

Released from his pipe, at least momentarily, he inhaled the morning air.

'*Sab el Kir*,' he boomed, to us, to the river. Good morning.

'*Hawaga*.' It was the way he would always address us: foreigner. 'Where are you going?'

'To Sudan,' I said.

'Al-Sudan.' He widened his eyes, and began to give us directions. 'We are going to Luxor. After Luxor, you will find Aswan. After Aswan, you will find a big lake. On the other side of the lake, you will come to Sudan.'

'How long will it take to get to Luxor?' Melinda asked.

'Two days,' he said, holding up two fingers. 'We are going home to Luxor. The journey home is always the quickest.'

We expressed mild surprise, and examined our maps.

He tapped me on the knee. '*Hawaga*. Two days. We are not a felucca.'

50

At midday Romany cut the engines, and Milhaez steered the barge into a narrow inlet where we moored between the bank and a low island of reeds and stunted palms. Our cargo of cement was destined for a factory at Tima, a town which lay a few miles back from the riverbank.

We spent five days moored in this inlet while the barge was unloaded. It was a pleasant interlude, and we did not mind the delay nearly as much as the captain did. In spite of all evidence to the contrary, he always believed that we were leaving *bokra*, tomorrow. But the unloading, all done by hand, was a slow process. The third *bokra* was a Friday, the Muslim holy day, when the labourers did not come at all.

Each morning trucks from the factory bumped along a dust road and turned down on to the low gravel bank where we were moored. All day long a team of labourers, pale with cement dust, streamed up a plank out of the hold with the bags of cement, like a trail of ants.

In the afternoons the owner of the factory usually came to visit and to check the progress of the work. The stream of barefoot labourers quickened their pace while he was on board. The owner was a fat boyish figure in a neatly pressed gallibaya. He had a fat shiny face and a smug smile. He sat on the bench sipping tea and described his wealth to me. He owned the factory. He owned many trucks. He owned so many *feddans* of land. He owned, it seemed, half of Tima. I made a show of looking bored with this recital of wealth.

To further aggrandize himself, he tried to supplant the captain as our host.

'I would like to invite you to come and stay at my house,' he said. 'I have a large house in Tima. You would be very comfortable there. Later I could arrange for a car to take you on to Luxor.'

'That is very kind,' I said, 'but we are happy here.'

'But you have no beds, no cushions, nothing.'

'We like the barge. We prefer to be on the river.'

The captain beamed with satisfaction, and the owner lost interest in us.

Like any Egyptian, the captain took his role as host very seriously. While the labourers were on the boat, he insisted that Melinda go into purdah. The labourers, he explained, were bad men. They would *look* at her. He pronounced *look* like a curse, and mimed the bad men *looking* by jutting his head forward and glaring at her like a demented goldfish. As a host it was his duty to protect a female guest from such horrors.

It was impossible to refuse his request; to do so would have been an insult. So for the potential crime of the bad men, all of whom seemed perfectly pleasant, sentence was passed on Melinda, who was duly imprisoned in the hold. There she languished throughout the hot hours of the day, emerging each evening only when the workmen had departed. She took it philosophically, and spent her days reading *The Seven Pillars of Wisdom*. When I went below for visits I found her eating dates and musing on Lawrence's alleged masochistic sexuality.

The life of the river and the riverbanks went on about us. Beyond the gravel beach where the trucks drew up, the bank was a mass of reeds and elephant grass, their ripe heads shot through with light. The women who came down to the river, no doubt fearful of *looks* themselves, avoided the barge. We could hear them laughing and chattering beyond the reeds, their dresses flashing bright glints of colour through the green stalks. Downstream an ancient felucca lay in against the bank, its hull the colour of granite. Early one morning a horseman appeared on the bank in rich blue robes, his horse caparisoned with coloured ribbons. He cantered back and forth on the gravel beach, then rode off through a corn field.

In the afternoons fishermen in small skiffs laid nets along the low island of reeds which lay between us and the main channel, returning to gather them at night. Through the day the river graduated from the silvery grey of the morning to the pale marine colours of midday to a deep velvety blue in the early evenings. The long desert ridges above the far bank looked like petrified pink brocade.

In the evenings the smell of cooking pervaded the boat. We ate at a low round table set out on the foredeck, splendid meals of hot *ful* beans, salads of tomatoes and onions, and fresh fish from the river. The meals were prepared by Milhaez and Romany while the captain smoked his *seisha*. His life aboard was entirely idle; the others waited on him like two wives, catering to his needs and bolstering his ego.

In the twilight after dinner he was like a Buddha on his bench, wreathed in tobacco smoke. They had been away from home for eight weeks, and one evening the captain showed us the presents he had bought for his wife. He kept them beneath a cushion at the end of his bench. There was a flimsy nightdress which seemed to consist only of feathers and ribbons, and a mysterious stick of what looked like fudge. We did not understand the word for this, so the captain resorted to mime. First he engaged in enthusiastic eating of the fudge, and then in even more enthusiastic kissing.

'Book, film or quote?' I asked.

'It's a very lovable sweet,' Melinda said.

'It's a kind of lipstick,' I said.

The eating and the kissing grew more abandoned.

'An aphrodisiac!' I cried.

He tucked it away safely beneath his cushion, smiling mischievously.

'*Hawaga*,' the captain said. 'Do you miss your home?'

'No,' I replied. 'What about you?'

In answer he quoted a boatman's saying: 'The sailors of the Nile have no home but the river, and the river is home to no one.' It sounded marvellous in Arabic.

52

One afternoon we went for a walk to a nearby village where we met an old man with a stick and a long grey moustache who invited us home for tea.

The old man sat next to us on the *mastaba*, a low adobe platform which ran round the walls of the front room of his house. He had a wan creased face and wore an old double-breasted suit jacket over his gallibaya. The room was empty save for a pile of cushions and blankets in one corner and an enormous television set on a stool in the middle of the earthen floor.

'Have you just moved in?' Melinda asked.

'I was born in this room,' he said.

Tea was carried out to us on a brass tray from the women's quarters. As news of our presence spread through the village, more and more people arrived to stare at us. The old man instructed his grandson to bring us cushions. Two enormous bolsters, as hard as planks, were produced. Perched atop these monoliths like exhibits, we towered absurdly above the old man. By now the entire village had crowded into the room. A sea of hushed and bemused faces stared up at us.

Our host was shy, and when conversation flagged he resorted to the television. He introduced it proudly as the only television in the village. It had been bought by his three sons who all worked in Saudi Arabia.

From atop our cushions we dutifully watched the television, while the assembly of villagers watched us watching the television. An American film was showing which I recognized as *Double Indemnity*. Physical attraction was drawing an insurance salesman into a web of murder. How was he to know, he mused, that murder smelled of honeysuckle?

The old man leaned forward on his stick and solemnly read the Arabic sub-titles aloud. He seemed to be doing this for our benefit, unaware that the sound-track was in our own language. The dialogue was quick-fire stuff, and he never got more than half-way through each sub-title before it was replaced with the next one.

After a time we were invited into the harem in the rear of the house. The women sat on a *mastaba* against a sunny wall with their legs drawn up into red velvet skirts. Children clustered round our knees. A plate of dates was produced and we threw the stones over a low wall to three black goats who munched them mournfully. The room smelled of animals and cooking.

There were three women, the wives of the old man's three sons. They were bold and animated and all talked at once, sometimes in unison. They asked us a stream of questions, and laughed and chattered about themselves and their children. Their husbands, they said, only came home once a year, to father more children. They did not miss them, they confided to Melinda. It was not easy when they came home. They were like strangers.

Later, when I returned to the old man, I found him alone with a few boys and the American film. It was reaching a murderous conclusion. The old man seemed to have lost interest in it. He patted the bench beside him, and I sat down.

He pointed at the boys in thrall to the film.

'They are not as we were,' he said. 'When we were boys, we wanted to be like our fathers. But our sons now do not want to be like us.'

On the afternoon of the fifth day the unloading was completed. We unlashed the mooring cables almost as the last bag of cement was carried down the gangplank. Coming out into the main channel, we made a wide U-turn and headed upriver. We felt elated to be on the move again.

In the late afternoon light, the banks glowed with colour. The faces of the eastern mountains, lilac pink, were deeply creased, and pockmarked here and there with ancient tombs. A group of acacias, standing above a village made golden by the late sun, blazed with crimson blossoms. In mid-stream the river was a deep sapphire blue while along its banks it was washed with green and ochre and fulvous reflections.

With sunset the colours drained away. The eastern mountains quickly faded to a sombre brown. The fields of the west bank darkened by stages. The river itself clung longest to the light, shining opaline blue between gloomy banks. Then it too faded to a greasy blackness.

We did not stop with nightfall. There was no moon, and in the pale starlight the river showed between the banks as a slightly thinner shade of black.

After a time Milhaez began to sing and the boat seemed to be carried upriver on his voice. He sang for miles and miles. The captain joined in with a long raucous song, beating time on the tea tray. In the moments of stillness between the songs, the hugeness of the night overwhelmed the boat.

Singing, we came upon Sohag. The bridge was a trail of lights between the two banks. After the dark river, the town looked as bright and brassy as Manhattan. But beyond Sohag we seemed to enter an even darker reach of the river. We saw no more villages, and the river, broken now into narrow channels by low islands, began to curve.

Milhaez stopped singing and the captain went forward in the bow to stand as look-out. The night was pitch black and we could see nothing. The huge boat cleaved the darkness blindly. Milhaez spun the wheel this way and that, negotiating islands that only appeared, at least to our unfamiliar eyes, at the last moment. I never knew how much Milhaez could see, and how much he steered from memory.

54

'You must come to our house,' the captain said. 'We will have a big meal, *mulikai*, chicken, rice, fresh bread. My wife is a very good cook.'

We were eating breakfast, crusts of petrified bread dipped in sweet tea. Morning mists curled across the surface of the river. The welcome we would receive at journey's end, and the fine meal we would have, was a recurrent theme of conversation.

'You will meet my mother,' the captain said. 'She is very big.' He leapt up from his bench and waddled across the foredeck like an enormous goose.

'You will meet my daughter,' Milhaez said. 'She is four, and she is very beautiful. When she grows up she will be a doctor and live in England.'

On the bank a line of children running through a field of clover were knee-deep in mist. Their voices across the water were dream-like. Ahead of us a headland loomed out of the mist like the prow of a huge ship.

The river was smooth as a pond. We sat on the bench and watched the sun come up above the eastern ridge and the mist clear like drifting smoke. Out of sight, on the edge of the desert beyond the wide stretch of cultivation, lay Abydos, one of the most sacred sites of ancient Egypt, where the souls of the dead gathered at the tomb of Osiris.

As the morning wore on the captain became preoccupied.

'There is a problem,' he said after a time. 'At Nag Hammadi there is a lock and at Qena there is a police check.'

'You could let us off,' we said. 'We don't want to make trouble for you.'

He became conspiratorial. 'At Nag Hammadi, you can go below. No one will see you. There will be no problem. But at Qena we will have to bribe the police not to check the boat.'

'How much?'

'Fifteen pounds.'

We gave him the money and he handed it immediately to Romany, the administrator of bribes.

The barrage at Nag Hammadi came into view in the early afternoon round a wide bend. It was a long, low-arched bridge with a lock at the west side.

We went below.

'Only half an hour,' the captain said. He closed the hatch. We sat in the darkness feeling the motion of the boat. After a time the engines slowed and we could hear the wheel turning. The engines reversed and cut out altogether, and we knocked gently against a mooring.

The men went ashore. We could hear their voices grow fainter. Then the boat was silent. We waited in the dark hold for an hour, then two.

Voices and footsteps above us heralded their return. The captain was complaining about something. There were other voices we did not recognize. We crept in under a low table and covered ourselves with a tarpaulin.

A moment later the hatch shot open and men in boots came down into the hold, their voices loud in the confined space. Their boots scraped on the floor; we could just see them from beneath our tarpaulin. They stopped near us, then turned and went up the ladder again. They left the hatch open, and we could hear them going about the barge, arguing with the bargemen.

Then they were gone. Presently the engine started, and from beneath the tarpaulin I could see the shadow of the wheel turning in a square of sunlight on the floor. The light dimmed and we bumped something hard. There was the smell of wet stone and water dripping. We were in the lock.

It filled slowly. We could measure the rise of the water by the gradual lightening of the hold and the change in the quality and volume of sound. We rose into birdsong and the evening call to pray. In a moment we were underway.

A few minutes later Romany pulled off the tarpaulin. He was squatting at our feet grinning his wide sheepish grin. From the deck above the captain was calling us.

The bargemen were in high spirits, the problems of the lock now behind them. The men in boots were inspectors who had taken an unusual interest in our barge. Romany mimed them going about the boat, looking here and looking there. Everyone laughed, and the captain clapped me on the back and called me a good fellow. Our hiding under the tarpaulin delighted them.

Above us on the east bank an enormous headland reared up, the colour of ripe apricots. Beneath it, at the water's edge, was a single *dom* tree, the split palm tree which is the first sign of Upper Egypt.

56

We travelled all night. The bargemen had scented home.

We passed towns whose mosques were lit up with coloured neon strips like amusement rides. In one of the darkest reaches of the river, we came upon a cluster of lights on the east bank. A faint hum, like insects, became music, a whining *narghil*, and drums. There were lights suspended in the trees, crowds of people, dust hanging. It was a wedding. The sharp shadows of branches swayed across the lighted crowds of dancers. Then the night closed in again.

At Qena we went below while the bribe was administered. We could hear the police launch coming alongside. They pulled away again almost immediately. We were back on deck in a quarter of an hour.

The river and the night seemed endless. We sailed on into a warm enveloping darkness. Far behind us our wake exhausted itself on the banks, and the river was still again.

Looking up at the stars I thought of the goddess Nut, her breasts spangled with constellations. Of all the gods one was happiest to see her, this beautiful figure, slim as a girl. The ancients thought of her as resurrection, giving birth to the sun each morning. One found her beneath the lids of coffins and stretched across the ceiling of tombs, hovering above the dry bones of dead men.

57

When I woke in the morning, we were drawing into the bank. The captain was at the wheel; Milhaez, who had piloted the boat through the night, lay asleep on the deck in a bundle of blankets.

The river was wide and empty. The sun was just coming up over the far bank, trailing a red reflection across the water. On our side the bank was slow and grassy and sloped up to trees. We nudged against it, and the engines cut out. The sweet stillness of birdsong stole over the barge.

'Home,' the captain said.

He and Romany ran a plank down on to the bank, then beckoned us to follow them. We took up our bags and left Milhaez still sleeping on the deck. The village lay a few hundred yards back from the river across fields of yellow stubble. We went up a narrow street where children peered out of doorways.

At the end, in the doorway of the captain's house, his mother waited for us, an enormous woman in black. She had a kindly face and smooth soft skin. When she moved she waddled just as the captain had illustrated. She welcomed us home as if we were lost children.

The mother was the centre of the household. Her husband was dead, her daughters had gone to live with their in-laws, and her two sons, Muhammad and Milhaez, had brought their wives home to her. They all lived together in two rooms and a courtyard. The sons with their wives had the rooms, and the mother slept on a wide divan behind a curtain in a corner of the courtyard.

Her sons were delighted to see her, and were as warm with her as they were distant with their wives, greeted, after eight weeks on the river, with diffident handshakes. Hovering in the background, like unwelcome neighbours, the wives eavesdropped on the tales of the river. The captain's wife, a woman of the most extreme ugliness, smiled toothlessly at me. I tried not to think of her in the feathery nightdress under the influence of the aphrodisiac.

We sat in a high vestibule between the street and the courtyard. White doves fluttered down through the doorway and children swarmed in and out. In the courtyard a chicken shrieked as one of the wives wrung its neck.

Milhaez cradled his daughter in his lap, the one who was to be a doctor in England. She was a thin sickly child with a tremendous head of dark curly hair, a tiny shrunken face and enormous eyes. Her limbs seemed lifeless, and she never spoke or uttered a sound. She lay in her father's lap like a limp doll, gazing at him blankly, as if in a trance.

Lunch was as the captain had promised, a grand meal of many dishes. The mother ate with us. She sat with the chicken pot in her lap, tearing off pieces of the bird and handing them round. The wives and the children would eat later.

In the afternoon a car was sent for. The family stood outside the house as we drove off. The children shouted after us, and the mother waved both hands like fat fluttering birds.

58

We stayed only one night in Luxor before turning downriver again to visit the great temples of Abydos and Dendera which we had passed on the barge.

At El Balyana we found rooms above a tea-house on the edge of town. The rooms gave off a dark upper hallway where an old man slept on a bench in his underwear. Presumably he had been locked out of his room, for the tea-house manager searched in vain for keys to the antique padlocks which fastened the tall double doors. Eventually he opened one for us by hitting it with an old chisel.

The keys must have been lost for some time. Our room appeared not to have been inhabited in living memory. It was furnished with an ancient iron bedstead and a wooden table so decrepit that it collapsed as I walked past it. There were sand drifts in the corners, and what I took for lace curtains at the windows turned out to be spider webs.

El Balyana was a town of dirt streets full of donkey carts and horse-drawn barouches. The men of the town carried long walking sticks of the sort one saw in the ancient temple reliefs.

59

On the walls of tombs throughout Egypt are boats sailing the Nile. The boats, and the journeys they undertake, are symbols of resurrection. Their destination is Abydos, the home of Osiris, one of the most ancient and venerable sites in all Egypt. It was the object of pilgrimage for the living and the dead, and the focus for their hopes for life beyond the grave.

The story of the resurrection of Osiris, like the resurrection of Christ, was the promise of resurrection for all. Once a virtuous king, whose subjects hailed him as a god, he was killed by his jealous brother Seth. With the help of friends, Seth lured Osiris into a coffin-like box. Then they sealed the lid and threw him into the Nile.

His body was eventually found by Isis, who was both his sister and his wife. She performed the funerary rites so essential to Egyptians, but not before conceiving a child by the corpse. Incest and necrophilia were as nothing to the amorous Egyptian gods.

Safely buried, Osiris now arose from the grave to train his son Horus for the punishment of Seth. After a terrific struggle, in which Seth lost his testicles and Horus an eye, Horus emerged triumphant.

It was a pivotal moment in the history of the Egyptian gods, the triumph of good over evil.

As the site of the principal tomb of Osiris, Abydos was a place of particular sanctity for the ancient Egyptians. Everyone wished to be buried there, or at least to set up a cenotaph on hallowed ground. After death, the deceased journeyed to Abydos to begin the process of resurrection. It is these metaphorical journeys that one sees on the walls of their tombs: the dead sailing the river in search of a promise.

60

Abydos lies to the west of El Balyana on the edge of the desert. The Temple of Seti, its principal monument, rose beyond the fields like a grey ship with shabby bits of Egyptian village clinging to the outer walls like barnacles.

The temple is a magnificent building, with some of the finest reliefs in Egypt. Out of the hard glare of the open courts we passed into cool, columned halls which offered the same inviting refuge as the palm groves along the banks of the river.

The gloom was cut by long thin shafts of light falling between the columns from ventilation holes in the high ceiling. They struck the stone floor in points of pure whiteness. Figures moving through the dark halls flickered like ghosts as they passed through these moments of light.

One vast hall of columns gave on to another as the temple rose in long slow ramps towards the inner sanctuaries: seven chapels dedicated to seven gods. They are high narrow rooms, their walls covered with reliefs depicting the rites appropriate to them. One of the rooms, the Osiris chapel, leads through to a further suite of rooms, dedicated to the Osirian cult. It is here that the sacred mysteries of Osiris's resurrection were celebrated.

In the gloom, temple attendants were sweeping. The dust they raised filled the room. Vertical shafts of light, full of dust, stood against the darkness like solid white columns. But when we plunged our hands into them, the dust-filled light ran through our fingers like water.

61

We went to Dendera in a carriage along a road lined with dusty trees. Wandering around the ruins of its outlying buildings, we found the rough foundations of a sanatorium. In the small cells the insane had waited on stone beds for the divinely inspired dreams which they believed would offer prescriptions for their cure. At one end were basins for water-cures. Patients were immersed in water from the Nile which had been poured over divine statues inscribed with magical spells.

The main building at Dendera is the Temple of Hathor. It is Ptolemaic and is rare amongst the buildings of ancient Egypt for being architecturally intact. It dates from the last years of Egyptian independence and was still being built during the lifetime of Christ.

The temple illustrates the animal fetishism that lies at the dark roots of Egyptian religion and which it never really outgrew. Hathor is depicted either as a beautiful young woman or as a rather sad cow. Sometimes she appears as a strange hybrid of the two: a woman's face with long cow's ears.

In the last century, before the Suez Canal was cut, when the Indian Army passed Dendera on their march from the Red Sea to Alexandria, the sepoys identified the figures of Hathor with Shiva's bull, Nandi, and much to the surprise of their British officers, worshipped in the columned halls of the temple.

A breeze passed between the columns of the Hypostyle Hall. High above us an elongated Nut stretched across the ceiling and swallowed the sun. Gods and goddesses sailed through the celestial oceans of stars scattered across her tunic.

The ceilings of the inner sanctuaries told another story. They had been colonized by bats, whose black dung crunched beneath our feet. In the furthest and most sacred rooms the smell was so intense it was difficult to breathe. Thousands of bats squirmed hideously on the ceilings. They had taken possession of the abodes of the gods.

62

We were sitting on a column base in the Hypostyle Hall reading when the first figure appeared. I did not see him come in but looked up to find him standing suddenly between two columns. He was dressed in white: white shorts, a white T-shirt which did not quite cover an enormous stomach, and a white floppy hat with a white handkerchief covering the back of his neck. Over his mouth and nose was a white mask of the sort that the Japanese wear in the streets of Tokyo.

He came well-equipped. He wore headphones and a yellow battery pack strapped to his arm. A camera hung from his neck, a small shiny backpack from his shoulders, and a plastic water bottle from his belt. He looked in that first moment like a spaceman who had landed suddenly and unexpectedly on a strange planet.

He stood for a moment between the columns, staring into the gloom. Then he moved on, stepping carefully in his heavy boots as if the floor might have been sown with mines. As he passed out of sight behind a column another strange figure appeared from the direction in which he had come.

She was short and fat. She wore a matching top and shorts of turquoise towelling stretched to breaking-point. She too was loaded with heavy equipment and wore a white mask.

'Elmer,' she whispered, peering through the columns. Then she plodded out of sight in his wake.

She was followed by another, and then another, and then many. They filed into the temple, a stream of garish colour and silly hats and bare white flesh. Most wore white masks and all of them bristled with equipment: fly whisks, cameras, binoculars, Walkmans, water bottles.

'Bus number two this way,' a guide called. They gaped at the massive columns and passed on. A few stragglers pointed cameras, and flash guns popped in the darkness.

We were curious about the masks, and asked a matron in a pink jumpsuit and a pair of bat-wing spectacles about them.

'Well, it seems I'm allergic to all the dust in the air over here. We're in Egypt for a whole *week*, you know.'

A row of masked faces went by. No one, it seemed, wanted to be left out of the allergy. And then, as suddenly as they had appeared, they vanished.

I remembered reading a quotation attributed to Hermes Trismegistus, a Ptolemaic deity linked with Thoth, the god of wisdom. It was a prophecy:

> There will be a time when ... all holy reverence for the gods will vanish and be made of no effect ... Egypt will be abandoned, and the land which was the home of worship will be stripped of the presence of the deities and left bare. Foreigners will fill this region and the land; and there will be not only a neglect of devotions but, what is harder, religion, piety, and divine worship ... Then this most holy land, the abode of shrines and temples, will be most full of graves and of dead men.

63

On the train to Luxor we witnessed an arrest. Just before it left Qena three policemen boarded. The first was a young officer with a well-cut uniform and a shiny vain face. In his wake were two older men in crumpled uniforms, unshaven clumsy fellows, carrying their rifles gingerly as if they feared they might go off unexpectedly. Their badges were pinned to their uniforms with safety pins.

The young officer advanced on the ticket collector at the end of the carriage.

'We are searching the train,' he announced. 'Do not let anyone off.'

The ticket collector shrugged, and the policeman passed up and down the carriages questioning passengers.

Just before Qift, they arrested a sheep. The young officer got down from the train and went into the station building. His subordinates followed, carrying the captive in a wicker cage. They put it down in a strip of shade and stood to attention on either side with their rifles.

The sheep gazed through the bars at the departing train with a look of woolly innocence.

64

In the old days Luxor and Aswan were favourite winter haunts of a wealthy and leisured class of Europeans. They came for the climate, the charm of the river, and the antiquities. Archaeological discoveries in the latter half of the nineteenth-century had caused a considerable stir in Europe. European newspapers avidly followed the adventures of antiquarians and treasure-hunters in distant lands, as workmen back home wrestled crated colossi from the temples of the Nile through the entrance halls of the British Museum and the Louvre.

The nineteenth-century tourists came upriver from Cairo in the new Thomas Cook steamers or, more grandly, in privately hired *dahabeeyahs*. They stayed in the splendid hotels of the era – the Old Winter Palace at Luxor, the Cataract at Aswan. They hired dragomans to escort them round the tombs and temples in the shade of parasols. They played croquet and bridge, had picnics in the Valley of the Kings, exchanged visiting cards and arranged dinner parties. In the evenings they rode out in carriages to see Karnak by moonlight. It was a pleasing interlude in privileged lives to which the alien shabbiness of the town beyond the hotel gardens, and the very remoteness of the place on the edge of the civilized world, added a whiff of adventure and glamour.

Luxor and Aswan still draw tourists up the Nile, but times have changed and standards have slipped. Their hotels are likely to be one of the faceless cement blocks which have sprouted in both towns. Their stay is far from leisurely. They are *doing* Egypt, and they are in a hurry.

The chief redeeming feature of tourism is that it adheres strictly to preordained patterns. In Egypt one will encounter tourists in Cairo, Luxor and Aswan, and occasionally in Alexandria. The rest of the country escapes their notice.

Luxor, next to Karnak and across the river from the Valley of the Kings, suffers most. In the winter season the town is awash with tourists. Their contact with the local population is largely commercial, and the agent of that exchange is the tout. Between them, the tourist and the tout manage to capture most of the worst elements of their respective cultures. They deserve each other.

We were fortunate to be in Luxor in mid-summer when the heat makes it off-season. The drivers of the polished and ornamented barouches which stood idle beneath the trees smoked and gossiped in the depths of the leather seats, and we were the only guests in our hotel.

65

Our hotel overlooked the Temple of Luxor and the river. After the more spartan conditions of the past two months, it seemed the height of luxury. There was a writing table and an adjoining bathroom, and clean sheets arrived each morning. For this, we had tourism to thank.

In the evenings from our balcony we watched the setting sun slant through the columns of the Temple of Luxor and lay a golden radial across the floor of the main court. Beyond, the river was a polished blue and the feluccas glided across it like pink-winged swans. Beyond the river were the ancient faces of the Theban Hills.

We grew very fond of the Temple of Luxor which we saw from our window in every mood of light. Visitors in the nineteenth century found its columned halls crowded with mean hovels, the slums of Luxor. Now cleared, it has a unity and humanity of scale not found at Karnak, its more famous neighbour. Its statuary is delightful. A smoothly sensual colossus of one of the Ramses guards a doorway. The face is serene, and almost smug. In the corner of one of the courts a small figure of Queen Nefertari is depicted standing by the feet of a colossus. On the column next to it a Greek tourist, visiting the temple over 2,000 years ago, carved the figure of Paris as a huntsman, a compliment to her beauty.

Karnak on the other hand is vast; the site could accommodate ten European cathedrals. The ruined columned halls seem endless. It is astonishing but lifeless, a parody of the worst of Egyptian architectural excess.

66

We spent a week in Luxor. To avoid the heat of the day we went out in the mornings, waking while it was still dark. By the time we had dressed the first grey light of the day had appeared at the window. In the streets the shops were closed and shuttered. The bicycle hire man, struggling with his lock, talked of Winston Churchill. He was a great admirer of Churchill, and remembered the cigars with particular affection. We pedalled off on our bicycles to a *ful* stall in the souk where the smell of the beans filled the street and the bread was still warm from the bakery.

The early mornings at Luxor were misty. The river was white, and on the ferry in mid-stream, it seemed we were adrift in a cloud. On the west bank we pushed the bikes up a steep slope and cycled along a long straight road towards the desert and the tombs past green canals, lines of heavy trees and slumbering houses. We passed the Colossi of Memnon in a stony field, their shins covered with the graffiti of Greek and Roman tourists. Long tails of mist were curling out of ditches and melting in the sunlight. Ahead of us, the Theban Hills, flushed pink in the early sun, looked creased and worn.

The Theban necropolis, which includes almost 400 tombs and a handful of major temples, lay scattered across a sloping swath of desert between the cultivation and the hills. The village of Gourna, a disparate sprinkling of houses, shared the dry slopes. Its inhabitants have lived off the dead for millennia, first as tomb robbers and then as tomb guardians. There are those who believe that their houses are built over tombs, unknown to archaeologists, and that the owners still supplement their incomes by selling off the contents bit by bit on the black market. Certainly it is the only Egyptian village I know where the houses are placed so far apart.

We had one social engagement during the week, with Sheikh Ahmed, one of the guards at the Temple of Medinet Habu. He was a friend of a friend, and gave us a warm welcome and invited us to lunch. His daughters emerged shyly one by one from the rear of the house to greet us as we ate our meal, each more beautiful than the last.

'They are looking for husbands,' Sheikh Ahmed said. 'In the village there are no good husbands. Take them to England with you,' he said casually, picking lamb out of his teeth. For a dizzy moment, I pictured myself at home in London surrounded by an entire harem of these dark-eyed beauties. Then Melinda kindly guided me outside into the harsh sunlight of the street.

At the Ramesseum, we met another old friend: Ozymandias who inspired Shelley's poem, known to more careful historians as Ramses II. His colossal statue lies toppled at the entrance to one of the courts of the temple. It was one of the largest free-standing statues in Egypt, 17.5 metres high. The index finger alone is a metre long. Diodorus thought the statue magnificent. It is a fine piece, and retains a remarkable delicacy for all its size. But unfortunately it has fallen face down and Shelley's 'shattered visage' is now pressed to the 'lone and level sands'.

67

The royal tombs in the Valley of the Kings concern themselves exclusively with the rituals required for a successful passage through the Underworld.

We left our bicycles at Deir el-Bahari and climbed the mountain track to the valley. Below us the broad terraces of Hatshepsut's temple were set into the curving amphitheatre of the cliffs. From the top we had a wide view of the valley with its bands of colour:

the blue of the river dotted with white sails, the green fields on either side, and the enclosing tan-coloured deserts. It had a striking symmetry, from dust to dust. Beneath us kites turned high above the temple.

We picked our way across the broken mountain heights. The air was rarefied and invigorating and one almost forgot the heat. For a time we could see nothing but high endless desert. Then the Valley of the Kings opened at our feet, a wide bowl. We slid down a steep path past a lonely long-eared donkey who snuffled at our backs.

Round the floor of the valley are set the entrances to the tombs. They are all variations on a basic pattern: long passageways descending underground to a series of antechambers and finally to the burial chamber itself. The walls are lined with paintings depicting the Pharaoh engaged in the rituals which facilitated his passage to resurrection.

The journey to the Elysian fields of the next world, so closely modelled on the world of the Nile, was undertaken at night. The deceased sailed along a river whose banks were crowded with mythical creatures and enemies of Re, the god of the sun. The illustrations and quotations from religious texts which line the walls are a kind of map, enabling the soul to navigate these treacherous currents and overcome the pitfalls and creatures which might impede his passage.

Royal barques, hawk- and ram-headed gods, rising suns, scarab beetles, crowd one upon another. The dark passageways of the tombs have been transformed into an ordered progress where the terrors of death have been subdued and banished. The whole is orchestrated towards the moment of resurrection, with the rising sun, in the domain of Osiris.

In their tomb portrayals the deceased are always seen as young and fit, the image of eternal youth. The Pharaoh is met by the lissom naked figure of Nut who takes his wrist gently and leads him forward to his tomb. Behind him is the god Horus who guides his elbow while patting him lightly on the shoulder. The dead king seems mesmerized by them as they lead him gently but determinedly down the long ramps.

Vultures fly down the ceilings into the depths of the tombs. Osiris presses an *ankh*, the symbol of life, to the lips of the dead king.

Fantastic creatures stalk the riverbanks. Blue vaults are painted with yellow stars, the constellations bright and distinct. In the depths of the night, in the presence of Osiris, the sins of the deceased heart are weighed against a feather. A dreadful creature, with the body of a hippopotamus and the head of a crocodile, strains forward to devour those unfortunates who fail the judgement.

But it is not the fear of this judgement which so pervades the tombs; careful preparation and knowledge of the proper formulae were all that were required. The horror of the tombs is a thing unspoken: the fear of total annihilation from memory. It crept in amongst the ordered ranks of hieroglyphics in a simple line of graffiti, scrawled in French, on the hull of one of the royal barques: 'You must not forget me.'

68

The tombs in the Valley of the Kings all date from the New Kingdom. Their occupants, who had seen the pyramids of the Old Kingdom looted and defiled, were paranoid about tomb robbers and took elaborate precautions against them. Their tombs, in a remote valley, were unmarked. Their design included hidden doors and false burial chambers. But in the end it was all in vain. Only Tutankhamun's tomb survived intact.

In the twenty-first dynasty the situation in Egypt had become so unstable that the Theban priests became seriously concerned about their royal charges. In secret, they removed the mummies from their tombs and hid them, some in the tomb of Amenhotep II, thought to be more secure, others in a cleft in the rocks high above Deir el-Bahari. There they remained until they were discovered in the late nineteenth century.

In the 1930s the royal mummies were taken to the Egyptian Museum in Cairo. Amenhotep, who had been found with a garland of flowers still round his neck, went by train, first-class sleeper, where he was given the top bunk. Others went by river steamer. As the dead pharaohs sailed downstream the fellahin appeared on the banks lamenting, the women crying and tearing their hair. The archaeologists accompanying the mummies remarked on the way these scenes echoed the mourning scenes in the tombs themselves.

But the archaeologists' obsession with the past had blinded them to the real cause of the lamentations they witnessed along the river. The annual floods had been low for some years, and conditions in the villages were very bad. Many people were dying from hunger.

69

In Luxor we hired a felucca with two crewmen to take us the 120 miles by river to Aswan. The journey took four days.

We left on a windless morning, and for a time the town seemed impossible to shake off. Hugging the bank we laboriously rowed and poled our way past the endless stone quays of riverside hotels and the flanks of cruise ships.

Our captain was Mahmud, a lad of 17, short and stocky with a face flattened like a boxer's. He had been working the river between Luxor and Aswan since he was 12. His crewman was his older brother, Ahmed. He had just finished three years of national service. He had been posted to the police in Asyut and had hated his time there.

'The police in Asyut,' he said darkly, 'are very bad men.'

A few miles upstream from Luxor we moored beneath a high bank. The two lads poured with sweat and our sail hung limply from its yard.

'We'll wait for a barge,' Mahmud said.

We spent the long afternoon reading and dozing beneath the boat's awning. About five o'clock we were roused by the distant thudding of an engine. A few moments later a barge hove into view. We hurriedly pushed off and rowed out into mid-stream. Mahmud waved his shirt and the barge cut its engines for a moment for us to come alongside.

When we were secured, we went aboard the barge to meet its captain. He sat cross-legged on his bench in front of the wheel, a piratical figure with an Errol Flyn moustache, a fancy turban which trailed down over one shoulder, brightly dark eyes and a flashing smile. His two crewmen were ancient decrepit fellows who hovered at his shoulder like ragged parrots. The captain spoke in a smooth torrent of words, ending each sentence with his wonderful smile. He was a man of the most terrible charm. With a wave of his hand he ordered chairs brought for us, and tea.

He was from Minya, and we told him of our stay in the town.

'Minya.' He glowed. 'I am from Minya. My mother is from Minya. My grandfather is from Minya. We are people of Minya.'

'And you,' he went on, 'you must be "the Foreigners Who Travel on Barges".' He had already heard of us on the river grapevine, about our journey upriver with Muhammad and Milhaez and Romany. He asked us where we were from.

'England.' He laughed heartily at this. 'England with the crazy Eden. How is the crazy Eden?'

'He is dead.'

'Ah,' he nodded with his wicked smile, 'this is good. This is good news. All Egypt will be happy to hear of the death of the crazy Eden.'

The sun set and a swollen orange moon rose through the tousled heads of palm trees. The captain lit a long cigarette and ordered more tea.

'Tell me,' he said, 'do you have a river and barges in England?'

At midnight we cut loose from the barge, and dropped astern. The orange rectangle of light from its engine room grew rapidly smaller and smaller on the wide river. We drifted ashore and the bow whispered on to sand.

When I woke once in the night I could feel the north wind blowing softly on my cheek, and knew we would have good sailing the next day.

In the morning the wind was up and we set off immediately. By mid-morning we had reached Esna, where there is a barrage. We walked into the town while our felucca waited its turn at the lock. It was a dusty, dreary place.

Flaubert, on his way up the Nile in 1850, found Esna much enlivened by the presence of *ulmeh*, literally 'learned women', prostitutes who had been banished from Cairo by Muhammad Ali some years before. Flaubert went to the house of Kuchuk Hanem, a famous Cairene courtesan reduced to eking out a living in this provincial backwater.

Brothels, Flaubert wrote, are 'a meeting place of so many elements – lust, bitterness, complete absence of human contact, muscular frenzy, the clink of gold ... One learns so many things in a brothel, and feels such sadness, and dreams so longingly of love.'

Kuchuk Hanem danced 'The Bee' for which the musicians were blindfolded. She was 'a tall splendid creature ... her skin is slightly coffee-coloured. When she bends, her flesh ripples into bronze ridges. Her eyes are dark and enormous, her eyebrows black, her nostrils open and wide; heavy shoulders, full apple-shaped breasts ... On her right arm is tattooed a line of blue writing.'

He spent the night. The *coups*, he wrote, were good, 'the third especially was ferocious, and the last tender ...' He lay awake much of the night in an intense reverie. When he slept, he entwined his fingers in her necklace as if to hold her should she awaken.

He loved the bittersweet aura of it all, the mixture of ecstasy and debasement that he felt lay at the paradoxical heart of life.

'How flattering it would be to one's pride if at the moment of leaving you were sure that you left a memory behind, that she would think of you more than the others.' But he knew this to be a delusion. Years later he wrote to his mistress that while he wove an aesthetic about Kuchuk Hanem he knew that he had vanished completely from *her* memory. 'Travel makes one modest. One sees what a tiny place one occupies in the world.'

71

The gods of Egypt were great travellers, and great lovers. Their journeys, from the stuffy confines of their temples, often had romantic motives. Each year the goddess Hathor came upriver from Dendera to Edfu for a conjugal visit with Horus. Happily she chose these occasions to appear in the form of a young woman rather than her more usual guise of a cow. Reliefs show the divine lovers sailing out to greet each other at this 'Feast of the Beautiful Meeting'. They spent every night together between the new and the full moon.

The temple at Edfu, which we reached on the morning of the third day, was dedicated to Horus, for this was the spot where he was said to have vanquished Seth, and thus to have established the ascendancy of good over evil, This is never a convincing concept, and the reliefs display the struggle and its happy outcome with an adamancy that seems to betray doubt. The pharaoh of the day is nobly shown as Horus's second. Seth appears in the form of a hippopotamus.

The inner sanctuary at Edfu was flooded with a green watery light. In a further room, Horus's Chamber of Victory, we found a huge sailing barque, a replica of the kind used to convey the statue of Horus to his assignation with Hathor. It loomed out of the darkness like a sunken ship.

72

We sailed on after sunset. In the darkness we passed through the defile of Gebel Silsila where the river narrows dramatically to a width of no more than a few yards. The moon was not yet up and in the darkness we could only just make out the rock face of the west bank above us, a cliff some thirty feet high. The east bank appeared to be the same. The wide and leisurely Nile, constant for over 600 miles, had contracted suddenly to a dark gorge.

Between the high walls of the banks was an eerie silence. Though the wind appeared to have died we were still carried gently forward.

After hundreds of miles of open river, the gorge seemed unreal. In the darkness we could hardly be sure what we were seeing. Peering into the night we could just discern the gaping portals of tombs in the rock faces.

Eventually we emerged from the defile, and the river widened again. The low, flat banks seemed deserted. After a time we came upon three moored feluccas, with only their masts visible against the sky. A group of men huddled round a fire, silhouetted against the orange flames.

Beyond the moored boats and the fire we drew up on the bank for the night. The men from the fire walked over to us. They were Nubians, tall and dark-skinned with elegant gallibayas and long turbans. They greeted us formally and elegantly, in a manner that suggested we were their guests.

The tallest of the tall Nubians spoke to Mahmud, enquiring about us, the foreigners. When Melinda answered him in fluent Arabic, they all looked at her as if they had seen a ghost, bade us good-night, and melted away into the darkness again.

73

With every day the riverbanks became more tenuous. We had left the endless reliable fields of Middle Egypt behind. A fresh north wind was carrying us into another Nile where the desert pressed close upon the riverbanks.

At Gebel Serag the cultivation on the east bank disappeared altogether and the desert came down to the river, leaving only the railway line and a few scrubby bushes clinging to the water's edge. Sandpipers stalked the dunes above the river in disciplined hunting parties. Herons abounded on the desert bank, rising awkwardly out of the reeds as we approached and flapping heavily away.

On the fourth day we passed the Temple of Kom Ombo perched heroically on a promontory above the river. Like Edfu and Dendera, Kom Ombo dates from the Ptolemaic period, the last spasm of ancient Egypt when a Hellenized dynasty ruled the country from

Alexandria. There is more than a hint of classical Greece in the architecture, and the blue river seen through the sand-coloured columns gives it a Mediterranean freshness. On one corner of the site the river had eaten into the bank and pulled part of the masonry of an out-building down into the current where it lay half-submerged, growing gardens of weeds.

Beyond Kom Ombo the mighty west bank, miles wide in Middle Egypt, shrank to a line of palm trees which tossed their heads and leaned towards the south. The great escarpments of the east bank had fallen away, leaving only distant reaches of desert sky. We saw few people, and when they appeared they were taller and darker than Egyptians to the north. They seldom waved or called to us, responding only when we greeted them with a most unEgyptian reserve. The dark children, swimming from the banks, stopped their play to watch us pass in shy silence.

We felt a long way from the Mediterranean. We were sailing into Africa.

74

We moored in the early evening against a low grassy bank which rose to a wood of tamarisk trees. Beneath the trees were paths of white dust. The evening smelt of dung fires.

Mahmud bathed from the stern of the boat and then went off through the trees to buy some food from a nearby village. The wind had fallen away and the evening was spread out across the river, still, languid, suffused with golden light. On the far bank white oxen were coming down to the water.

Ahmed sat in the stern looking at the river. Throughout the journey he had seemed withdrawn and preoccupied. To make conversation now, we asked him about Asyut.

'*Mish kwiss,*' he said. 'Not good.' He had said this before. It was not unusual. Egyptians usually spoke badly of anywhere other than their own village and district.

'You didn't make any friends there?' we asked.

He shook his head. He seemed depressed and we wanted to cheer him up. On the far side of the river the oxen stared down at their reflections in the orange shallows.

'It must be an easy life, a policeman. What do you do? Stand on the street corners and watch the cars?'

He shook his head, looking at the river.

'Not like that,' he said. 'It is not like that. Asyut is a very bad place. There is much trouble there.'

'What sort of trouble?'

'There is fighting.'

'Who is fighting?'

'Students. They fight with each other and with the police and the army.'

'Were you in the fighting?'

He nodded. He sat in the stern, half-turned away from us so we saw only the side of his face. The length of the boat was between us. I wanted to hear about the riots in Asyut and found myself leaning forward, anxious that he should not clam up. He said nothing for a time.

'The fighting was very bad,' he said after a time. His voice was higher and his shoulders had risen.

'What did you see? What was it like?' I asked.

He sat looking at the river with his shoulders hunched up. The sun had set and the colours were all draining away. On the far bank the oxen had become ghostly.

'Was there much shooting?' we asked after a while.

'Yes,' he said. 'There was a great deal of shooting. They gave us ammunition for the guns, and many people were shot.'

'Where was that?'

'In the streets. Near the railway station.'

'How did it happen? The shooting.'

'They came up the streets towards the station, crowds of people, young men. They had banners and they were shouting.' He needed no prompting now, and he spoke with a rush of relief. 'There were many of them, hundreds, coming up the street towards us shouting. The officers ordered us to draw our guns on them. We thought they would stop, with the guns drawn, but they kept coming, shouting. Then the shooting began. We were all shooting at the

99

crowds, as if the guns were not loaded, and only meant to frighten them. The front row of people seemed to trip and fall. Then the crowds were running, and the ones who had fallen did not get up.'

His voice was strange. The darkening river made it sound hollow.

'They made us carry the injured into the station. There was blood everywhere. When the hospital people came they shouted at us too, and called us dogs.'

I suddenly realized he was crying. He stared at the river with his shoulders shaking and his hands clasped tightly in his lap. Tears ran down his face.

We sat in silence. The tears were entirely unexpected. Nothing in our four days on the felucca with this sullen boy had prepared us for this, as nothing could have prepared him for that afternoon in Asyut. He was a country innocent from a world of dust lanes and riverside villages. The events of Asyut seemed to belong to another world.

'*Maleesh*,' I said at last. 'Never mind.' It seemed wholly inadequate but it was what Egyptians said in the face of any crisis. *Maleesh. Maleesh.* The words were a kind of balm.

He nodded, his face turned away from us.

Later, when the boys had gone below deck to sleep we sat in the bow and trailed our hands in the warm water.

'The stream mysterious glides beneath,' Melinda quoted, 'green as a dream and deep as death.'

'What is that from?' I asked.

'I can't remember. I've had it on my mind all week.'

75

Early legends, blithely ignoring the further river, often located the well-springs of the Nile at Aswan. Immediately above the town lay the barrier of the First Cataract, and for millennia Aswan was the boundary of Pharaonic Egypt and the known world. Beyond it lay Nubia, and beyond that the Land of Punt, an almost legendary region which the Egyptians penetrated only briefly in the imperial years of the New Kingdom. Right down to the middle of the nineteenth century travellers to Aswan felt they had reached the limits of civilization.

Today it is even more emphatically the end of Egypt. A few miles upstream is the High Dam. Behind it lies Lake Nasser, which stretches to the borders of Sudan, and beyond, covering all of what was once Egyptian Nubia.

Aswan has none of the melancholy transience of most end-of-the-line towns. It is a delightful and civilized place and nowhere in all Egypt is the Nile in more picturesque form. It threads through the town, full of islands and reflections and white-sailed feluccas, between banks of smooth red granite and yellow sand. The river breezes fan the town, and in the evenings the tree-lined Corniche is one of the finest promenades in the world. It is no wonder that the former Aga Khan, with the whole world to choose from, spent his winters at Aswan and chose to be buried there.

Opposite the town, high up in a sandy ridge, lie the Tombs of the Nobles, ancient Egyptian border officials and governors of Aswan. Most date from the Old and Middle Kingdoms, and were already ancient when the first tomb shafts were sunk at Thebes. The inhabitants of these tombs were some of the earliest explorers of the upper reaches of the Nile. Inscriptions refer to expeditions upriver into the Land of Punt, the Sudan. Harkhuf, a governor, lists the treasures he brought home: incense, ebony and leopard-skins. On his fourth journey, he seems to have reached equatorial Africa, perhaps even the sources of the river. He returned, he reports, 'with a dancing dwarf . . . from the land of spirits', probably a pygmy.

In one of the tombs we peered through a dark gap and saw a broken mummy lying exposed at the bottom of a shaft. It was in two pieces, both black, as if they had been thrown up charred from the fires of hell. For ancient Egyptians the careful preservation of the deceased and his tomb ensured success in the after-life. But no one succeeded in escaping the tomb robbers. The Nile was one long cemetery of desecrated tombs, and Egypt, for the followers of Osiris, a land of restless and tormented souls.

The construction of the High Dam just above Aswan in the 1960s created a vast reservoir to regulate the flow of the Nile, and to lift forever from Egypt the threat of flood or drought. The result was Lake Nasser, 250 miles long, covering almost a fifth of the Egyptian Nile, and stretching some 70 miles into Sudan.

At the time the world's attention was caught by the drowning of the antiquities along this stretch of river, and the heroic efforts made to save temples like Abu Simbel. The plight of the many thousands of displaced Nubians seemed to go almost unnoticed. Most were resettled in government housing in the Kom Ombo basin downstream of Aswan. Traditional Nubian society was torn up by its roots. But it is not just population displacement that has made the High Dam at Aswan such a controversial issue.

For thousands of years Egyptian agriculture was dependent on the annual flooding of the river. Drought in Ethiopia and Sudan often meant famine in Egypt. The dam has broken this threat. It has secured and increased the supply of water. Two crops a year are now taken rather than one, and extensive desert reclamation schemes are underway. It seemed the only salvation for a country with a burgeoning population and limited arable land, wholly dependent upon irrigation.

But Egypt has paid a heavy price for its hubris. The annual flooding replenished the soil with silt. Now Egypt is dependent upon imported fertilizers which drain foreign currency reserves. Fishermen blame falling catches on the dam, and the loss of the silt has accelerated the river's flow. It has begun to erode the banks which it built up over millennia. Some military strategists see the lake as Egypt's sword of Damocles. Should an enemy ever bomb the High Dam, Egypt would be washed into the sea by the very waters which have created it.

The bleak shores of the lake remain uninhabited. For years there has been talk of building a road and railway along the shore to link Aswan with Wadi Halfa, the first town inside Sudan. But nothing has come of it, and the only way to reach Wadi Halfa from Aswan is by a regular boat service that plies the lake.

In the afternoons in Aswan we collected our post and wrote letters home. We wrapped packages of film and journals and sent them to Cairo and to England. Sudan did not have the facilities of Egypt and we would be out of touch for at least six weeks, until we reached Khartoum.

In the evenings we would stroll along the Corniche and have dinner at a riverside restaurant where we could watch the feluccas passing through the reflections of the lights on Elephantine Island. The knowledge that we would not see restaurants or hotels for some time gave a poignancy to our days in Aswan. On our last night a new crescent moon arose above the town. It was the Muslim New Year.

After dinner we went back to our hotel and threw open the shutters to cool the room. On the balcony we spread out our maps. They showed the Sudan huge and blank, and the river curving through empty spaces.

The idea of the Sudan had followed us up the Nile like a rumour. Suddenly here in Aswan, we realized it was well-founded: incredible but true. We were leaving in the morning.

BOOK II
SUDAN

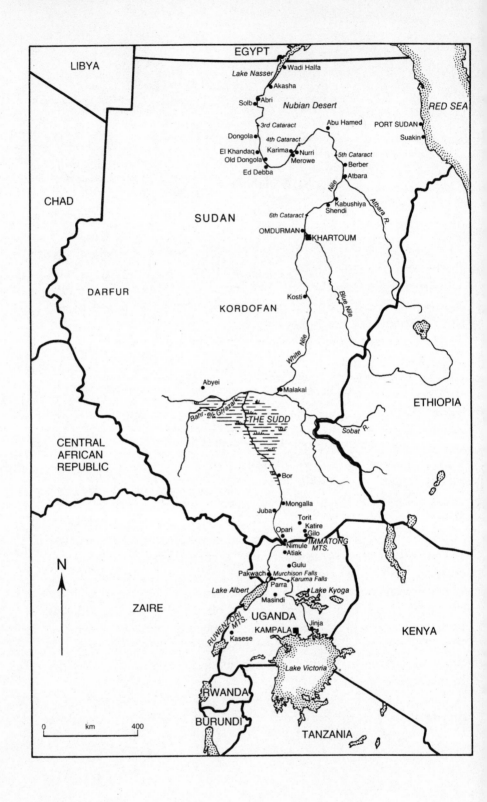

1

The boat left from a quay near the High Dam. Rattling through the broken no man's land between the town and the dam, the dark windows of the train showed only our own reflections. After a time it stopped. We cupped our hands against the window and peered out. We could see nothing.

'Do you want the boat?' a man across the aisle asked us.

'Yes.'

'This is it. Quickly. The train does not stop long.'

We threw our bags down into the darkness, and climbed after them. Almost immediately the train jerked and moved off. We found ourselves in the middle of nowhere. We could see neither station nor buildings.

At some distance was a cluster of lights. We made towards them, picking our way over a welter of tracks. Eventually we came upon an empty railway shed with a paved road and a line of street lamps along one side. Between the shed and the road were rows of white tents and a miscellaneous assortment of huts and gas-lit stalls. Encamped on the ground around them, behind high walls of baggage, were a couple of hundred people, mainly Sudanese.

Music wailed from the stalls, and the smell of onions and *ful* filled the air. The soft drinks sellers tapped out rhythms on the sides of their coolers with bottle-openers, keeping up an incessant chant of Peps, Peps, Peps, although Pepsi was the one drink that none of them had. A warm wind blew newspapers between the stalls like heavy erratic birds.

Along the broken kerb of the road stood a line of taxis, their drivers dozing in the back seats with their legs dangling out of the

107

open doors. In one direction the road disappeared into the darkness, presumably towards Aswan. In the other it ran a few hundred yards to a high chain-link fence with a locked gate, and then on to another distant cluster of lights, the harbour buildings. Beyond lay the lake, invisible in the darkness.

We turned back to the sprawling baggage, so profuse and various it seemed organic, mushrooming in the rich compost of arrivals and departures. The great mounds were the trappings of lives not just of journeys. They overwhelmed their poor owners and gave them the air of refugees, caught between the darkness and the high wire fence.

At about 1 a.m. word passed through the encampment that we would not be boarding until the morning. We carried our own humble bags across the road, and lay down to sleep on a gravel slope in the lee of a hut.

2

In the morning we could see the lake. It lay below us, still and blue, between bleak desert hills. The dam lay off to our right, a low gravel embankment. It seemed far too insignificant to be holding back a lake large enough to stretch from London to the Scottish borders.

We waited all morning. As the sun climbed higher, people moved into the narrowing band of shade along the wall of the railway shed, and when that shrank to nothing, they stretched sheets between the walls of baggage and crawled beneath them.

In the early afternoon the gate finally opened, and the crowd arose as one and began loading each other with boxes and sacks. The baggage was on the move.

The boat was a modern German vessel with fittings so basic it looked unfinished. Nearby was moored an old wooden riverboat, one of two such boats which until recently had served the run between Aswan and Wadi Halfa. The previous year fire had broken out on its mate which sank with great loss of life. The remaining boat was taken out of service for fear of a repeat disaster, and new German boats were ordered.

'Everyone died,' a man next to us said. 'Three hundred and thirty people. The unlucky ones who didn't drown were eaten by crocodiles in the water, and by scorpions and snakes if they reached the shore.'

We were travelling steerage and had secured a place on a bench on a port deck. From a deck above us, a row of anonymous bare feet dangled. All about us our fellow passengers were camped amidst their prodigious baggage. On the open deck in the stern, between life-jackets and coiled mooring ropes, prayer mats were laid out and men came and went throughout the day to pray towards the eastern shore. The Sudanese were already proving far more devout than the Egyptians.

Our neighbour looked out across the lake. The barren shores were tinged with the red of Aswan granite.

'So many people in Nubia said they would rather die than move. But when the time came, they all moved. What choice did they have? The flood was coming.'

3

In the night the shores of the lake were dark. This was the Empty Quarter of the Nile.

The night was cold. A myriad of green long-legged insects danced crazily around a light which shone all night above our heads. In a fitful sleep I dreamt I was swimming through drowned villages. Palm trees waved like underwater weeds. I swam through houses where the sodden relics of habitation floated in the middle of rooms, a child's shoe, a disintegrating book, a scrap of carpet, its red dye still leaking into the green water. At one house the door was jammed and when I pushed against it a body floated up weightlessly. Then more bodies appeared, drowned children with bleached faces, their long hair brushing hideously across my face. I woke with a start to find one of the green insects fluttering on my cheek.

In the morning we passed Abu Simbel. The seated statues stared unblinking into the sun, their hands laid rather primly on their knees. At this hour the stone was amber-coloured. From the lake the temple looked smaller than I had expected, and terribly neat, like a life-size model of the real thing. It was saved from the flood by being cut into blocks and moved piece by piece to higher ground. Some say they left its soul behind.

At midday, we were standing in the stern when a voice hailed us from an upper deck. We looked up to see an old man in a flapping gallibaya pointing to the eastern shore.

'*Hawaga*,' he called, 'Wadi Halfa.'

He was pointing to a completely barren shore.

Binoculars revealed a low quay against the dark sand, and off to one side figures standing about on a bare slope with piles of baggage. There were no buildings, no trees, nothing.

We dropped anchor offshore, and passengers and baggage were off-loaded on to a barge. The quay, which acted as the customs shed, was three rusting barges lashed together and covered with a roof of corrugated iron. We walked down an unsteady plank into the Sudan: a desert plain, dotted with scrub, stretching away to steep hills which rose from the sand like islands from a sea. Away to the left was a small encampment of black nomad tents, their side flaps hoisted to catch the afternoon breezes.

Wadi Halfa lay a few miles inland. A collection of jeeps and small Toyota pick-ups waited to ferry the arriving passengers to the town. Standing in the back of one of the pick-ups as it sped across the hard sand, with the dust spiralling out behind us across the vast plain, it seemed that a whole new world was opening up. The air smelt differently, and the feeling of space was overwhelming. It felt like Africa. The sedentary instincts that we had begun to feel in Aswan were swept away in the wind.

4

Old Wadi Halfa had been a delightful riverside town full of palm trees and fine houses. It had a population of 11,000 people. It lies now beneath the waters of the lake, about ten miles out from the shore. Its inhabitants, with the inhabitants of all the drowned villages of Sudanese Nubia, were transported to Khashm el-Girba, east of Khartoum, almost 600 miles away.

A few people remained to take up lives in the new Wadi Halfa, a bleak tenuous place which sprang up where the railway line from Khartoum comes to an apparently arbitrary end against a low wall of sleepers. There are no streets and no trees. The plain-faced buildings sit in the desert like tents, and straggling flocks of goats wander among them searching for scraps.

The bleakness of the place was exacerbated by the heat. From eleven in the morning until four in the afternoon nothing stirred. We were there in September when the daytime temperatures never fell below 100°F, and at midday were closer to 110°. We longed for the arrival of autumn, but began to doubt that such a season existed in Sudan. We were to wait another six weeks before the fierce summer heat showed any sign of breaking.

The buildings of Halfa all face north to avoid the worst of the sun and to catch the northerly breezes. In the souk were dim shops which sold batteries and bottles of scent and boxes of safety pins. The tea-houses were poor places with earthen floors and blackened walls, and the fruit and vegetable sellers, squatting beneath awnings, were all specialists who sold only one kind of produce each. They arranged them on the sand – lemons or onions or oranges – in careful little piles and sold them for so much a pile. The prices were fantastic, far higher than in Egypt. Sudan was a land of scarcity where fresh vegetables, and much else, were luxuries.

Of tailors, Halfa had no shortage. There seemed to be scores of them in the town. In the mornings they worked outside in the streets on their ancient pedal machines, raising a loud chorus of whirring. At midday they retreated into the cool darkness of their shops. They worked only in white, for unlike the Egyptians, Sudanese men wore only white gallibayas and pantaloons. The women made up for this restraint. In the streets, over their house clothes, they wore splendid full-length wraps, called tōbs, of the most startling colours and patterns.

At one end of the town was a bank where we went on our first day to change some money. It was a big dusty room with a wide counter. The clerk looked at us uneasily, torn between his duty and his better instincts. He glanced over his shoulder then leaned towards us.

'Do not change money here,' he whispered. 'Go to the shops. They will give you a much better black-market rate.'

5

We stayed in a hotel near the railway station, a humble place of three adjoining courtyards. The hotel was blue. The floors of the rooms were covered with cracked blue and white tiles, the walls were a pale blue wash flaking on to the sand and the doors a bright sea blue. In the centre of each courtyard were large earthenware water jugs which sweated gently in the breeze under the shade of thatched canopies. They were replenished each evening with barrels of muddy water brought from the lake on donkey carts.

We ventured out only in the mornings and the evenings when the sun was low and the shadows of the tall robed figures stretched to impossible lengths across the sands. The afternoons we passed in the hotel courtyard where we ate, read, played cards, and slept like cats in a paradise of shade, northerly breezes and birdsong, while the town outside baked.

The terrific heat of northern Sudan is the inspiration for the peripatetic bed. Life in a Sudanese hotel revolves around the court-yard and the bed, usually a light metal cot with a thin mattress. The room is of no consequence. It is unfurnished and used only to store your baggage.

During the day the bed is moved into the shade of the arcades around the courtyard where you sit or lie upon it outside your door, and catch whatever breeze is going. In the evening the beds move out from under the arcades into the courtyard itself where you spend the night sleeping under the stars with your fellow guests. In the morning the beds return to the gentle shade of the arcades.

What this arrangement lacks in privacy it gains in congeniality.

112

Friendships quickly develop as guests help each other carry their beds back and forth.

We shared our courtyard with a large colony of sparrows, who resided in two stunted trees, and a company of merchants from Berber. The merchants were a cheerful but rather mysterious lot. In answer to our enquiries they said they were waiting for goods coming from Egypt to receive customs clearance. We thought we detected more than a hint of irony in this answer, and we suspected that they were smugglers. They dressed well and were seemingly unconcerned about their long wait in what was not Halfa's cheapest hotel. Like everyone else they spent their days lounging in the arcades of the courtyards. In the mornings we would see them in the souk holding hands with strange men.

The merchants were devout Muslims and their prayers in the patchy shade of the two courtyard trees, prefaced by elaborate washing, punctuated the day. They were dismissive, however, of President Numeri and his introduction of Sharia, Islamic law, which demanded the amputation of the hands of thieves and forbade all alcohol under threat of public flogging.

'You must not worry about these laws,' they said. 'They apply only in Khartoum. Here in Wadi Halfa, in Dongola, in Berber, everywhere else, these laws do not matter.'

In the evenings the merchants invited us to join them as they sat chatting on their cots in the middle of the courtyard. Gas lanterns at their feet threw deep shadows across their faces. The oldest reminded us of the barge captain. Next to him were two brothers, tall beautiful men with liquid eyes and graceful hands. Opposite them was a small elfin fellow who wore a shiny blue waistcoat over his gallibaya.

The merchants were handing round a five-litre plastic jug of the kind normally used to carry petrol. Each drank from it in turn. They handed it to us, and waited for our response. It was *seiko*, a clear spirit made from dates which tasted rather like home-made grappa without the subtlety.

I blew through my lips as if I was breathing fire.

'Very good,' I said.

They laughed and clapped me on the back and handed the container round the circle again.

'If you throw it up in the air,' the elfin one said, 'it will evaporate before it reaches the ground. But we will not try it. It is a sin to waste the gifts of Allah.'

Later the men began to sing for us, sitting forward on the edge of their cots. The songs were slow and melodic. They sang very softly, at times almost whispering the words. The songs were about love and loss, aspiration and disappointment, but the men smiled as they sang, as if the melodies and the sheer pleasure of singing overcame the tragedy of the words.

6

Wadi Halfa was a town of transients, waiting on the boat to Egypt or the train to Khartoum. Both appeared about twice a week. They were meant to coincide so that travellers would have a smooth connection, but they rarely did, and the tea-houses and cheap hotels of Halfa were swollen with travellers who invariably had to wait for days.

We became regulars at a tea stall in the open desert between our hotel and the souk which served the delicious spiced and milky Sudanese tea. There were no tables and one sat on the sand to eat. At night the stall was lit with gas lanterns and the sands beyond their uncertain light were crowded with shadowy figures eating and drinking. In spite of the sacrifice it had made for the High Dam at Aswan, whose turbines generated megawatts of electrical power, Wadi Halfa still had no electricity.

The owner of the stall reminisced about old Wadi Halfa where his father had owned a big tea-house on the Corniche. It had been a most beautiful place, he said, before the flood. 'There were fine buildings all along the river, a long avenue of palm trees, perfectly straight, beautiful mosques and many beautiful houses. Not like here.' He gestured towards the darkness beyond the circle of light. 'You could have stayed in the Nile Hotel. All the rooms looked over the gardens which ran right down to the river. The flood took

114

everything. The last part of old Halfa to disappear was the minaret of the Tawfikia mosque.'

7

Fifty thousand Sudanese lost their homes to the rising waters of Lake Nasser. Twenty-seven villages, as well as the town of Wadi Halfa, were submerged. The administrator in charge of compensation and resettlement was Hassan Dafalla, an intelligent and sensitive man who managed a difficult task with considerable skill. He was one of the last people to leave the old town of Wadi Halfa after its inhabitants had been transported south, and he has left a chilling account of the empty town's last days.

The deluge began on the first day of September 1963. Dafalla woke to find the railway station yard covered with water, and half a mile of track submerged. In the early afternoon the river breached its bank opposite the Tawfikia mosque and invaded part of the market. Later in the afternoon the embankment at El Geiger was overwhelmed and water surrounded the Ismaili mosque.

The following day the entire market area was submerged, and the shops, built of mud-brick, melted like biscuits, leaving islands of rubble in a brown lake. The hospital was encircled and parts of it began to collapse. Water rushed across the road to the Nile Hotel, carrying scorpions and reptiles into the drowning rooms.

In the evening Dafalla found the waters were seeping into the gardens of his own house. Shrubs, which had been dying from lack of water since the supply had been cut off, were suddenly green and straight again in a brief moment of health before the rising waters overwhelmed them. Rats living in the storerooms of his house emerged from their holes, carrying their young in their teeth, and ran to higher ground.

That night, worried about the water entering his house as he slept, he left the edge of his bedsheet dangling on the ground so that the water would awaken him. In the morning he found the Nile had reached his garden parapet. Soon only the groves of palm trees,

115

the waters rising up their trunks, showed where the houses had stood.

I was reminded of Isidora whose mummy we had seen at Tuna el-Gebel and of a recurring paradox, destruction by the forces of creation. The further we went up the Nile, the more the river seemed to express some awful ambivalence.

8

In the deserts of northern Sudan the Nile describes a huge S-curve. At Abu Hamed the river turns back on itself and runs south-west for some 200 miles before it turns again and reasserts its northerly course. It is a considerable diversion. Following the river, it is almost 1,000 miles from Wadi Halfa to Khartoum while as the crow flies it is less than 500. The railway, built by Kitchener in 1897 as part of the reconquest of the Sudan, takes the shorter route and cuts across the desert. The much longer route along the river, which we chose to follow, has neither a railway nor any proper roads.

The first leg of our journey was to Abri, a village on the river almost 100 miles to the south. The only means of transport was by truck. We tracked down the drivers in the tea-houses of the souk. They were vague about dates of departure, and only shrugged and said *bad bokra*, a phrase which literally means 'the day after tomorrow' but is generally understood to imply something rather more indefinite.

The drivers' uncertainty was due in part to the vagaries of the train from Khartoum, on which half the town seemed to be waiting. The trucks would leave only after the train had arrived.

We searched out the station master at the station.

'When is the next train arriving from Khartoum?' we asked.

'Probably on Monday,' he replied. He was a morose man hunting flies in a stuffy office beyond a grille.

'What time on Monday?' we asked.

'In the morning,' he said, bringing his slipper down on his desk with a crash. 'If not in the morning, then in the afternoon.'

116

It did not let him down. Late on Monday afternoon the long owlish hoot of the train whistle was heard throughout the town. We stood outside the hotel and watched for it. It appeared, coming across the desert, as a long trail of dust.

It was dark by the time the arriving passengers began to fan out through the town in search of lodgings. Many came to our hotel, arriving on donkey-cart taxis laden with baggage. They emerged out of the darkness into the gas-light of the doorway like ghouls, their black faces powdered white with the dust of their journey.

9

Sudan is Africa's largest country with an area of almost a million square miles, ten times the size of Great Britain. It is also one of the continent's least populated, with just over 20 million people. But a final statistic captures even more eloquently the nature of the country: in all its million square miles, there are only a thousand miles of paved roads.

On the rough tracks which criss-cross the vast distances of Sudan, lorries are the only reliable means of conveyance. They carry both cargo and people; the two travel under much the same conditions, and are generally indistinguishable by journey's end. The interiors of the cabs, which represent a kind of first-class, are decorated like seraglios with floral upholstery, tasselled curtains, quotations from the Koran and heavily retouched photographs of Sudanese pop singers. But sadly they are small, and there is room for only two or three passengers beside the driver; everyone else travels steerage in the open back of the lorry. Heaven only knows what kind of pull is required to secure a seat in the cab, probably direct descent from the Mahdi at the very least.

The morning after the arrival of the train, we found a lorry in the souk preparing to leave for Abri. We climbed into the back, already full of people perched atop a deep pile of cargo, and squeezed into a rear corner, hoping there was no one else to come. This proved naïve. A never-ending stream of people kept climbing over the sides and lowering themselves and their tremendous baggage into the sea of bodies. It was becoming increasingly difficult to move.

When at last the influx appeared to have slowed to a trickle, the engine was started. At this signal, another fifteen men climbed over the sides and squeezed in. The crush was appalling. There were over sixty people in the back of the lorry. Twenty would have been crowded.

Despite the conditions the journey began in jaunty mood. Bumping along the rough track out of the town towards the range of red hills to the south, everyone joked and laughed like children on a school outing. The rows of young men perched atop the slatted sides sang snatches of song which no one could hear above the noise of the engine.

The track turned and twisted through the desert hills. The town was soon lost from view but the lake appeared off to our right. After a time we dropped down from the hills on to a flat gravel plain where the track ran straight as a drawn line.

The route to Abri took us across the western edge of the Nubian desert, known as the Batn el-Hagar, the Belly of Stones. It is an uninhabited and notoriously hostile desert, which has contributed as much as the Nile's cataracts to the historical isolation of Sudan.

We crossed contorted ranges of hills between the empty plains, the lorry thumping over rocks and labouring in its low gears. Occasionally I saw birds, huge buzzards, squatting on rock outcrops, and once a small antelope, far off across an expanse of stones. The sky was huge, and as pale as porcelain. The sun seared down on us through the thin air, and when we slowed and turned our own cloud of dust enveloped us. The lake had long since disappeared from view.

10

'I am living in fear of my internal organs,' said the man pressed between my shoulder blades. I turned my head. Like myself, he was clinging to the side of the lorry like a shipwreck victim. Between the fearsome jolts he released one hand from the lorry and clutched his side in pain.

The lorry bumped and shuddered mercilessly through the rutted desert tracks. At the back we took the worst of it. The battering was violent and continual. Time and again the bumps lifted us off our feet. Crowded against the other passengers and against the sides of the lorry it was impossible to cushion the landings. As we pounded up and down, sharp stitches developed in our sides.

The only relief was occasional stretches of soft sand in which the lorry was in danger of getting stuck. We went slowly through them in low gear, rolling like a ship in a heavy sea, our rigging of ropes, which lashed all the bags in place, creaking loudly. A tense silence fell on the passengers as they peered over the sides. But our driver was expert and we always emerged safely.

The continual jolting and the cramped conditions made for unexpected hazards. Thrown high into the air by one bump, one of our closer neighbours, a young man in a gallibaya, lost control of his bowels. The result was deposited on one of Melinda's shirts which was draped over my camera bag at my feet. It was a narrow escape. A moment before Melinda herself had been sitting on the bag.

We stopped twice at primitive tea-houses, the only buildings we saw in over eighty miles of desert. Both were run by wizened old men who passed their days listening for the distant whine of approaching lorries. When they heard one, they put the kettle on.

The first tea-house was a low straw hut; the second occupied a corner of an abandoned building by a well. We huddled in its dark ruinous rooms sipping bitter tea while gusts of sand blew in at the doorways. A row of men were praying in the shade of the lorry. I spotted the incontinent Nubian slinking off into the desert to squat behind a hill.

At Akasha we reached the river again. We rose over the shoulder of a hill, and suddenly it was there beneath us, looking glorious with the afternoon light sparkling on its rippled surface. We had not seen the Nile proper since Aswan, only the lake. Here at Akasha it was its old self again. After the desolation of the Batn el-Hagar and the physical exhaustion of the lorry ride from Wadi Halfa, I felt almost tearful at the sight of it.

119

We stopped by an empty building and disentangled ourselves from each other. The men from the lorry picked their way through a graveyard of broken stones to pray at a sheikh's white-domed tomb, while we made our way across a wide flood plain of gravel and cracked mud to the river.

We washed on the bank. The water was brown and fast-moving, spilling over a bed of white gravel. The river turned through a wide bend and we could see no other habitation either upstream or down. There was a thrilling emptiness about the place. On both banks steep hills were darkening with the sunset. The light in mid-river was silver, and the current stronger than any we had seen in Egypt. Only a few miles upstream was the Dal Cataract.

The water felt silken on our hot cheeks. We sat entranced on the riverbank, until we heard the hoot of the lorry's horn signalling our departure.

11

We left Akasha as the sun was setting beyond the hills on the far bank of the river, and travelled another four hours in darkness. We were never far from the river now and our route alternated between the straggling hamlets along its banks and the stretches of desert further inland.

The last hours of the journey were torture. The constant pounding of the lorry had left me dazed and exhausted. The stitches in my sides stabbed with pain at every jolt. Melinda had long since been called forward to join a group of women sitting near the front on soft sacks of flour. I clung to the sides of the lorry in one of the rear corners, between the incontinent Nubian and the man with the fearful internal organs, where I was thrown about like a rag doll. I fell into a kind of pained trance from which I was eventually rescued by voices shouting at me to get down.

We had reached Abri. The journey, just over 100 miles, had taken twelve hours.

The other passengers melted away towards palm groves and

1. Twilight at Akasha, the Nile in the Nubian Desert

2. (ABOVE) City of the Dead, Cairo   3. (BELOW) An Egyptian gentleman, Luxor

4. Adrift in Middle Egypt, the barge pilot and the author

5. Melinda on the train to Kabushiya

6. (OPPOSITE) The furthest extent of Egyptian influence, Meroe, Northern Sudan

8. (ABOVE) A dervish, Omdurman

7. (LEFT) Nubian architecture, Abri

9. (OVERLEAF) Storm clouds over the source of the Nile, Lake Victoria

houses. We passed down a dark lane between low buildings, and found the river at the end. There seemed to be no one about. We washed and lay down to sleep on the bank. Two boys passed in the moonlight. One carried a stringed instrument like a lute. They sat down a little apart from us and began to play, serenading us with gentle tunes. To these lullabies, we fell asleep.

12

The morning was bright and calm. We woke to the familiar sound of voices on the riverbank, elongated and hollow. It was a sound we had not heard since our journey on the felucca to Aswan. The river was slate blue and as wide as anywhere in Egypt. On the beach beneath us a group of men in white gallibayas were unloading sacks of dates from a boat on to a donkey cart. The river lured their voices out across its surface and returned them disembodied.

We went in search of breakfast. The main square of Abri, set back a little from the river, was a wide expanse of sand imprinted with donkey hooves. In one corner was a splendid shade tree, as wide as it was tall, beneath which a group of men gossiped. There were a couple of shops which sold even less than the shops of Wadi Halfa, and a tea-house full of wood smoke. Round a corner was a *ful* shop, a humble place of rough wooden benches set out on an earthen floor.

We had hoped that Abri might expand our diet. But, like those at Wadi Halfa, the eating houses sold only *ful*, a dish which consisted of cooked beans occasionally enlivened by raw onions. We ate *ful* for breakfast, lunch, and dinner, and began to reconcile ourselves to the fact that we would have little else until we reached Khartoum.

In the *ful* shop we met Muhammed Salih, the boatman who had been unloading dates on the riverbank. He was a small, elfish man with two long buck teeth. When he smiled, they emerged from his upper lip like a conjuring trick. We asked about Amara, an ancient site on the far bank of the river, and he agreed to take us there in his boat.

At the boat we met Muhammed's crewman, a tall gangling fellow with an oblong face. At the mention of Amara, he nodded feverishly and leapt aboard.

'He is a lunatic,' Muhammed Salih said simply. 'A good man and a very good boat man, but sometimes they must come and take him away in handcuffs.'

We pushed off. The lunatic took the tiller and chatted amiably to himself. Muhammed Salih crouched in the bottom of the boat and began to tear up pieces of rag which he stuffed with a knife into the cracks between the planks of the hull where the boat was leaking.

He was intrigued to hear that we were from London. He had heard of London.

'A very rich city I believe,' he said. 'There must be many date trees, and mangoes and guavas and bananas and oranges.'

On this fine morning adrift on the Nubian Nile, it was impossible to disillusion him.

13

The ruins of Amara are known locally as Abu Chinesa, Father of the Church, in the mistaken belief that they are Christian remains. Nubia was a Christian kingdom for almost a thousand years from the middle of the sixth century. It is remarkable that the Islamic conversion of Egypt in the seventh century took so long to penetrate up the Nile, and more remarkable that Christianity has vanished so entirely from northern Sudan in the space of 400 years. In Egypt the Copts remain as a substantial reminder of Christian ascendancy some thirteen centuries after its demise. In northern Sudan it is as if the Christian kingdom never existed.

Amara is an ancient Egyptian site. It dates from the imperial days of the nineteenth dynasty in the New Kingdom. Among the ruins is a temple built by Ramses II.

Muhammed Salih had moored the felucca short of the site, and the lunatic, who knew the ruins well, now led us across the desert. He was a scarecrow figure with his short gallibaya flapping about his knees. It was midday, and the sun bore down like a heavy weight.

The desert has engulfed Amara. Nothing remains but a low mound littered with pot sherds. The sand had drifted to expose the foundations of a few walls, the shafts of two or three columns, a length of cornice and a floral capital.

The two old men were fascinated by the place. They crossed back and forth over the mound recreating a town, here the houses, over there a road, here the church. It became a game and they competed with one another to conjure buildings from the broken and half-buried stones. Their interest in the place seemed to increase as ours waned. The heat felt like treacle, and the sun drilled into our skulls.

At the river I stripped off my shirt and trousers and dove in. The sensation of the cool water closing over my baking head was one of indescribable ecstasy. I wanted to bury myself in the river, in its cool dark depths. The water enclosed me, and I felt a delightful sense of surrender. I wondered if this was what it felt like to drown, if at the last moments the fatal waters felt like cool and friendly hands.

14

In Nubia it was the season of weddings.

Muhammed Salih invited us to a wedding on Arnata Island. The fact that he was only a guest himself did not seem to matter. We moored against a shelf of cracked mud where we were welcomed ashore by a small boy in a brown smock who shook our hands as formally as if he was there in an official capacity.

Arnata was a paradise of shade beneath a high canopy of date palms. At midday it seemed deserted. Insects droned in the stillness and goats nosed through the dust. The air smelt of straw. The houses were set apart between yellowing fields of corn and durra and walled orchards of apricot trees. With their high windowless walls and painted crenellations, they looked like small forts. Between the trees you could see the muddy blue of the river and the hard shadowless light falling on Abri on the far bank.

We had lunch in a house with a large courtyard where a circle of dates, dark against the swept sand, were drying in the sun. In a cool, bare reception room, we were joined by two young men, Daud and Fayek. They were cousins. Daud was a darkly handsome fellow with flashing white teeth, a student of agricultural science at an Egyptian university, home on holiday for the wedding. Fayek lived in Abri. He had a sensitive face with a slightly wounded expression, and sucked his moustache with his lower lip. Both were in a state of excitement about the wedding. It was a rare opportunity for contact with young unmarried women.

'There is no way to meet them,' Daud said. 'You see them at a distance. You see them all your life. They are your neighbours. But you cannot meet them. To stop and speak with a girl alone is thought very bad.'

We chatted about weddings. Sudanese weddings are elaborate affairs. In the old days the celebrations lasted for forty days. But ritual everywhere is in retreat, and three days is now thought sufficient.

They enquired about weddings in Europe. The white dress and the elaborate cake pleased them but our description of the reception was a disappointment. They were entirely disbelieving when we told them that the prospective groom did not have to reach any financial settlement with the bride's family.

In Sudan the groom is obliged to pay a bride-price to the bride's father, as well as bestowing an agreed standard of material wealth upon the bride herself. In recent years the bride-price had suffered from terrible inflation. It was a subject which regularly cropped up in conversation with young Sudanese men.

'You have to be very rich to be married in Sudan today,' Daud said. 'The wedding itself costs a great deal. And you must pay the bride's father three, four, five thousand Sudanese pounds. It is too much. Before long a wife will cost as much as a lorry.'

The inflation of the bride-price was an imported phenomenon. It came from Saudi Arabia and the Gulf States where more and more Sudanese men went to work for wages which were unheard of in Sudan. They returned to their villages to marry with sums of money far beyond the means of their brothers at home. The result was that many Sudanese men, who did not have the opportunity to work abroad, had to save fifteen or twenty years before they could contemplate marriage. It was the cause of much bitterness.

'It is no longer the man who is important,' Fayek said, 'only the amount of money.'

Both Daud and Fayek shook their heads in disgust, but one could see already that their own fortunes would be quite different. Daud, with his qualifications, would go abroad. Fayek, without such opportunities, would spend the rest of his life in Abri, much of it saving for the distant prospect of marriage.

Later in the afternoon we went to call on the groom. Tonight was his wedding party, which the bride would not attend. She would hold her own celebrations the following night.

We found the groom in a neighbouring house with a group of friends in attendance. He was having henna applied to his hands and feet. He sat on the edge of a bed with his feet propped up on two chairs, their soles covered with a mass of sticky red paste. His arms were extended and he clutched the henna mixture in his closed fists. He appeared to be confined in invisible stocks.

The groom had a weak and anxious face and he looked sheepishly up at us, unable to rise or to shake our hands. His elder brother, a customs officer from Port Sudan, came forward to greet us. Their father was dead and he was the head of the family. He had a proprietorial air about the proceedings which indicated he was paying for them.

'I have come home for three weeks' holiday,' he announced. 'And I have decided it was time my brother was married.'

The brother smiled foolishly at us. He was well cast as the bridegroom of jokes, a nervous frightened figure, alarmed by his impending appointment with the world of woman.

15

In the evenings a huge meal was served for all the guests in an open space between the palm groves. The men and women sat in separate groups.

After speeches, the dancing began. A generator started up and neon strips blossomed in the trees. There were three musicians: a singer, a drummer who played a light drum which he carried beneath his arm, and a man who played a stringed instrument whose strings were stretched across a triangular frame. They played standing beneath the trees on the edge of the open ground.

A row of young men soon formed, including Daud who proved to be a fine dancer. They danced in unison, shoulder to shoulder, clapping their hands and stamping their feet in time to the music, swaying back and forth. The row became a curve, the men clapped and swayed, and the dust rose from beneath the hems of their gallibayas. Their dance was like the music, strident and flamboyant.

After a time a few women came forward to dance. They came two or three at a time and shuffled about self-consciously within the men's long curve, hardly dancing at all, just moving their feet in the dust. They came and went without regard to the music, turning their backs suddenly and walking away to where the women all sat together in a loud group beneath one of the trees. When one trio left it was immediately replaced by another, as hesitant as its predecessor.

With the arrival of the women, the men's dance became more aggressive. On the strong down-beats of the drum the line of men now surged forward with a kind of leap, stopping a foot or two from the women, then retreating slowly to their original line, bent forward from the waist and clapping their hands above their heads.

The women seemed to take no notice of them but stared at the ground as if they were looking for something in the dust. The male dancers circled them like birds of prey with great white wings.

The groom provided the evening's comic relief, turning up as regularly as a circus clown, never failing to get a rise out of his audience. He had the gloomy face of all great clowns, his hang-dog eyes at odds with the foolish grin. At intervals he went walkabout through the crowds. A ritual accompanied each appearance. As he approached one of the small knots of men or the larger groups of seated women, he held a short carved stick above his head and shook it at them as if threatening them with it. The men responded by raising their arms and clicking their fingers over his head, and the

126

women by breaking into high-pitched ululations. Everyone enjoyed these mysterious rituals inordinately.

The dancing went on unabated. At some point Daud appeared at my elbow, wide-eyed and dishevelled, his teeth gleaming in the shadows. He looked over towards the women chattering beneath the trees. Melinda, in their midst, had been brought another child to hold.

'There are no beautiful women in Sudan,' he said.

I was so surprised by his assertion that it was a moment before I protested.

'No, no,' he said. 'They are ugly. They are too dark. Not beautiful like European women.'

He smelt of perfume, and something stronger, date liquor.

'Do you know Egyptian women?' he asked.

'In what sense?' I asked. It turned out to be the biblical sense.

'They like sex very much,' he said. 'Especially with Sudanese students,' he added, flashing his teeth.

He hurried back to the dancing, joining the end of the line, his head bare, his turban flung over his shoulder like a long scarf. Clouds of dust hung like a mist about the dancers beneath the trees, curling up around the neon lights. The row of men surged forward and back, forward and back, their eyes on the women. It was a chance to observe them openly. On the curve of a girl's neck or the line of her cheek, whole lives would turn.

16

The absent bride, in her father's house, was no doubt listening to the distant music as well. We knew nothing about her except that she was 16. The groom was 30.

Though her entire upbringing will have been directed towards marriage, she will have played little part in choosing her husband. The match will have been arranged for her by her family, perhaps years ago. She and her fiancé will know each other only as acquaintances; they may never have had any opportunity to speak privately with one another. Though marriage is the crucial event of her life, it is thought seemly for her to affect unhappiness about it. As the wedding approached she will have stopped eating, and will appear morose.

The bride will have been prepared for her wedding by older female relations. For some weeks she will have been taking smoke baths by sitting over smoking and scented embers. Her hands and feet will have been decorated with intricate henna patterns; her body massaged and oiled with a traditional blend of perfumes; and all her body hair removed so that she is as smooth as a child before puberty.

The marriage contract will be officially sealed when a holy man recites the opening lines of the Koran. The contract is between the two families and neither the bride nor the groom will be present at its signing. While this ceremony is taking place seven women will go down to the riverbank with a bowl of food. They will eat a little of it, and then throw the rest into the river for the angels. Then they will return with the bowl full of Nile water with which they will wash the bride's face.

After the contract is sealed there will be more festivities and dancing. In the evening the bride will dance for her husband and he will lift her dress to cut the thongs of her underdress.

The concept of female modesty is so strict in Sudan that the new bride is expected to resist her husband's first sexual advances. The marriage will be consummated only when he overcomes her defences and takes her by force. But the pantomime of resistance may well be more real than mock, due to the particularly brutal form of female circumcision practised in Sudan.

Circumcision of girls is widespread through a band of countries right across the centre of Africa, and up into Egypt. The forms vary considerably from the removal of the hood of the clitoris to the excision of the whole clitoris and parts of the labia. In Sudan they practise what the Sudanese call 'Pharaonic Circumcision'. This is a severe form of excision and infibulation which involves the removal of the external genitalia, the outer and inner lips of the labia as well as the clitoris, and the sewing up of the sexual orifice leaving only a small opening for urination and menstrual flow. On the wedding night the opening has often to be enlarged with a razor or a knife.

128

Though the practice has been illegal for many years, the law has had no impact on custom. It is thought that over 80 per cent of Sudanese girls still suffer infibulation. In rural areas of the Arab north, like Abri, this figure is more likely to be 100 per cent. An uncircumcised woman is thought ugly and unclean. Circumcision and particularly infibulation are meant to ensure virginity and chastity. The belief that it has religious origins is consistently disputed by Islamic scholars who point out that the custom is nowhere sanctioned by Islam, that it predates Muhammad and that it is practised by non-Muslims as well as Muslims.

The irony of female circumcision is that it is perpetrated and maintained by women. Men play no direct part in it, and are largely ignorant of the anatomical details and their implications. It is women who carry out the operation and who are most resistant to arguments against it.

17

We found Fayek's 80-year-old father Amin in a room above the courtyard of his house in Abri where the windows were open to the northerly breezes from the river. He had soft full lips, beautifully smooth cheeks and watery eyes with whites the colour of tea. His hair, white and brittle, grew in a startled fringe around a polished bald crown.

Amin greeted us in English. He had worked in Egypt for years with English people, and though he faltered at first, the language slowly came back to him. He was going deaf, and I sat with him on a cot, speaking loudly into his good ear. He was overjoyed to be speaking English again.

He had been born on Arnata. His father had died when he was a child and his mother, who was Egyptian, had taken him to Egypt. There he had learnt English and French and had worked in a foreign shipping company. He had loved Alexandria. It was then a city of Europeans, he said, so beautiful and clean. Not like Cairo, a filthy place. The Egyptians, he sighed, are not a tidy people.

The Second World War had disrupted the shipping business, and Amin had lost his job. One day, walking in Alexandria, a stray bullet had just missed him, hitting the wall behind him. It was probably fired, accidentally, by a drunken soldier. But he took it as an omen. His mother was dead so he decided to go back to his father's people in Sudan. He was 33.

In the date groves of Abri he had realized how much he had missed the country of his childhood. 'I left Sudan as a boy of ten,' he said. 'But always in Cairo, in Alexandria, I was talking of Abri and the island, Arnata. Places to the Egyptians which might have been in a fairy tale. I had begun to think they were a fairy tale too. And my own childhood was part of the fairy tale.'

But now, in his old age, he dwelt on reminiscences of Egypt, as if the habit of a lost fairytale land, once acquired, could not be broken. He remembered the harbour at Alexandria, the trams to Abu Qir, and the lighted shops along the Rue Rosetta. He asked about a tea shop in Sharia Sa'ad Zaghoul but we did not know it.

'We always had tea there,' he said. 'On our way home in the evenings. Tea and ...' he searched his mind for the word, 'and pastries. Beautiful pastries.'

18

In the afternoon Abri was suddenly engulfed by a *haboob*, one of the notorious dust-storms of northern Sudan.

We had been out walking along the river with Fayek when the eastern horizon had darkened dramatically. A fierce wind blew up. The sky seemed to sink, and within minutes the storm was upon us.

We started back to Fayek's house. The wind rose to a gale, and we leaned into it to keep our feet. The desert seemed to have lifted and occupied the air. Enveloped in clouds of grit and sand, we could hardly see three paces in front of us. The choked air glowed with an infernal orange light. The world had dissolved into a whirling nightmare.

At the house we found the courtyard so thick with sand that we could not see the far wall. We felt our way up the steps into the main room. There, transfixed by the gale, stood Amin. The shutters banged wildly against the walls, and a bottle of pills was swept off the table and broke at his feet.

The storm subsided as quickly as it had come. Then a remarkable thing happened: it began to rain. Fat drops were falling in the courtyard. The old man stirred, and stumbled down the steps. He stood in the middle of the courtyard with his face uplifted. Raindrops spattered in the dust about him.

We too went out to stand in the rain. It was sparse and fitful and only lasted three or four minutes, but it was the first rain we had seen since coming to Africa six months before.

When it passed Amin stumbled up the steps and sat on a cot.

'In Alexandria it rained every spring,' he said.

His cheeks were wet with raindrops.

19

In the evening we went to another wedding. Sometime after midnight we left Fayek to the dancing and made our way back to the house where we found Amin roaming from room to room like an unquiet ghost. In the main room above the courtyard the radio crackled. It was the BBC Arabic Service.

Amin came up the steps into the room and sat down abruptly on one of the cots. He rubbed his knees, breathing heavily as if he had been exerting himself.

'I have been listening to the radio,' he said, 'the news from London. People are starving.'

'Where?' I asked.

'Here in Sudan,' he said. He shook his head. He was panting, and seemed almost on the verge of tears. 'I remember how it used to be. It was a fine country. The people were happy. We were all happy. Now everything is turning bad. What has happened to us? Everything has gone so wrong. In the south there is war. And now there is not enough food. People are starving. We hear these things not from our own government but from the British radio.'

Sudan was not yet equated in the world's mind with drought and famine. We had not heard any news ourselves and such was Amin's state of agitation that we thought this talk was some delusion of his.

20

We spent another five days in Abri, waiting for a lorry going south. We stayed in a cheap hotel by the river without ever meeting the owner or the manager, or anyone whom we could pay. Most nights we slept outside on the riverbank in a watery moonlight. We took our meals in the *ful* shop. The owner had one of the town's few generators but he complained of the expense of petrol, and invariably we ate our dinner in darkness while the other patrons came and went, bumping against the tables.

In the evenings the square and the lanes of Abri were littered with reclining figures, men stretched out on the ground, enjoying the cool air, chatting with friends. In the darkness one had to pick one's way warily. We were grateful for the white gallibayas. After a time the men would rise, one by one, and make their way homeward. By eight o'clock the village was empty. By nine, it was asleep, except for stray dogs patrolling the darkness and the old man in the bakery kneading the dough for tomorrow's bread, *ayesh* – the word can mean both bread and life in Arabic.

On late-night strolls in the empty streets, we sometimes passed the low door of the bakery. It was a subterranean room, its air white with flour dust. Beyond the old man we could see the fires beneath the stone ovens, the flames leaping in their blackened hearths. Waves of heat wafted up through the doorway into the cooling evening. The old man in his loincloth was bathed in sweat. Twisting and kneading the great balls of dough in his underground chamber, he seemed to be wrestling with some amorphous devil while the village slept.

132

21

The six men prayed in the moonlight, their bottoms turned up towards us, and their heads bowed in the direction of the river, ghostly between the palm trees.

When the prayers were finished we all climbed into their Landrover. They had agreed to give us a lift to Solb, the site of an ancient temple.

They were genial but secretive men. They wore white gallibayas and shiny black shoes, and they all carried black briefcases. They had the air of men engaged upon some mission too serious to speak of, at any rate to foreigners. When we asked them where they were going they replied only 'Towards Dongola.' We had no idea why they were travelling at night.

We sat in the back of the Landrover and suffered the usual battering. The men all held their briefcases across their knees. Between the bumps, the conversation turned to politics. Sudan, they all agreed, was a 'tired' country.

'The government is interested only in its own preservation,' said the man next to me. 'This is what happens when people are in power for too long. They arrive with fine ideals. The problems overwhelm them. And soon they find all their energies are directed towards standing still. To keeping themselves in place.'

'They must keep everyone happy,' another said. 'They must keep the army happy. They must keep the Muslim brothers happy. They must keep the businessmen happy. To keep them all happy, they are bleeding the country.'

'They will not last,' a third man said ominously. 'Trouble is brewing.'

This last comment was followed by a terrific jolt which threw us all against the roof of the car. We landed in each other's laps. For a moment the briefcases were askew.

Beyond the windows the desert was desolate. We came upon a vast camel herd being driven north. We were on a route known as the Forty Days' Road, one of the longest droving tracks in the world. Huge herds were gathered in Darfur and Kordofan in the west of Sudan, and driven to Egypt, to Edfu and Esna, and to Asyut where many would be loaded on to trains to be taken to the big camel market in Cairo.

For a time the night was full of camels, hundreds of them parading out of the darkness. Their leering heads craned forward in the headlights, peering disdainfully at us. An endless stream of undulating legs and flanks moved past the windows. Dust rose like a yellow fog. Finally we saw the herders, mounted on tall caparisoned camels, their faces swathed against the dust. They whistled and yelped warnings to each other, trotting back and forth around the edges of the herd. And then they were gone, camels and herders, as suddenly as they had appeared, leaving a thick pall of hanging dust.

Further on the headlights picked out bones and ravaged carcases. The camel tracks to Egypt were littered with skeletons.

Sometime later the driver stopped the Landrover. Outside all was dark. Solb, one of the men said. We got down, and all the men climbed down after us to stretch their legs. Off to the left against the sky we could see a cluster of columns, and beyond them a line of trees marking the river.

The men drew water from the goatskins hanging on the outside of the car. We all waited our turn for the metal beaker. Evaporation through the porous skin had made the water deliciously cool.

'So you are going to Dongola,' I said.

'In the direction of Dongola,' one of the men replied.

They nodded solemnly in unison.

'We are doing a feasibility study,' another said.

'What are you studying?' I asked.

'The feasibility of road or railway construction through Nubia.'

The men all looked at us as if waiting for our opinion. Being without an opinion, we too nodded solemnly.

'Why do you travel at night?' Melinda asked at last. 'Surely you need to study the landscape to get some idea of the feasibility.'

'It is too hot to travel by day. Besides we know the landscape. It is not feasible. And whatever is feasible cannot be afforded.'

'It is only a study,' another said. 'Of feasibility. The government has no intention of building roads. It is bankrupt. It cannot afford such projects. It can only afford feasibility studies, which they are hoping will keep the Nubians happy.'

'So are the Nubians happy?' I asked.

The men shook their heads. 'They are not happy. They know it is only a feasibility study, and that there is no intention of building anything.'

'So it is better to travel at night for this too,' another said. 'We meet less people. It is difficult for us when they ask so many questions, and do not believe any of the answers.'

The men stood in a half-circle with their briefcases. They were a forlorn lot, passing through Nubia by night, with the guilt of a government they did not support around their necks.

We shook hands, and thanked them for the lift. Then they climbed back into the Landrover and their tail-lights bounced away into the darkness of the empty desert.

We picked our way through a field of boulders and then climbed the huge stone blocks on to the floor of the temple, still warm from the heat of the afternoon sun. We slept in the shadow of a wall, but in the night the moon stole round and found us.

22

Solb was an imperial outpost of the Egyptians. The temple was built by Amenophis III to commemorate his victories over the Nubians. It has survived for over three millennia as a reminder of Egyptian domination of Sudanese affairs.

We woke at dawn to find the columns washed pink with the first light. It was a splendid ruin, with the same fluted columns as the Temple of Luxor. The two temples are contemporaneous, and it seems probable that the craftsmen of Luxor were sent into the wilds of Nubia to plant the flag in mortar and stone.

In the long run Solb was more of an artistic than an imperial triumph. Originally the temple had been guarded by a pair of reclining granite lions. Some centuries later they were removed to Gebel Barkal, and from there they were taken to the British Museum where they still flank the entrance to the Egyptian gallery. When Ruskin saw them, he hailed them as masterpieces.

A herd of black goats passed through the forecourt, their bells tinkling. After the fenced and guarded sites of Egypt, with their busloads of tourists, we were grateful for the untamed and solitary ruins of Sudan which allowed us to be alone with the ancient world.

23

In the nearby village we met an old man wearing two wrist-watches. He explained, without any enquiry from us, that he had found one of the watches, and wore it so that if the owner ever returned he would see it on his wrist and be able to claim it.

We asked him about transportation to Dongola. Someone had told us that there was a weekly bus between Abri and Dongola. But as we were now on the west bank, we would have to re-cross the river to intercept it and we did not know its schedule, or even if it had one.

'There is a bus,' the old man said.

'Where from?'

'From here. Going to Dongola. But it comes only once a week.'

'What day does it come?' we asked.

'Today,' the old man said.

Our hearts rose. 'What time?'

'At seven o'clock.' The old man looked at both his watches. It was eight o'clock. Our hearts sank again.

'But it is always late,' he said. 'Usually it comes about nine.'

24

To our great surprise, the bus was in fact a bus; we had assumed the word to be some gentle euphemism.

A long spiral of dust, like a horizontal tornado, appeared, spinning across the desert. It came to rest on the edge of the village, and when the dust cleared there was a bus, albeit of primitive construction. A long wooden compartment had been bolted on to the chassis of a lorry. Inside were seats and sliding glass windows. Our bags were strapped to a rack on the roof. Dusty goatskins full of water hung along the sides.

Naturally there were drawbacks. We had the last two seats at the very back of the bus. The bumps were no less dramatic than on the lorry and, with a metal roof a couple of feet above our heads, rather more dangerous. A woman opposite us was knocked unconscious somewhere beyond the Third Cataract.

The only other passengers to board the bus at Solb were a young woman and two older companions. A large crowd of women had seen them off, standing tearfully around the bus wiping their eyes on the corners of their tōbs. As the bus started an old woman, presumably the young woman's mother, began to wail.

The young woman had paid no attention to her party of well-wishers but had sat in the bus, while the bags were strapped to the roof, examining her hands. She wore a tōb patterned with ludicrous purple flowers. Her face was huge with a thick jaw and traces of a moustache.

As the journey progressed she took a particular interest in Melinda, coming back to sit and talk with her whenever I got down to stretch my legs at one of the stops. She was going to Khartoum, she explained, because she was ill in the head.

Her minders, the two older women, watched her warily and tried to call her gently back to her seat.

'They are witches,' the young woman said. 'They have kidnapped me and are taking me against my will.'

The two witches, out of earshot, smiled and nodded at Melinda over the backs of the seats.

'In Khartoum there are many witches, all ill in the head.' The young woman leaned forward and whispered in Melinda's ear. 'Some of them are my friends.'

25

In all the villages of Nubia, Dongola was held up as an earthly paradise. In Dongola there was electricity. There were shops, Pepsis

137

and cars. In Dongola, the merchants of Berber had said definitively, there is *kula haga*, everything.

Dongola did not disappoint us. There were Pepsis, but even better, stalls which sold beakers of freshly squeezed iced lemon juice. The market was rich in fruit and we spent our days eating fleshy pink grapefruit and green oranges. In one corner of the market was an open pavilion full of tailors, pedalling their machines like cyclists, and in another a butcher's shed where men in bloody aprons wielded long knives amongst the hanging carcases.

The eating houses allowed us to add dishes of lentils and okra to our diet of *ful*. Once I had a chicken, a wizened and ancient bird whose life, I suspected, had not been easy. In the hour before sunset when the shadows lengthened throughout the town and the heat of the day subsided, the tea-houses all served a delicious spiced coffee in small china cups.

Dongola was located on a side channel of the river. At this season the channel would normally have been full of water, with moored boats knocking along the wall of the Corniche. But this year the river was low, and Dongola's channel was dry, its bed of cracked mud baked as hard as concrete. Boys rode across the channel from the island opposite on thin donkeys, and ibises stalked the lingering pools of water for stranded fish. On the island a man ploughed the banks with a pair of white oxen, and the turned dust blew away behind him.

26

On our first morning in Dongola we were hailed in the main street by a man in a *ful* shop. He left his table and came hurrying out into the road to intercept us, a half-eaten piece of bread in one hand. He was dressed, anonymously, in the regulation white gallibaya. He finished his mouthful of *ful* and asked if we had registered with the police. We had.

'Where have you come from?' he asked suspiciously.

'Abri.'

His eyes narrowed. 'Where are you going?'

'Karima. And then Khartoum.'

He searched his mouth for renegade bits of *ful* and chewed the finds thoughtfully. 'What nationality are you?' he asked.

'British,' we said.

'Have you come from Libya?'

'No. Just from Abri. And before that from Egypt.'

This seemed to disappoint him. 'Israel?' he asked hopefully.

'No.'

He looked about him then leaned towards me conspiratorially and tapped my chest. 'I am a secret man,' he said in English.

I nodded, as if to say that his identity was safe with me.

'I will visit you later at your hotel,' he said, returning to his breakfast.

It was our first encounter with the Sudanese secret police. They were independent of the regular police and the army, and were meant to serve as the government's ears and eyes.

Later in the day the secret man appeared at our hotel door, knocking softly in a kind of Morse code. He came in and sat on the edge of a cot. We lent him a pen and he wrote our heights, under the impression they were our passport numbers, on the back of a cigarette packet.

'We must be vigilant,' he said, closing the door silently behind him.

27

Our hotel was more conventional in form than the hotels of Nubia. There was no courtyard, and the rooms had tall shuttered windows and ceiling fans. Tradition however dies hard, and the guests still carried their cots out of their rooms to sit and lie in the communal passageways.

We shared the hotel with three honeymoon couples who filled

the place with the heavy scent of wedding perfume. The first couple were very young and very happy. The bride, who was ravishingly beautiful, could not have been more than 15. The groom may have been in his early twenties. He was a bashful figure with a shambling adolescent walk. They spent their days and nights closeted in their room from which came gales of hilarity. Occasionally the young man appeared, shuffling down the corridor in a short tunic which revealed his bony knees, to fetch bowls of water from the water cooler for his bride. Her thirst, apparently, was insatiable.

The second couple were older and very unhappy. The groom was a loutish fellow who spent his days eating sunflower seeds and fiddling with a transistor radio on a cot outside their door. Whenever he ventured inside the room, we could hear his bride shouting until he returned to his cot in the passage.

The third couple, whose happiness was not to the exclusion of others, invited us to dinner one evening in their room. The groom, Sadiq, worked in Saudi Arabia and had come home to marry Ipti. They were on their way to Khartoum where she was going to finish her secondary education. She would conceal the fact that she was married. Secondary schools did not take married women, though women traditionally marry very young. Ipti's determination to complete her education received full support from her husband; he hoped that she might go on to university.

Sadiq and Ipti both spoke English, but they loved to hear Melinda's Arabic. Her Egyptian accent sent them into fits of giggles.

'It must be very easy to learn Arabic in Egypt,' Sadiq said. 'All the Egyptians do is talk.'

We discussed the river. Throughout Nubia we had heard people complaining about how low the river was this year. The failure of the rains in Ethiopia had meant that the Blue Nile, which brings down two-thirds of the annual flood, had fallen far short of its usual input. Egypt, with its High Dam, has a buffer to make up for any such shortfall. Sudan has no such advantage. The low river meant that the water was further and further away from the fields it was meant to irrigate.

There was also the problem of erosion. In the region of Dongola, Sadiq told us, the river was shifting its course eastwards. People on the west bank watched the river retreat while those on the east saw their fields slowly being eaten by the current.

'You cannot depend on the river,' Sadiq said. 'It does not give you anything. It only lends it.'

28

Dongola is the terminus for the boats which take advantage of the open river between the Third and Fourth Cataract. A regular service runs between Dongola and Karima, 175 miles upstream. It is one of the few river-boat services left on the Nile. The journey takes four or five days, depending on the state of the current.

The boats leave Dongola once a week. On the appointed day, we had an early breakfast with a rowdy gang of boatmen in a makeshift café on the riverbank. When we went to pay, we were told that one of the boatmen had already paid for us.

The boat did not appear until mid-morning, coming downstream from Karima. It was an ungainly-looking vessel with two double-decker barges lashed on either side. But when it had shed the barges to facilitate the unloading, it emerged as a slim and elegant craft of a kind which had plied the river rather more regularly fifty years ago. Its name was the *Kirbekan*.

It arrived with a cargo of grapefruit, piled in sacks on the lower deck of one of its barges. A team of Africans from the south, barefoot men in ragged shorts, unloaded them. Pouring with sweat in the hot sun, they ran down a gangplank, with the sacks across their bent backs, to heave them on to one of the lorries on the bank. Arab merchants, cool and magisterial in their gallibayas, clutched fat wads of notes, and shouted and bartered theatrically with one another, jockeying for position in the now bullish grapefruit market.

Some of the sacks were faulty, and split open with the rough handling. In this atmosphere of surplus, no one bothered with the strays. Soon there were grapefruit everywhere. They littered the banks. They fell in the river and floated downstream. Children played football with them, and the waiting passengers filled their pockets. One of the Arabs presented us with two heavy bags of them. It was a grapefruit heaven to which everyone was admitted.

We got underway at midday, with the two barges securely lashed to the sides. The *Kirbekan* turned through a wide arc and headed upstream. A group of figures stood waving on the floating dock. Our wake set it pitching like a raft in a high sea, and one of the waving figures tumbled headfirst into the river.

29

The *Kirbekan* was a colonial vessel. She was named after the site of a battle between the British and Mahdist forces during the Gordon Relief Expedition. The outcome had been indecisive, which is presumably why the Sudanese did not bother renaming her after independence in 1956. She had been built on the Clyde and had the leisurely but earnest air of another era.

There were two full decks and an upper forecastle which housed the wheelhouse set forward of a blue funnel shaped like a pillar-box. The upper deck consisted of cabins set back to back which opened on to gangways running the length of the boat on either side. The second-class cabins were furnished with two narrow bunks, a small set of shelves, a fogged mirror and an array of brass hooks. The first-class cabins were better-appointed with wash basins and small chests of drawers. The first-class bathroom boasted a vast antique bath with brass fittings. Only the lack of a plug spoilt its magnificence.

On the lower deck were the boat's offices. The crew's quarters were in the bow, and aft of them was the galley. It was a cramped dark room with an old wood stove. Food and tea were passed through two hatches on either side of the boat. The supply was fitful and seemed to depend on the mood of the cooks, two temperamental old men as thin as famine victims. I courted them assiduously, and always managed to elicit something even when the atmosphere in the galley was at its most difficult.

In the passageways around the galley were bedraggled chickens tethered to pipes. As the journey progressed they disappeared one by one, but mysteriously never reappeared in the food, which was the usual bowls of *ful*. Given their sorry condition, this was probably a blessing.

Aft of the galley was the engine room set below deck, an inferno of heat and noise and diesel fumes. Aft again was the post office. The *Kirbekan* was a post boat, and the villages along the river between Dongola and Karima depended on it. Grilled windows announced their business on brass plates in English: Sale of Stamps, Parcels, Money Orders, etc.

The steerage passengers travelled on the upper decks of the two barges. They brought everything with them – bedding, cooking stoves, food – and camped on rugs spread across the open floor of the deck. The barges were segregated. The starboard barge was the women's barge and the port barge the men's. The women's barge was full of children and colour while the men's was a sombre place. Every mealtime a procession of white-robed men crossed the middle gangway of the *Kirbekan* to the women's barge.

30

There are thirty-five 'stations' or stops between Dongola and Karima. Most of the villages are set back from the river, and nothing on the riverbank marks the 'station'. The captain knows them all from memory.

The arrival of the boat was always a great event, and crowds gathered to watch the rituals of arrival and departure. Many had to run aboard to do business in the post office, and get ashore again before the boat pushed off. Stations were often heralded long before we reached them by the sight of figures in bright tōbs and flapping gallibayas running along the banks to be present at our docking.

For us the boat had a different attraction. Afloat on the river we were removed from the heat and the dust and the traumas of the banks which passed at a picturesque distance. Running in against the bank was always an uneasy moment: the plank being thrown down, people running up and down, voices raised, goods being loaded. One felt the rough hands of the wider world, and it was always a relief when the engines reversed and the river intervened again between us and the banks.

31

The Nile in Sudan is a very quiet river. The emptiness of the country was reflected in the emptiness of the river and its banks. The villages, when they appeared, were spacious. There were no men in fishing boats laying their nets, no barges, no naked boys swimming from the banks. Only occasionally did we see women washing or drawing water, or feluccas ferrying people from one bank to another. There were no high desert bluffs framing the river valley, only a narrow fringe of growth between the water and the flat desert.

In the high banks you could see the gifts of the river, the strata of earth as clearly delineated as the rings of a felled tree. Swallows had made their nests in this soft soil, creating long lines of holes like miniature cliff tombs. As the boat approached they emerged, great clouds of birds rising from the riverbanks.

The banks were steep and given to subsidence. The brown water sucked and tugged at their base, which crumbled and fell piece by piece back into the river from which they had come. Even vegetation did not save them. Huge trees, perched on the edge of the water, had had the earth eaten away from around their roots, leaving them hanging uselessly in mid-air, bleached and skeletal. In places where yellow dunes had broken through to command the banks even the sand could be seen sliding slowly into the Nile.

One afternoon we passed the ruins of Old Dongola, perched on a bluff above the east bank. Once a great city famous for its royal palaces and cathedrals, the capital of the Christian kingdom of Nubia, it was now abandoned as completely as the religion. One Arab historian had likened it to Baghdad. Another wrote of its many churches, fine houses and wide streets. Nothing remains but the shells of a few adobe-brick buildings, sprouting from the sands like tough weeds.

At sunset the starboard side of the boat glowed with orange and pink light. On the port side it was already twilight, with waves of coolness coming off the water and the bank. Later the moon rose above the trees on the east bank, a three-quarters moon rolled over on its back, tipping silver light across the black river.

That night the boat moored after we had retired to our cabin. The low river made navigation tricky, and the captain had decided on caution. From my bunk I could see a mud bank in the moonlight.

Once, when I woke, I could hear a splashing sound, something heavy falling into the river. I listened, and after a time it came again. I got up and went out into the moonlight of the gangway. All was still. Then a clod of earth broke away from the crumbling wall of the bank and fell into the water below. Upstream another fell.

The river was stealing away with its own banks.

32

Karima was full of requiem birds. In the morning they sailed above the souk in ever-decreasing circles, landing heavily on the corrugated roofs of the butcher's shed and the line of shops nearest the river. They were big bedraggled birds, buzzards and vultures, with bald foetal heads. Perched in baleful rows above the eaves, they surveyed the market beneath them with stony eyes.

In the souk the only bargains were cheap Chinese imports – razors and combs, tiny mirrors and torches, toothbrushes and folding scissors. They were packaged in brightly coloured boxes with brand names like Lotus Blossom and White Pigeon. The local produce was the luxury end of the market. Fruit and vegetables were scarce and expensive. We found a vendor with a few miserable piles of tomatoes, the first we had seen in Sudan. They sold for £4 a kilo, a day's wage for a well-paid labourer. The souk was almost deserted.

In the eating house where we took our breakfast on our first morning in the town, the owner apologized that there was no bread.

'We have no flour,' he explained. 'We are waiting for flour to arrive on the train from Khartoum. *Inshallah bad bokra.*'

We ate a murky stew at a table by the doorway. Across the glare of the souk, buzzards adorned the rooftops opposite like malevolent icons. The bill for breakfast was three times what it would have been in Dongola.

We stayed in a brand-new hotel set in empty ground near the radio mast. The walls were bright blue with fresh paint and the courtyard was laid with paving stones and raked gravel. In the lavatories were taps and showers which worked. The toilets, the usual hole in the ground, smelt only of freshly dug earth. I shone my torch down one of the holes. The pit beneath it was vast. The hotel was perched above an abyss awaiting the excreta of generations to come.

The north wind blew without break in Karima. It blew through the streets banging doors and shutters and hurling stray pieces of paper into the air. In the souk it rattled the corrugated roofing like thunder. The trees along the river danced in the wind.

Night and day it blew through the open window of our room, covering everything with a thin layer of grit.

33

On our first evening in Karima, we went in search of a *ful* shop for dinner. The town was in darkness. Here and there circles of light, accompanied by the thud of generators, illuminated a few houses and shops. We stopped to ask directions of a shopkeeper standing on his porch beneath a neon strip.

He shook his head. 'Everywhere is closed. There is no bread.'

In a back street we found a corner eating house at the end of a row of dark houses. Outside were a couple of tables and chairs. The metal shutter over the door was half-closed but a group of men and boys stood about in the road waiting. No one looked at us as we came into the circle of light.

We asked one of the waiting men if there was any *ful*.

'*Mafi*,' he said. 'There isn't any.'

But the fact that the men were waiting seemed to contradict this. We were hungry and there was nowhere else to eat. We waited for whatever the men were waiting for.

After a time the shutter opened. Across the doorway was a counter. A short fat man looked at the waiting circle and at us, then closed the shutter again. The men did not stir.

After a time the shutter opened again, and the fat man carried out two small bowls of *ful* and laid them on one of the tables. From an apron pocket he lifted two bannocks of bread and set them beside the bowls. He turned to us and motioned for us to eat.

We looked round the circle of men.

'Who is first?' we asked.

They looked at the ground and said nothing.

'*Itfadel*,' we said. But no one moved. No one would eat before the foreigners. To do so would defy all the strict mores of Sudanese hospitality. And for us to refuse the food would have been deeply insulting to them all.

'Come, come, eat,' the owner said.

We sat down and ate. We shared one of the pieces of bread and left the other on the table. Then we paid at the counter and hurried away up the dark street.

34

In the desert to the west of Karima lies the isolated hill of Gebel Barkal, a long, narrow spur, flat-topped with precipitous sides. The ancients knew it as Holy Mountain, the throne of Amun-Re, Lord of the Winds. Beneath its southern flank, facing the river, are two ancient temples, and near its northern end is a cluster of small, steep-sided pyramids.

We walked to Gebel Barkal early one morning, skirting a large graveyard on the edge of the town where buzzards squatted amongst the stones like old women come to mourn. In the empty desert we found ourselves dreaming of food. A month of *ful* and now the shortages of Karima had bred obsession, and the morning air seemed to be full of the hallucinatory smells of cooking. In such revelry we came to Gebel Barkal.

Napata, the ancient city which had stood somewhere near Karima, was the furthest south that the ancient Egyptians had come in their brief colonial venture in Sudan. Almost nothing of the city has been found except the temples and pyramids at Gebel Barkal. It had been a magnificent city; pharaohs, eager to impress the local population with the benefits of Egyptian rule, had enriched and endowed it. Its temples were said to have been the southern counterpart of Karnak.

Their ruins are engaged now in a slow metamorphosis from building to desert. Deep sand had drifted through the Hypostyle Halls. The columns were stumps, so eroded that they looked like a row of rock formations. A double rank of rams were weathered smooth and featureless, blind dumb hulks. The wind rattled the thorn bushes which grew in the courts, and hares started out from behind the blocks of masonry and bounded away across the desert. On one block we found, crudely carved, a row of Egyptians with bony knees. They looked lonely, so far from home, from the verdant busyness of Egypt.

The westernmost of the two temples runs inside the mountain. Its sanctuary was a cave. Across the entranceway was a gate which bore a weathered sign in English, barely discernible:

Visitors who do not find the *ghaffeir* present are asked to assist in the preservation of this monument by reporting the matter to the District Commissioner, Karima. 1944

On cue a very ancient man appeared from behind a bush where he had been asleep on a blanket. He seemed to be part of the desert, his ragged clothes were covered in sand and his eyes, opaque with a white film, were encrusted with grit. Perhaps he had not dared to leave the site since that fateful day in 1944 when the white men had come with their sign to make spies of all visitors.

With an enormous iron key he opened the gate. Clouds of bats flew out over our heads, and the air reeked of their dung. The wall paintings were crude and blackened with age. The cave sanctuary reminded me of the subterranean church at St Paul's with its dis-

148

turbed faces leering down from the dome. There was the same look of horror and derangement. The smell of bats was suffocating and we fled outside.

The pyramids, which stand just to the west of the mountain, are much smaller and slimmer than their famous predecessors, the Egyptian pyramids of the Old Kingdom. Little is known of their occupants. E. A. Wallis Budge, the great Egyptologist, excavated the shafts of one of the pyramids in 1897. At a depth of twenty-five cubits he found three chambers, one of which contained the bones of sheep, sacrificed over 2,000 years ago. They turned to dust at his touch. Nearby were pieces of an amphora which held traces of Rhodian wine.

Another shaft led deeper still, presumably to the mummy chamber. But further exploration was soon frustrated. At forty-five cubits he found the shaft full of black water, the water of the Nile, invading the tombs through the underground water-table.

35

We met Michael on our way back from Gebel Barkal. He was driving a new Toyota Landcruiser which floated up the street between the camels and the donkey carts like a spaceship. It slowed and stopped as it came abreast of us. When the window slid down a cool shaft of air-conditioned air pierced the layered heat of the afternoon.

Michael was a German engineer working on an electrical project which was part of an aid package funded by the West German government. They were installing electrical lines running through the villages on both sides of the river along the Karima reach. The project displayed admirable optimism for the supply of electricity was already chronically overstretched. Power cuts were so frequent that we were three days in Karima before we realized it had electricity at all.

Michael was as startled to find us in the streets of Karima as we were to find him, and even more startled to learn that we had come round the river from Wadi Halfa. He was so pleased with his find that he took us home.

Home was a compound in the desert beyond the town, where the expatriate staff of the project lived in prefabricated units behind a high barbed wire fence. The units were aligned in straight rows like suburban houses. Some of the men had tried a little gardening, and their box-homes differed only in the state of the few dusty flowers which grew by the front steps. In the far corner huge generators thudded. German optimism did not extend to depending on the local electrical supply themselves.

Michael led us into one of the office units. We crossed its threshold into Europe. Even the climate was duplicated by air-conditioning. There were swivel chairs, co-ordinated office furniture, concealed lighting, wall charts, venetian blinds, a thick carpet. Germans passed up and down the corridor carrying folders and mugs of coffee. Most startling of all were the telephones, until Michael explained that they could only ring other units.

He had come abroad, he told us, to escape the dreadful routine of life in Germany. But Germany had come too. The desk lamp, the air-conditioning, the year planner, the high fence, the community of fellow expatriates, were all anchors which kept him safely moored in German waters. He knew this and felt rather foolish about it, yet he clung to these symbols. He was lonely for home.

36

Michael asked us to dinner. It was served, at six o'clock exactly, in a prefabricated cafeteria. The food was laid out on counters for the men to help themselves. After a month of *ful*, it was a staggering display. There were dishes of creamed and buttered vegetables, carrots and corn and mushrooms and asparagus and baked potatoes. There was roast beef, fried chicken and sausages. There was a rice salad, a green salad and a tuna salad. There were sauces and condiments, slices of wholemeal bread, dishes of butter. We felt faint with anticipation.

Waiting in the queue, I tried to appear relaxed and normal. The men in front of us seemed to be taking forever. When my turn came, I piled food carefully on to my plate, trying to get a little of everything, until buttered carrots began sliding off the sides. I had a moment of panic when I realized that I had not left any room for mushrooms. My heart was pounding.

At the table I tried to eat slowly. The knife and fork, implements we had not used for months, felt clumsy and I feared I would send the whole glorious lot scattering across the table, into Michael's lap. I smiled weakly at him. His face seemed angelic.

'Everything is flown in from Germany,' he said, 'right down to the table salt.'

I nodded, my mouth full. I could see the men were going back for seconds: bliss. Melinda, normally the most modest of eaters, was clearing her plate for the next onslaught.

Dessert was a choice of fruit trifle, apple pie with fresh cream, or a three-flavoured ice-cream served with hot chocolate sauce. I had them all.

After coffee we retired, exhausted, to the club-house. It was supplied with videos, tape-cassette players and piles of the latest German magazines. We had only just settled into chairs when there was a light knock on one of the windows. Michael opened it and handed an envelope out into the darkness. A jug of clear liquid was passed in. It was the evening araki run. The spirit was still warm from the still.

'The people here are living in the fourteenth century,' one beefy young German said. 'The biggest part of this job is not building the electrical line. That's nothing. It's making the place habitable for us. There aren't even any roads. To get to Khartoum is an eighteen-hour drive across the desert.'

They all looked forward to the end of their contracts, and like schoolchildren awaiting the holidays, knew how long they had to run to the day. The ones who were new hoped for a transfer. There were rumours of a big job in Haiti, another in the Philippines. Michael, who had grown maudlin under the influence of the araki, had his heart set on Haiti.

151

'The climate is beautiful. The sea is just outside the door. The women are friendly. It is paradise.' It seemed a perverse view of one of the world's most disadvantaged countries.

We walked back through the desert to the town and our hotel. I thought of the men standing outside the *ful* shop the previous evening. The compound was a blaze of light in the darkness. At a distance it looked like a space station floating in a void.

37

We crossed the river in the morning in a ferry full of noisome and ill-tempered camels. At the landing stage tea-ladies squatted on low stools with glasses and sugar bowls laid out on blankets about them, shaded by great dusty umbrellas.

We trudged up the bank into the sandy lanes of Nurri. It was early and they were still cool and full of shade and people. Mango trees billowed above high blank walls. White-robed men astride tall camels cantered past, flickering through the bars of sunlight as they went. Water chattered through raised irrigation ditches into the orchards, and the lanes smelt of camel dung and wet earth.

When we emerged on to the edge of the desert the light was blinding. Out of the glare appeared the Nurri pyramids, a group of about thirty-five. They were tall and slender and elegant, and looked magnificent in the white light and empty spaces of the desert. Like those of the pyramids at Gebel Barkal, the occupants are unidentified though they are thought to be Kushite kings and queens, buried here before the capital of this home-grown dynasty moved south to Meroe.

The wind had sculpted exquisite ripple effects in the slopes of sand around the bases of the pyramids, and in the desert emptiness it seemed that the wind, howling around corners, had sculpted the pyramids as well. They huddled together in solidarity against the long forgetful centuries.

A small girl and a smaller boy came past wearing ragged tunics. She was carrying an empty sack, and explained that they were on

152

their way to cut prunings of desert scrub for their goats. She pointed to a distant cluster of miserable structures, half-tent and half-hut, where a few black goats could be seen wandering aimlessly.

The boy and girl, brother and sister, were very solemn children. The little boy said nothing but watched me with a steady, serious gaze. The girl had a still and beautiful face and a firm, polite manner. Both were encrusted with sand. It filled their hair, lay in the cracks of their skin and beneath their fingernails, and clung to the moistness about their eyes.

The girl wanted to know everything about us, where we were from, why we were there, what our names were, whether we were very old. In answer to our own enquiries she told us that they were from the desert but that they had come to camp near the river because their goats were dying. There was nothing for them to eat. She herself was the goat-herd, and every morning she had found more of them dead. They had had forty goats but now there were only seven. She held up seven fingers. She told us about the goats in a serious child's voice, without any sense of distress. She was not old enough to realize that her dead goats were part of a much greater tragedy.

38

The departure of the twice-weekly train for Khartoum was a great event in Karima's social calendar. The train left at midday and people gathered around the station and along the platform from early morning to see and be seen. By mid-morning it seemed as if the entire town had turned out.

We had reserved seats the previous day, and we found our names, written backwards, on the door of one of the compartments. We sat by the open window watching the promenading crowds.

The baroque rituals of Sudanese greeting were an endless fascination. Two men meeting on the platform could spend five full minutes in salaams and salutations before any real conversation began. The phatic formulae were spoken in a singsong chant, accompanied by much hand-shaking and head-nodding and laying of hands across hearts.

From the crowds on the platform there emerged many of the people that we had met not only in Karima but also elsewhere in northern Sudan. The boy who had sold us beakers of lemon juice in Dongola appeared smiling out of the crush of people, his turban falling over his eyes. The postman from the boat came into our compartment to exchange pleasantries and wish us well. An old man from Nurri arrived and pumped our hands feverishly.

The train surprised everyone by leaving on time. When it jerked and started there was a moment of panic as passengers on the platform rushed to get on while relatives and friends fought to get off. The train picked up speed slowly, and people were still climbing out through windows past other people climbing in when we were well out into the desert.

Sudanese trains are of an antique vintage. The windows have no glass, and the toilets, being waterless, are abandoned to baggage. In the second-class compartments the seats are upholstered but broken, and the dislodged springs are a considerable threat.

Our progress was fitful with much stopping and starting. Once under way, top speed was not much more than 25 miles per hour. Even at this pace, the train managed to kick up whirling storms of sand which blew through the windows and filled the compartment. Thick layers of grit covered everything. It became difficult to breathe and like our fellow passengers we swaddled our faces in turbans. We looked like a compartment of bandits.

Not far from Karima the track left the river and we rode through pure desert. Nothing relieved the level sands, neither scrub nor trees. Through the brown veils of dust and sand we could see a line of telegraph poles following the track. On the tops of the poles huge buzzards sat watching for desert snakes.

At El Kab we followed the river again for a time. We could see the rocks of the Fourth Cataract protruding from the water like the ribs of a famine victim.

'It is the lowest Nile in eighty years,' one of the men in the compartment said. 'The whole country is suffering.'

39

Dawn found us standing in a siding. A couple of hundred yards from the track was a nomad camp of black oval tents. A few goats and donkeys and hobbled camels moved amongst the tents. Children squatted by the early morning fires feeding the animals with twigs. The rising trails of smoke were pale blue in a brown landscape. Away to the right the sun lay just above the horizon, fat and dull. After a long wait a north-bound train passed, the train to Wadi Halfa, enveloping us in sand. Then we started again.

The landscape was changing. The desert had become the Sahel, that band of semi-arid country which lies between the pure Sahara to the north and the savanna country to the south. The sand was replaced by a gravel surface which was dotted with flat-topped acacias and thorn bushes. It was a landscape of nomads who moved between watering holes and thin pastures, and further south, of agriculturalists dependent on wells and sparse rainfall. But in recent years climatic change and overgrazing had contributed to the dramatic desiccation of the Sahel and the consequent growth of the desert. Right across Africa the Sahara was creeping further south every year. This year the rains had failed completely and the process had accelerated. Along the railway line we could make out the ghostly outline of abandoned canals and fields, just discernible in the sand.

The nomad encampments became a regular feature of the landscape. They were a sorry spectacle. Drought had forced them to the riverbank. It was a considerable humiliation, for the tribes were proud people who believed their nomadic existence to be far superior to the sedentary riparian life of the Nile.

We found Atbara in the grip of a *haboob*. The sky was nicotine yellow and we could not see the end of the platform for thick veils of sand. We crossed the Atbara river on an iron bridge. The water below was as grey as the girders. The Atbara is the first tributary of the Nile that one reaches coming upriver from its mouth. It is a seasonal river. At this time of year, October, it is normally in spate, supplying the Nile with over a fifth of its total volume. But drought in the Ethiopian highlands had reduced it to a thin stream.

Beyond the town, the *haboob* cleared and the desert began to shimmer with mirages. The acacias stood knee-deep in water and the nomad tents floated on wide silver lakes.

As we went further south, the distress of these encampments became tangible. Children in rags ran out towards the train begging for scraps. People threw down bits of bread, bananas, biscuits, and the children scooped them up without breaking stride, running with the train until they tired. Their starved faces had a terrible intensity, a mixture of determination and fear. They seemed to cling to the train and flinch from it at the same time.

This was the fate of the great nomadic tribes of Sudan, feeding their goats the last of the thorn bushes, unravelling the very landscape on which they depended, and begging for scraps from passing trains.

40

We got down from the train at Kabushiya, a sprawling village straddling the railway line about a mile from the river. In its streets camels snoozed in the afternoon sun like cats.

One of our fellow passengers on the train had given us the name of a friend of his, a teacher. We found the school behind high walls at the edge of the open desert. Jadallah emerged from a side building, a young man with a drooping moustache and a melancholy face.

In a moment we were transformed from weary travellers to visiting dignitaries, a role difficult to perform when so much in need of a bath. Our treatment made me think of films in which garage mechanics are mistaken for presidents of banks, setting in train a series of delightful misunderstandings. Jadallah showed us round the school like visiting royalty. As we entered each class the boys leapt from their seats and greeted us in unison as if they had been rehearsing for our visit for weeks. I found myself fingering an unseen tie and pulling at my shirt cuffs. Melinda, beautiful as ever despite twenty-four hours on a dusty train, was well cast as a princess.

In the evening we were guests of honour at an assembly in the schoolyard at which the boys sang songs and gave recitations. They had clear pure voices, and accompanied the songs by clapping the most elaborate of rhythms. The evening was concluded with speeches by Melinda and me. We told them about our journey and about London where we lived. Under the stars in the Sudanese schoolyard, the journey seemed oddly dull. But London arose from the desert night as an enchanted city. We told them of buildings forty storeys high which held more people than all of Kabushiya, of shops as big as palaces, of a bridge which opened for boats to pass, of buses as tall as houses, of trains which ran underground, of streets and streets of electric lights so bright you couldn't see the stars. In the rows of wide-eyed faces we saw home as a destination more fabulous than the Mountains of the Moon.

Later we carried our cots into the courtyard of Jadallah's house. Jadallah brought a pot of tea and we lay in the dark talking and looking up at the stars.

He was a disappointed figure, and lamented the poverty and limitations of Sudan and of his own life. He longed to go to England, to the enchanted city of London. He longed to leave all his sorrows behind like a pile of abandoned clothes.

Suddenly I felt ashamed of my speech. I was all too aware of the corrosive effect that the superficial glamour of the West had on less wealthy and more traditional societies. It was not something I wanted anything to do with. The sad truth however is that one's very presence is part of that baleful influence.

41

The next morning we set off across the desert to walk to the pyramids of Meroe which lay on the horizon like a distant cluster of witches' hats.

Above the sound of the wind, a mile or two from the school, we thought we heard someone call, but when we looked round we saw nothing but the empty desert and a few bleak tents. We walked on. A moment later a little girl appeared at our sides and tugged at our hands.

She led us to a single tent hiding from the wind in a hollow. We peered beneath the low flap, and as our eyes adjusted to the gloom, we saw a woman inside lying on a wide bed. She waved at us to enter. We stooped and went inside. The woman sat up on her elbow and slipped a heavy breast back inside her dress. Curled beside her on the bed, close against her bosom, was a tiny baby wrapped in dark cloth with only the back of its head visible. Its sleek dark hair was plastered to its scalp.

'*Itfadel*,' the woman said.

We squatted inside the doorway. The woman's bed, a wide wooden platform strung with gut, occupied almost the entire tent.

'Where are you going?' she asked.

'The pyramids,' we replied.

'*Sharap chai*,' she said. Drink some tea.

We tried to refuse but she insisted, and we did not want to offend her. Tea, and the sugar to sweeten it, would be a major expense for her. From her bed she called outside to the little girl to boil a kettle.

The tent was round and snug and womb-like, a refuge from the vast spaces and the glare of the desert. It was no more than five feet high at the apex of its curved roof, far too low for anyone but the children to stand upright. The walls and the roof consisted of layers of sacking and coarse black cloth made from goat hair hung over a frame of twisted branches. These layers came down to within a foot of the ground where they met a low skirting wall of raffia matting. Pots, a gas lantern and large camel bags hung from the framework of the roof. Across the bed were strewn a confusion of blankets and dark cushions of camel leather. Beneath the bed small red and black chickens pecked the sand. Three children, all smaller than the little girl who was making the tea, stood on the far side of the bed, in against the wall of the tent, staring at us wide-eyed, their hands resting reassuringly on their mother's leg. The tent smelt of incense which was burnt to keep the devil away from the new-born.

The mother reached into a box at the end of the bed and produced a bowl of dates. She had a large strong face, a full mouth and skin like dark satin. Her eyes were huge and outlined with kohl. The whites were the colour of fresh cream. Her hair beneath a tasselled scarf was tightly braided.

Her name was Miriam. When we told her our names she laughed

and refused to repeat them, thinking them too foolish.

The baby, a girl, was only four days old, and was as yet unnamed. She would not be named until the Naming Day, the seventh day after birth. They did not always survive, the mother explained. It was better, if they died, that they were not named at all. She had had ten children, she said, but only six had survived.

The little girl brought a tray of three tea glasses, and set two down on the sand before us, giving the third to her mother.

They were from the desert. 'Times are hard and we live here now, all the year round, near the river.' Her husband was 'at the river', working or looking for work in the fields. 'We have lost our animals. We had a horse to bring water from the river but it died. Now we use the donkey of a neighbour. If it dies we must carry the water ourselves.'

She waved flies away from the baby's head. Though we expressed interest in it, she did not lift it or turn it so that we might see its face. The menace of the evil eye is a powerful concern in Sudan. Praise is thought to attract harmful spirits, and mothers are reluctant to show off their new-born, particularly to foreigners ignorant of such anxieties.

'The new-born are a promise,' she said, 'a promise from Allah.'

42

In the afternoon Melinda accepted an invitation to visit the women teachers at the girls' school. She found them seated on metal cots in a darkened room, eating dates and spitting the stones on to the floor. A crowd of girls' faces stared in at the window.

The status of women teachers is not very high in Sudan. Girls are brought up to consider marriage the only fulfilment, and women teachers are likely to be those who have not fared well in the marriage stakes. Where there is little social contact between un-married men and women, a woman's physical beauty is far more important than the virtues of her personality.

The women teachers were all unmarried. One was very fat,

another had a badly pock-marked face, a third had a squint, and another was very dark. They tended to hilarity, and their conversation was full of fantasy.

The youngest, a shy woman, told Melinda that she was going to the University of Khartoum at the beginning of the year. The others spat out their date stones and hooted with laughter. 'She has a *desire* to go. She has a *desire* to go,' they chanted. 'Nothing more.'

Another told Melinda that she was going to marry the brother of Nafisa, one of the other teachers, and that he was going to take her on a honeymoon to England. When Nafisa came into the room the other teachers enquired after her brother.

'But I do not have a brother,' she said. And there were more gales of cruel laughter.

The teachers shouted for tea, and two little girls in white smocks brought a tray of glasses.

'In England I think you do not beat the girls,' the teachers said. 'But in Sudan the girls are very stupid. We must beat them. They are donkeys.' The teachers all shook with merriment, spilling their tea into the saucers.

At the assembly before the beginning of evening classes, the shy teacher who desired to go to the University of Khartoum harangued the girls, then beat a number of them with a short length of electric cable.

43

At the beginning of the nineteenth century, Shendy was the largest town in the Sudan with a population of 6,000. When John Lewis Buckhardt arrived there in 1814 disguised as an Arab on his way to Mecca, he found a thriving market with spices and sandalwood from India, swords and razors from Germany, writing paper and beads from Genoa and Venice, and slaves from the upper reaches of the Nile. Five thousand slaves a year were said to pass through Shendy on their way to Arabia, Egypt and Turkey. A healthy man fetched fifteen Spanish dollars and a woman twenty-five. The traders slept with the women they bought, and enjoyed getting them drunk first in the town's taverns.

We went to Shendy on a desert track, a two-hour run from Kabushiya in the back of an almost empty lorry. We lay lolling on sacks of flour with all the contentment of executives in a chauffeur-driven Rolls.

With the exception of Atbara, through which we had passed on the train, Shendy was our first Sudanese town. By comparison, even Dongola paled to the status of a mere village. Outside our hotel was a stretch of paved road, the first we had seen in Sudan. It ran for a couple of hundred yards, as far as the crossroads, before it foundered and surrendered to the sand again. There were buses for Khartoum in the square, and a fleet of taxis which cruised through the town like parodies of 1950s Americana with tinted windows, low sun visors, angled aerials, flame decals and mud flaps. In the evenings their drivers, immaculately robed and turbanned, parked outside the juice stalls in the square and lounged behind their wheels with their doors open and their radios blaring.

In spite of Sharia, Shendy manages to retain something of its former notoriety. In our hotel sin and sanctity co-existed uneasily. We were woken early each morning by the sound of prayers in the courtyard as the guests took their turn on the prayer mat by the wash-basin. One of the more devout inhabitants never left his room. Whenever we passed his door, always slightly ajar, we could hear him chanting. No doubt it was atonement.

Our nights were always disturbed by the late return of an elderly gentleman who occupied the room next to ours. He was a man of considerable girth and in his unsteady condition had difficulty negotiating the narrow doorway. Once inside, he invariably found his room a dull place after the evening's entertainments and re-emerged moments later to wander about the courtyard amongst the slumbering forms, looking for someone to talk to. Finding no one he talked to himself. Seated on the wash-basin he conducted incomprehensible but moving monologues in the moonlight.

Another of our fellow guests was an elegant young man with a beautifully groomed moustache which turned up at the ends. He wore a white turban woven with bands of gold and purple thread. Each evening he paid us courtesy calls as we lay on our cots in the

161

arcade before supper, greeting us with elaborate compliments. He was, he announced proudly, a shoe polish salesman.

The Sudanese have developed a taste for proper leather shoes, unlike the Egyptians who preferred the convenience of plastic flip-flops. From beneath the salesman's own gallibaya an ostentatious pair of platform shoes protruded. He wiped at them with his handkerchief.

'The dust,' he sighed. 'The dust is a terrible problem.'

Shoe polish was the coming thing in Sudan, he assured us. He was lucky to be in on the ground floor. He unwrapped his samples from an old newspaper and laid them carefully on my cot: three battered tins of Kiwi polish. Shoe polish had taken him all over East Africa, he said. He talked with great excitement of Nairobi. Juba was a beautiful town. We would be happy there.

We asked about the civil war in the south; the rebels were always threatening to take Juba. He assured us that this was not a problem. It was a town for honeymooners.

44

The train to Khartoum was a dust-bowl. Near the front we found a restaurant car. It was like stepping suddenly on to another train, in another country. There was glass in the windows, comfortable chairs and green table cloths on the tables. We took refuge here from the crowds and the dust and the disintegrating carriages, and drank quantities of tea.

Beyond the windows the desert was full of illusions – mirage lakes and long shimmering marshes. Trees threw reflections across the glistening shallows, and banks of reeds stood along the receding shores where camels and goats wandered contentedly.

We fell into conversation with a German at the next table. He was the Khartoum representative of a large European agrochemical firm, dealing in fertilizers and insecticides. In the mid-1970s there had been brave talk of making Sudan the bread-basket of the Middle East. Those dreams had come unstuck in a tangle of bad planning, rising oil prices, the flood of skilled Sudanese labour to the Gulf, crippling foreign debts, and profiteering. The agrochemical company saw no future in Sudan; it was closing its office. The German was to be transferred home in four months' time.

'I count the days,' he said. 'Sudan is a tragedy. When I came here there was some hope. There was investment, a strategy for development. It was to be a meeting of Western know-how and Arab money. Now they can't even pay their debts.'

'There were terrible shortages in Karima,' we said.

'Shortages,' the German snorted. 'The west of the country is in the grip of full-scale famine. How long have you been away from the news?'

'Six weeks. Longer really.'

'You won't have heard then. Sudan has become this year's Ethiopia.'

'We have seen the encampments along the track.'

'They are alright. They have just come to the river because they have run out of pasturage in their own areas. In the west conditions are much worse. They are starving. They are coming to the river too, but for them the journey will take weeks. Someone was saying the other day that there are already big refugee camps outside Omdurman.'

'What is being done?' I asked.

'Nothing, I should think,' the German said. 'The government has completely lost its way. Look at this Sharia. A disaster. It was bound to provoke the Africans in the south. The civil war there is ruining the country. Chevron were prospecting for oil, and had found big reserves in Bahr al-Ghazal. Now they have pulled out. The Jonglei Canal was going to increase the supply of Nile water. Now that's been abandoned. Forget it. The country's going down the drain.'

'What are our chances of getting to Juba?' I asked.

'Impossible. Six weeks ago one of the boats to Juba was sunk by the rebels. 280 people killed. The south is too dangerous. There is no law, and no one to enforce it if there was any. The people will kill you for the few pounds in your pocket. A few weeks ago a German couple disappeared. No one has heard anything about them. Forget the south.'

163

He stared out of the window at the mirages, his mouth fixed in a grimace.

'Facilities,' he said. 'The country lacks facilities.'

It grew dark. We reached Khartoum about ten o'clock. In the forecourt of the station we looked for a taxi. The drivers all quoted exorbitant fares. Khartoum was suffering another petrol shortage.

45

Khartoum is a tenuous city. Set down in the middle of the desert in one of the world's poorest countries, it seemed as unreal as the German compound at Karima. The office blocks, the modern avenues, the wealthy suburbs, the shops with their wide glass windows full of modern goods, all belonged to another world. Few capital cities are a reflection of the countries they govern, but the gap between Khartoum and Sudan can be measured in centuries.

Its life-blood is imports. They arrive fitfully from Port Sudan along an antiquated railway regularly engulfed by sand. Should the flow of imports ever dry up, the modern city would quickly disintegrate.

Fuel is the most crucial and the most uncertain of the imports. The city was in the grip of a perpetual petrol shortage, and long lines of cars queued for days outside petrol stations. Lengthy power cuts were common, and every shop and office had its own small generator to fill in when the supply failed. More than the muezzin and the car horns, the sound of Khartoum was the sound of generators pounding away on the pavements outside the shops.

The city's lifeline is the airport. The paved streets peter out almost before they reach the city limits. Khartoum abounds in travel agencies whose only trade is airline tickets. Outside their doors linger black marketeers, eager for dollars, the currency of imports. The Sudanese pound changes value almost daily, sliding irrevocably downward.

46

We lived in a small room set like a cabin among billowing lines of washing on the flat roof of our hotel. Hotel rooms were at a premium in Khartoum. Melinda found it, and she made me close my eyes as she led me up the narrow stairs on to the roof.

The view over the city was splendid. We could see from the Anglican Cathedral near the river right round to the airport where the planes descended gently into the haze at the desert's edge. Immediately beneath us was UN Square where the high-speed arrivals and departures of a scrum of buses and taxis gave the city its only moments of Cairene frenzy. At the far end of the square was the El Kabir mosque with a sad little string of coloured lights hung between its two minarets.

Khartoum was full of beggars, and their numbers seemed to increase daily. In the early mornings bands of ragged boys and men scavenged through rubbish piles. The fleet-footed loitered outside eating houses, darting through the doors when the coast was clear to seize left-overs before the waiters cleared them away. Lepers squatted on street corners, their ravaged faces hidden by shawls, holding up the stumps of their hands in supplication.

Only the Corniche, lined with sober colonial buildings and with the old banyan trees planted by Kitchener, was free of their mournful presence. Modern Khartoum seemed to turn its back on the river. From the bank you look across to Tuti Island which lies in the mouth of the Blue Nile. With its banana groves, irrigated fields, goats grazing across swathes of stubble, and dark men in white drawers bending over their hoes, the island could have been almost anywhere on the Nile except Khartoum.

Just downstream is the confluence of the two Niles. We were following the White Nile, the senior partner which rises in the region of the great lakes of East Africa. It emerges, a full-grown river, from Lake Victoria which serves as a reservoir to keep its flow relatively constant throughout the year. The Blue Nile, like the Nile's two main tributaries, the Atbara and the Sobat rivers, is more temperamental. Fed by seasonal rains in the highlands of Ethiopia, it contributes at its high season almost three-quarters of the water of the combined river, while at its low season it manages less than a fifth.

From the confluence at Khartoum one can see the two streams flowing side by side in the combined river for some miles downstream, particularly during the summer spate. The names are hardly accurate. At Khartoum the White Nile was the colour of sand while the Blue Nile was the colour of rotting hay.

Across the river from Khartoum is the adjoining city of Omdurman. It is an Arab not a colonial town, a labyrinth of dust lanes and adobe walls. When the Mahdi captured Khartoum in 1885 from General Gordon, he turned his back on the colonial buildings and recrossed the river to make Omdurman his capital. His tomb, with its silver dome, remains its finest monument.

47

Khartoum was full of relief and development agencies whose Land-rovers shunted about the town between each other's offices: Oxfam, the United Nations High Commission for Refugees, Unicef, Médecins Sans Frontières, the Red Cross, the Red Crescent, the Islamic African Relief Agency, the Save the Children Fund. Talking to their representatives we clothed the rumours and stories with some depressing facts.

In northern Darfur and northern Kordofan huge areas had been left almost entirely unpopulated as the inhabitants, threatened with starvation, fled south and east. Malnutrition levels were four times the normal level in Africa and livestock losses were in many cases 100 per cent. Already there were thousands camped in a pitiable state outside Omdurman. The rising tide of beggars in Khartoum was part of this migration. Sudan's problems were aggravated by the influx of over a million refugees who had fled from war and famine in Ethiopia and from turmoil in Uganda.

Foreign relief agencies can only operate at the invitation of the host government, and Numeri's regime, beset by problems, was reluctant to face up to disaster on this scale, fearing that it might undermine their hold on power.

The Oxfam representative told us about a member of the French embassy who, in these early days of the famine, was mounting a virtual one-man relief effort, bringing food and supplies out to the camps beyond Omdurman each day in the back of his own Landrover. His name was René Richard. We went to see him, and he invited us to accompany him to the camps the following morning.

48

When we turned up the next morning at René's house we found a crowd of people, mainly children, camped in his garden.

'When I brought them here they were like skeletons,' he said. 'What can I do? There are thousands of them. I can only help a few.'

René was a stocky Frenchman with a round frank face. He was direct, and wasted no time on small talk or frivolous formalities. He suffered the elaborate etiquette of Sudan in good-humoured silence.

We drove out across the bridge to Omdurman. Behind us in the back of the Landrover was a mountain of bread and bananas which René was taking to the camps. At a police station we collected a young officer who acted as his escort. He had a sensitive face and an immaculate uniform, and dusted the Landrover seat with his handkerchief before getting in.

'We must call first at the house of a Sudanese musician,' René said over his shoulder. 'He is a pop singer. Very famous here in Sudan. We are trying to organize a concert to raise money for the refugees. He wants to help.'

We found the house in a narrow lane, and knocked on the blue metal door. A wizened old man motioned us across a courtyard towards a doorway where a curtain hung limply in the heat.

Inside was a small room made smaller by large items of Western

167

furniture: a huge double bed with a pink cover, two armchairs and a sofa ranged round a low table, and a set of shelves with a television, a video and a stereo. The curtains were drawn, and an electric light burned in one corner. Vases of improbably coloured plastic flowers sat on every surface and there was a smell of sickly perfume. As for the walls, they were papered from floor to ceiling with photographs. The photographs all showed the same man, singing, posing with a band, greeting celebrities, accepting awards, waving to crowds. They spanned a whole lifetime, and one could trace across the walls a shocking physical decline.

After a time our host appeared from behind a curtain. He was the singer in the photographs, but older and thinner than even the latest pictures. He wore a dressing-gown and slippers. His face was drained and his eyes cloudy. He held out a bony hand to each of us, and smiled nervously. The hand was cold, and he withdrew it the moment we touched it.

He sat on the edge of the bed, picking at its cover, and we made awkward small talk. He wanted to offer us breakfast and was unwilling to discuss the concert until we had eaten. He spoke in an abstracted way, as if he had difficulty in concentrating. Conversation soon lagged. He rose suddenly from the bed to put on a video for us.

'I think you will like this one, a European film,' he said, fumbling amongst the cassettes on a shelf. 'It is very good. A friend has just brought it from Europe for me.'

The film began with shots of naked corpses laid out on mortuary slabs. Long close-ups lingered on the grey faces, many of them stiffened in expressions of agony. A doctor appeared in a white coat. As the titles came up – the film was called *Faces of Death* – he began to cut one of the corpses open. It was quite clearly a real corpse.

The doctor, a middle-aged man with seedy matinée idol looks, was our cicerone through every manifestation of violent death. The film had no plot, just a parade of horrors. Nothing was faked. We watched real dog and cock fights. One bloodied dog tore another's throat out to the cheers of an assembly of hillbillies in a Kentucky barn. We moved on to China where a couple were eating the brains of a live monkey. A camera recorded the monkey's agony in its

168

cage beneath the table while another showed the top of its skull being sliced off.

We looked away. René was examining his shoes. The policeman looked ill. Only the singer, perched on the edge of his bed, gave the film his full attention. He was transfixed by it, and his face suddenly looked younger.

After a time there was a stirring behind the curtain. The singer got up and went out, returning a moment later with a tray of food.

'Mummy says breakfast is ready,' he announced.

<h1 style="text-align:center">49</h1>

Later in the Landrover, holding the photographs of himself which the singer had given us as farewell presents, the policeman said, 'He is an alcoholic. He is very ill.' He was visibly upset by the morning's visit. The singer was a great Sudanese hero.

We drove through the narrowing lanes of Omdurman. The journey to the refugee camps proved to be a descent through different levels of poverty, each of which we thought was the camp itself.

Beyond the slums of Omdurman lay a wasteland of adobe huts and tin shacks and ragged cloth lean-tos. Children with swollen bellies stood impassively in the road. But this was not the camp. These were the poor who were always with us.

Out in the desert we drove for a quarter of an hour over hard tracks before reaching an encampment of shabby black tents. Thin dogs skulked between them and faces stared out through the open flaps. But this was not the camp either. A toothless old woman in rags pointed us towards the horizon. 'God have mercy on them,' she said.

On the horizon, we now saw what we had not noticed before. It looked like a desert mirage, a vast expanse of small bushes. It was the refugee camp.

The first thing we noticed as we approached was the smell. It was the smell of death, of putrefying flesh. Then we began to see the animals, the carcases of donkeys and camels and goats scattered across the sands, swollen and stiff.

'When their animals die, they are finished,' René said.

The 'tents' of the camp were ragged pieces of cloth and matting draped over a framework of sticks. Hundreds upon hundreds of these makeshift dwellings stretched away into the distance. We drove through them, past shuffling figures, to a compound behind a high fence. A soldier waved us through a gate, and we stopped in front of a row of temporary sheds.

A trickle of relief had begun to reach this camp. When René had first come here, only weeks before, there had been nothing, no food, no water, no medicine. He had pestered government ministers and relief agencies to act. Now Médecins Sans Frontières, a French health agency, visited the camp regularly, the Islamic African Relief Agency were distributing sacks of flour, and the army was supplying water. The fenced compound set up by the army in the middle of the camp, was the headquarters of this effort, and soldiers with long whips were stationed at the gate to keep the starving recipients from overrunning it. They were hardly required, for no one would have had the energy for such aggression.

A soldier brought us into one of the sheds to meet the two headmen of the villages in Kordofan from which most of the refugees had come. They were skeletal old men sitting on a bench. One was nearly blind, the result of malnutrition. Plump soldiers came forward deferentially and helped the two old men to their feet to shake our hands. They greeted us as formally and as warmly as if we were visiting them in their own homes. In the midst of the squalor of the camp, they had lost none of their grace or dignity. Their hands in ours were weightless, like a collection of hollow bones.

'Relief is coming now, a little,' René said. 'But there are many camps.' He gestured to the north and the south. 'This is only one. In each camp there are thousands of people. Their predicament is very serious. Many people are dying. The men who are still able go into the city to find work. But because there are many men and only a few jobs, the wages have declined. Before, a labourer earned £5 a day. Now it is less than half that. And because of the shortages, food prices have soared. The laws of the market-place have no mercy on the starving.'

While the soldiers distributed the food that René had brought, Melinda and I walked through the camp. In the shade of their flimsy shelters, people moved about listlessly or squatted amongst what was left of their life's belongings: a couple of pots, an old blanket, a torn mat. Their clothes were in tatters. They seemed to exist in a trance, a state of numb shock; homelessness, illness and hunger were compounded by bereavement. They greeted us politely and correctly in light dry voices and enquired from where we had come and what had brought us to this place, and then drifted off into a haze before they had heard our answers.

The whole camp was gripped by a terrible calm. It was as quiet as death. There was no frenzy or agitation, no outward sign of grief. Their agony was silent. It was the most peaceful place I had ever known.

A woman in the doorway of a patchwork tent waved to us. She took our hands and led us inside. We were met by a thin sour smell.

On mats round the tent three women lay on their sides, holding their heads in their hands, their faces entirely expressionless. A fourth woman wearing only a thin shawl over her shoulders sat holding a small child. The child had a distended stomach, and flies crawled undisturbed over its face. The woman held up long bony hands to us. We went over and spoke to her. When we bent to stroke her child's leg, we found that it was stone cold. The child was already dead.

50

No one spoke of the war in the south. Many people genuinely knew very little about it, others preferred to ignore it.

The British embassy was more forthcoming. They strongly advised us not to proceed upriver. The activities of the SPLA, the Southern People's Liberation Army, were threatening all the links with the north. The rail bridge across the Lol river, a branch of the Bahr el-Ghazal, had been destroyed, breaking the only railway link

171

with the south. The river steamers had come under fire from the banks, and it was now feared that the rebels had anti-aircraft missiles with which they would begin to attack planes coming into Juba airport from Khartoum. Many southern troops had defected to the rebels who were now thought to control most of the province of Upper Nile. Juba, the capital of the south, was considered vulnerable.

The origins of the civil war lie in the ethnic differences between the north and south of Sudan, differences which reflect a cultural and geographical divide that stretches across the whole of Africa. The people of the arid north are Muslim and Arabic-speaking, while the southerners, inhabiting lush regions of considerable rainfall, are Negroid African. They speak a variety of tribal languages and are generally animists or mission Christians. In previous centuries northern Arabs raided the south for slaves. Southerners argue that the exploitation of the south by the north continues on almost every front. The north has always dominated the political leadership of Sudan, and the south, one of the least developed areas in all Africa, remains severely disadvantaged.

The latest conflict is not the first between north and south. Civil war began with the birth of an independent Sudan in the mid-1950s, and lasted seventeen years. It was brought to an end ironically by Numeri in 1972 with an agreement guaranteeing the south a measure of autonomy. All was well until Numeri abrogated this agreement in 1983 in order to divide the single southern province into three smaller regions. The situation was further exacerbated when, later in the same year, he declared Islamic law or Sharia and attempted, unsuccessfully, to apply it to the south as well as the north. Sharia, someone said to us, was the best thing that ever happened to the SPLA. By the end of 1983 a new civil war had begun for which there is still no solution in sight.

51

In spite of the difficulties we were determined to continue our journey upriver. The Sudan is a huge country, and the fighting was isolated and spasmodic. According to our own sources, life in the south went on much as before. Juba, though possibly in danger of rebel attack, remained relatively quiet.

In the Aliens Office near the Corniche we applied for permits to travel to the south. The army captain behind the counter advised us that we could only go by air.

'There have been a few problems with bandits attacking the river boats,' he said. 'We cannot be assured of your safety on the boats so I am afraid you must go by air to Juba.'

I had long been looking forward to the river journey through the great swamps of the Sudd. But expectations were narrowing and we felt grateful now to be getting to the south at all.

'Arrange for your air tickets,' the captain said. 'When you have purchased them bring them to me with your application for a permit. There will be no problem.'

52

In the Sudan Air office chaos reigned. Crowds of prospective travellers stormed the building every morning and fought with each other to gain and command the attention of a small but valiant force of counter staff who steadfastly refused to sell any tickets. Their defence was that the computer had broken down. They could not sell any tickets because they did not know what tickets had already been sold. They had no idea when it would be fixed. As for Juba, they said, there were no seats for three months, even with a functioning computer.

This impasse called for a flanking operation. A side entrance led up a flight of stairs to the management offices. An armed soldier guarded the door to keep customers at bay. I learnt the name of the managing director, and the following morning breezed past the startled guard brandishing this name like a password.

In the upper suite of offices I bluffed my way into the managing director's presence. He was a plump jocular man who enjoyed a quiet air-conditioned room far removed from the sweaty battle-scenes on the ground floor below him.

I told him of our long journey upriver, through Egypt and Nubia, and the way in which it had all come to an end in his Sudan Air office in Khartoum. He was from Dongola and I reminisced shamelessly with him about the tree-lined streets, the beauty of the river, the wonderful hospitality of the Dongolawis. In the mellow grip of homesickness, he picked up his phone.

'You have your permits for Juba?' he asked me.

'They have assured us that there will be no problem once we have the air tickets.'

He spoke briefly to someone on the other end of the line, then hung up.

'I have arranged for tickets on Wednesday morning. Collect them on Tuesday.' Then he smiled, remembering that I had been in Sudan for two months. 'And that is for certain.'

53

We collected our tickets the following Tuesday and took them to the Aliens Office. The captain at the counter seemed a little startled to see us again, and even more startled to see our tickets. But he was entirely confident about the permits, and helped us fill in our applications.

'Come back in the evening,' he said. 'Your permits will be ready.'

In the evening he was crestfallen. Our applications had been refused by the security forces, he explained. The army, who issued the permits, had passed our applications without question, but the security police, who vetted them, had turned them down. There was nothing he could do. The security forces were controlled from the Presidential Palace and were a law unto themselves.

'It has not been easy to arrange these tickets,' I said. 'Our flight leaves in the morning at 6 a.m. You said there would be no problem about the permits.'

'There is nothing I can do,' he said. 'My hands are tied. How was I to know the security forces would take such an interest in your applications? Their word is final.' He seemed as upset as we were.

We argued and cajoled, in the hope that if we made enough of a nuisance of ourselves some solution might be found. When the solution came, it was not what we had expected.

The captain glanced over his shoulder at his colleagues working at desks behind him, then leant forward across the counter as if to point out something to us on our applications.

'Never mind about the permit,' he whispered. 'The permit is a sham. You will not be asked for it at the airport. And in Juba no one will care about permits from Khartoum. Go to Juba. Don't worry about our permission.'

Then he straightened up and said in a loud voice for the benefit of anyone listening. 'I am sorry. There is nothing I can do. Your permits have been refused.'

54

The fact that only a hundred years ago virtually nothing was known of the Upper Nile was almost entirely due to the Sudd, the great swamps which clog the river between Malakal and Bor. They cover almost 9,000 square miles, an area larger than Wales. The word Sudd means barrier, and so for at least 2,000 years it was, blocking every attempt to reach the source of the river since a survey expedition sent by Nero was turned back in AD 60. Speke, the man who was eventually to reach the source of the Nile, mounted his first expedition from the coast of East Africa rather than try to brave the horrors of the Sudd.

In the early years of this century the British succeeded in cutting a permanent channel through the swamps, and a boat service now plies between Kosti and Juba. Travellers speak of the Sudd's utter monotony. For days from the deck of the steamer all one can see are endless papyrus swamps. It is a watery primeval waste, reminiscent of the waters of chaos from which the ancient Egyptians believed the world began.

Sir Samuel Baker, who hacked his way through in 1871, described the swamps in terms of a nightmare.

> Some evil spirit appears to rule in this horrible region of everlasting swamp ... No dependence can ever be placed on this cursed river. The fabulous Styx must be a sweet rippling brook compared to this horrible creation.

55

We saw nothing of the Sudd. It lay beneath a thick cover of cloud over which we sailed in the oblivious sunlight of air travel. In a couple of hours we passed from the arid landscapes of the north into equatorial Africa, a landscape of rain.

It was my birthday, and as the breakfast trays were handed out Melinda surprised me with presents collected surreptitiously from the markets and shops of Khartoum, all wrapped in blue tissue paper. The stewardess, impressed with this Western ritual, gave me an extra slice of fruit cake. But being on the plane at all seemed the best present: no one had enquired about permits at the airport.

Arriving at Juba reminded me of arrivals at small Irish airfields in my childhood. We came down out of clouds which shredded over the wings. There were glimpses of wet fields, wet trees, muddy lanes and red ditches full of water. As we broke beneath the clouds, the rain streamed across the window. The runway shone beneath us. We banked and this new world of green came up fast. Then we were down on the runway, bumping over its uneven surface, the engines roaring.

We got down from the plane into a thin drizzle. The airport building across the wet grass looked like a country schoolhouse. Damp stains spread up its yellowed walls. The morning smelt of wet grass and wet earth. Wisps of cloud streamed up a hillside of drenched colour.

A lorry unloaded our bags in a yard of puddles at the rear of the airport building. The northern Arabs, picking their way across the muddy yard in their white gallibayas, looked as forlorn as wet birds.

<h1 style="text-align:center">56</h1>

The Sudd was first breached by outsiders in 1840 when an expedition was sent by Muhammad Ali, the Egyptian ruler who twenty years before had conquered northern Sudan, with the intention of extending his suzerainty over the lands of the Upper Nile. In its wake came government officials, traders and missionaries who established settlements at Gondokoro and Lado and Rejaf and Mongolla, all sites along the Juba reach of the river. English officers and governors seconded to the Egyptian government arrived to put down little outposts of European civilization in the bush. General Gordon was the governor of the province of Equatoria for two eventful years, a decade before his last stand in Khartoum. His predecessor had been Samuel Baker, the first European to reach Lake Albert.

If they were honest, the government officials battled with the Arab traders who ravaged the countryside for ivory and slaves. If they weren't, they took their bribes and looked the other way. The missionaries, who had official sanction in their search for souls, brought their own problems. Conversion threatened the cohesion of families and alliances, and cut the tribal societies off from their own religious roots. The condemnation of polygamy threatened to deprive large numbers of women of family protection and any respectable means of support.

The Africans watched the foreigners come and go with a detached cynicism. Impermanence is in the very grain of the country. In these sodden regions, the damp rots everything and the riotous vegetation swallows the best intentions. Juba, which is said to have a population of 57,000, seems long ago to have abandoned this unequal struggle against the climate and the vegetation. We had expected something substantial, and found instead a place so elusive and fragmentary that for some time we thought Juba was elsewhere, that the collection of dust streets near our hotel was on the outskirts of the real town.

The air of Juba, malarial and corrupt, was heavy with the smell of rot. Buzzards flew low over the rooftops, their shadows gliding smoothly across the dirt streets and the stained walls, before they came to rest on the smouldering piles of rubbish and compost which littered the town. The langorous silence of mid-afternoon was broken each day by the taped muezzin of the mosque where the Arab merchants worshipped. Due to some defect, the tape ran at half-speed and the call to prayer was reduced to a slurred and ridiculous monotone in the afternoon heat.

Juba ignored the river. There was no waterfront, only a clearing of beaten earth where in the early mornings boys sold papayas and green bananas brought across the river by naked tribesmen in piroques, narrow canoes hollowed out of single logs. Upriver a little way were a couple of old warehouses, a floating dock and two abandoned steamers engulfed by reeds.

The river was narrower than we had known it, and the current stronger. The tribesmen poling their piroques kept close to the banks. The water was grey and greasy-looking. Smooth rocks broke the surface like the backs of rising hippos. Birds fluttered among the bushes that grew up from the shallows, hunting insects at the water's edge.

After months with the desert Nile, the river at Juba seemed sadly peripheral. There were no water pumps and no irrigation channels chattering away towards carefully tended fields, none of the elaborate husbandry of water which gave the riverbanks of Egypt and northern Sudan their vitality. The riotous vegetation of Juba flourished without any help from the river or any threat from encroaching desert. The total dependence on the river which had prompted the ancient Egyptians to elevate the Nile to the status of a god was broken. In the lands of rain the river had been humbled.

57

Our hotel consisted of a couple of low buildings along two sides of an earthen yard where a cock terrorized his small harem of hens. In the rooms the lumpy mattresses were stained with blood from the bites of bedbugs. Large patches of damp spread across the sagging hardboard ceilings and geckos scampered across the screened windows.

The hotel housed a transient population of Arab traders from the north, and Africans trying to get somewhere else. A group of enormous Tanzanian boxers were hoping to get to Denmark. The boxers' sense of geography was hazy but their faith in the pugilistic possibilities of Copenhagen was unshakeable. It was, they confided, a paradise for boxers.

The only permanent inhabitant of the hotel was a mad woman who lived alone in a small room at the end of one of the buildings. Though she had lived in the hotel for years no one knew anything about her; even her name was unknown. She never spoke, but no one even knew if this was a psychosomatic condition or if she was a deaf mute. She spent her days wandering between her room, where she slept on a pile of sacks, and a broken chair in the yard. Occasionally she made brief forays into the streets around the hotel, walking quickly and purposefully, as if she had somewhere to go.

Refugees fleeing Uganda in the wake of Amin's fall had brought her to the hotel in 1979. They had found her wandering on the road near Nimule. People assumed that she had been attacked and perhaps raped by some of Amin's fleeing soldiers. Costa, the owner of the hotel and the kindliest of men, took her in. Three months after her arrival she had suffered a miscarriage, and the dead foetus had to be taken from her by force.

Sometimes, sitting bolt upright in her chair in the yard, she would begin to rave, mouthing a silent torrent of words. Her hands flew up from her lap and performed a convoluted dance of gestures in front of her face. Her eyes were wild and her throat bulged. But no sound ever emerged except, occasionally, a strangulated whimpering like the sound of an animal in pain. Between these sporadic fits, her face bore an expression of complete disinterest.

58

In the evenings the patrons of the hotel sat out in the yard on a collection of broken chairs. As the twilight fell a company of toads emerged from beneath the buildings and hopped lumpily across the beaten earth towards a stand of corn opposite. It was at this hour that Jerry brewed himself a cup of Greek coffee in his room, and the smell drifted out to us on the evening air.

Jerry was a Greek trader who had come to Africa in the 1930s. He was between houses, so he lived in a small room in the hotel with all his life's belongings piled high to the ceiling. There was barely room to open the door.

Each evening after the march of the toads he appeared in the yard with his little cup of coffee and strolled amongst the other guests on their broken chairs, chatting and joking in his heavily accented English. He smoked strong-smelling cigarettes through a long ebony filter and always carried a fly whisk. His favourite was made from a giraffe's tail and had been given to him, he claimed, by a chief of the Ashanti tribe.

Jerry's face had the exaggerated quality of a mask: a great hooked nose, a wide, mobile mouth, narrowed eyes which depended for their expression on thick and very active eyebrows. His skin seemed to have been affected by the climate. It had the appearance of something mouldering and, depending on the time of day, was either yellow or grey.

In this remote outpost of equatorial Africa Jerry nursed sybaritic dreams. He was always waiting for some delicacy from abroad which one of his many contacts was sending to him: Imperial Leather soap, Frank Cooper's marmalade, a box of Swiss chocolates, a bottle of sherry. They rarely arrived, but it hardly seemed to matter.

The evenings found him in reflective mood. He was a cheerful, enthusiastic character with a quick, hard laugh. But he was an old man and his enthusiasm turned a great deal to the past when Africa, for Europeans, had been another country. Business had been good then. The barges went north full of cargo. There were many Greek traders in Juba in those days. Men even brought their wives and families.

'Such parties we had. All the food shipped in from Greece. Olives, retsina, cheeses, sausages. Things you never see here now. So nice. Everyone was happy. Business was good. Now it is finished. What can we do? Nothing.'

Parties featured largely in Jerry's reminiscences. In Port Sudan, where he had lived for many years, there were famous parties on board the P&O liners when they docked on their way to and from India. One night an Englishman had called for champagne for everyone to celebrate the fact that he had just become engaged on the high diving board of the ship's pool.

'Oh, we were drinking so much champagne. All night. Everyone was so happy. The Englishman took a case of champagne up on the diving board and was dropping the bottles into the pool one by one. We were swimming out for them. In our evening dresses. It was very drunken.'

Jerry was fond of the English. In the war he had joined the Catering Corps of the British army.

'It is better to be on one side or the other in a war. Never in the middle.'

In Ethiopia the British had arrested all the Italians after news came through that Italy had entered the war.

'That was very sad. They were all my friends. We hated to see them being taken away like that in the trucks. But what could we do? Nothing.'

59

When it grew dark Jerry took his torch and went up through the town to the Greek club. Juba had no electricity and at night the town was plunged into a quick warm darkness through which fireflies glowed and winked like errant stars.

The Greek club, which had once been a notorious casino, was no longer a club nor particularly Greek. It was a bar with a mixed clientele of expatriate aid workers, Greek traders, Sudan Air staff, army and security officers, and the floating population of our hotel.

181

Any attempt to apply Sharia in Juba had long been abandoned, and the town's bars were thriving.

The Greek club ran its own generator, and neon strips cast a ghoulish blue light into an outside yard where we drank Zairean beer at metal tables. Long steps led up into the main room which felt like a long-abandoned dance hall. The lighting did not extend beyond this, and one groped in the darkness for the urinals.

Jerry was dismissive about the rumours of rebel activities that made the rounds at the tables of the Greek club each evening. He had a way of turning his head aside when he spoke of things he did not like, and wrinkling his face, as if there was a bad smell.

'What is all this talk? Bandits. That is all. People exaggerate. There are always stories in Africa. When the first trouble came here in the 1950s everyone was at the airport immediately.' He laughed his loud hacking laugh. 'Now we are used to these things. It is nothing.'

For a town which was the greatest prize for either side in the civil war, Juba had the most desultory defences. At the bridge there was a gun emplacement and a small tank. The soldiers, checking the passes of people and vehicles which passed, listened to the rebel radio station. The rebels, it seemed, had all the best tunes.

60

At the Juba office of a forestry company we found a lift to the Immatong Mountains. The Immatongs lie about a hundred miles to the south-east of Juba, along the border with Uganda, a high forested range which contains Sudan's tallest peak, Mt Kinyeti at 10,456 feet.

The journey promised comfort. The lorry left its depot almost empty. Melinda had the luxury of a seat in the cab and I stretched out on some sacks of flour in the back. But in the market, after the loading of more sacks, the hordes descended. I found myself in a crush of bare-breasted women and restive babies who wrestled with their mothers' nipples in a manner so fierce I could hardly bear to look.

At the bridge everyone was ordered out, and the soldiers searched amongst the sacks for guns. On the west bank of the river, the Juba side, there was a clutter of tukals – circular mud huts with thatched conical roofs – and the bright colours of African clothing. On the east bank was a small army encampment where off-duty soldiers sat smoking in the doorways of olive-green tents. The tank sat under a tree like a display model. Grass grew up around its tracks.

Then we were off, picking up speed, rolling a cloud of red dust towards the south. The Juba plain, as flat as a sea, was full of sunlight. The huge African sky was crowded with enormous pewter-bellied clouds, high baroque creations, marble-white in the sunlight. In the far distance, in the direction of the mountains, columns of rain marched back and forth across the plain. Behind us we could see the line of the river, marked by a thickening of scrub and trees, a denser green.

Scattered along the road and back across the plain were tukals ranged round circles of swept and beaten earth. Women with flat breasts squatted by cooking fires sifting through pans of grain, and naked children, munching on cobs of roasted corn, waved as we passed. Marigolds grew around the doorways.

Occasionally we passed long clapboard buildings. Handpainted signs on the roadside announced them as schools and churches, for southern Sudan was still missionary country where eccentric Europeans spent lifetimes trying to call the native heathens to God, and to get them to put on some clothes. Through the open doors we could see the rough pews and white crosses painted on the walls.

At each village there were army checkpoints with barriers across the road. While we waited to pass, vendors crowded round the sides of the lorry holding up their wares: bananas, glasses of tea, paper funnels of nuts, single cigarettes.

The crowd in the back of the lorry were good-humoured and infected by the excitement of the wind and the journey. The red dust of the road which spiralled up around us had coated the black faces so that everyone looked rusty. In one corner a group of soldiers cradled their ancient rifles. In another a dreamy young woman in a blue smock, turned a home-made handle which had been inserted in a cassette machine whose motor no longer worked. She cranked it like an organ grinder and held it up to her ear to hear the music above the sound of the engine. In the midst of the bare-breasted women near the front sat a Muslim woman from the north, enveloped from head to foot in her tōb.

We plunged through a long tunnel of trees, the branches swishing just above our heads, and emerged where a huge sheet of rock reared up to the right of the road. The light was failing now and against the black rock I could just make out black figures, tribesmen dressed in loincloths, standing slightly apart from each other, looking down on the road. They stood motionless, watching us, their spears sticking up against the fading sky, alert and indifferent.

At Torit the soldiers would not allow us to proceed. They deemed the road too dangerous at night, vulnerable to rebel attack. Our fellow passengers climbed down and melted away into the town. One of the soldiers showed us to an empty tukal where we could sleep.

'I am sorry,' he said, embarrassed by its primitiveness, 'but in Sudan we are going backwards.'

61

In the morning the sunlight came through the trees like fresh spring water and the road was striped with bars of shadow and sun.

We had a breakfast of milky tea and balls of spiced and deep-fried dough purchased from a small boy who ran a breakfast stall from a blanket on a grassy bank.

A soldier came by in a baggy uniform and an old pair of broken boots which flapped like sandals as he walked.

'Gilo?' he asked, pointing up the road towards the east.

'That's right,' I said.

He drew nearer and became conspiratorial.

'We are going up there soon with bullets,' he said. 'We will finish things off. So when you hear rat-tat-tat, you will know everything is okay.'

He winked and moved off up the road, his intended swagger much impeded by the condition of his boots.

His reference to bullets may not have been entirely eccentric. I had heard that soldiers in the south were not given ammunition, until it was required for a particular action, for fear of mutiny or personal vendettas.

The previous civil war had begun in Torit, with an army mutiny in August 1955. It had been a vicious and largely unreported conflict which had ravaged the south for seventeen years. No one knows how many people died but foreign doctors who examined refugees from the war estimated that three out of four children never reached the age of 15, victims of malnutrition and disease, both greatly exacerbated by the fighting.

On this bright morning in Torit it all seemed incredible. Yet the road to the Immatongs, peaceful and inviting in the morning sunshine, had seen unspeakable horrors, and would do so again.

62

Coming out of the town on the rising road, we could see the mountains for the first time, blue in the distance, their folds just discernible as a deeper blue. A long scarf of cloud unfurled from round their shoulders.

The endless grasses were studded with flat-topped acacias and a tree whose leaves had turned a dark rust colour. Light and shadow swept back and forth across the plain, illuminating and darkening the colours, the brick-red road, the gold and yellow-green and auburn-brown of the blowing savanna and the blue mountains. There were few signs of human habitation now, and each fresh wave of light made it seem a new-born world.

The lorry plunged up and down steep slopes, rattling across plank bridges at the bottom of each ravine. We stopped by one bridge and the women got down to fill their gourds with red water. Flowing beneath a canopy of extravagant trees, by a red road where naked tribeswomen stopped to drink, this same water would flow through the wide deserts of Nubia and Egypt past the temples of Luxor and Karnak, beneath the tombs of Beni Hassan and the pyramids of Giza, entirely indifferent to the metamorphosis.

In Katire a band of men appeared, naked but for skin loincloths. Their bodies were decorated with patterns of dried mud, ash grey on their glossy black skin. They carried spears and banged skin drums. A crowd surged along in their wake drinking gourds of milky beer. They danced and whooped their way up the road beneath the trees, throwing handfuls of durra over each other. It had been a good harvest.

63

Gilo, at 6,000 feet, had been a hill station for British administrators from Juba. The lodge, built in the 1930s, is a fine stone building with a high porch at one end and tall green-framed windows. The bedrooms smelt of pine.

The lodge is owned by the forestry company which operates in the Immatongs, and they were happy to let it out to anyone who cared to make the trek up to Gilo. But few people came. The watchman who unlocked the doors and swept out the rooms said we were the first guests for some months.

The road from Katire to Gilo had climbed 3,000 feet in less than ten miles, twisting its way upwards through endless forest to emerge in a clearing before the lodge. A village of wood and thatch tukals lay on an open slope a couple of hundred yards away. Above the lodge was a meadow of wild flowers which sloped up to a pine forest where the sun only ever penetrated the first few ranks of trees. Beyond was the deepest gloom.

We stayed five days. They were cool and fresh and the light was always changing. In the mornings I woke early and lit the fire in the main room on which we cooked our meals. On the stone porch, with its view of mountain peaks, we read and watched the rain squalls coming from the west, the direction of Juba.

Our days at Gilo were haunted by a little girl, the daughter of

186

the watchman. She was 10 years old, but the poor diet of the mountains had so stunted her growth that she would have been small for a child of 6. Her head, which was shaved to prevent an infestation of lice, seemed huge compared to her body. It was an extraordinary shape, a long oblong from crown to chin, which reminded me of the Amarnan portraits of Akhenaton and Nefertiti with their elongated and rather bulbous heads. The child's name was Becky.

Becky appeared the first morning at the corner of the house, watching us as we took our tea on the porch, a grave, silent presence. With a little encouragement she came and sat with us and shared our breakfast, and from that morning she followed us everywhere at Gilo like a shadow. She sat on the porch in the mornings waiting for us to emerge. When the afternoon thunderstorms blew up she would appear shyly in the hallway and we would bring her in to sit by the fire while the rain lashed the windows. She never spoke to us, but watched everything with the same silent neutrality.

64

One day we walked to Itibol, following the road which ran past the lodge into the high forests. The weather was fitful and threatened rain. From the stone porch Becky watched us go without responding to our waves and farewells.

In the green gloom of the forests, the trees were festooned with trailing vines and grey lichen. Splendid but unidentifiable birds darted back and forth across the road, and pink and purple wild flowers grew along the banks. After a time we heard a shaking sound in the trees and looked up to see a tribe of blue monkeys swinging through the high canopy of branches. They retreated to a safe distance then sat contemplating us through a screen of leaves with the same thoughtful but uncommitted gaze as Becky. Later we saw colobus monkeys perched high up in small groups, looking self-conscious in their fine black and white coats.

Itibol smelt of ash and fermenting beer. The houses, built of timber scraps and wreathed in blue woodsmoke, were windowless. Heavy bonnets of grey thatch overhung the low doorways where palaeolithic figures were grinding durra, beating it with a rock in the worn hollows of flat stones. Far up near the top of the village a man with bloated cheeks was blowing a horn as long as an alpenhorn with its end resting on the ground. The deep melancholy notes rolled down the hillside like boulders.

At the bottom of the village, beneath a ragged canopy of thatch, was a massive steam engine which had once driven a saw in the days when the logs were cut on site before being taken down the mountain. It was a magnificent piece of baroque Victorian technology with endless knobs and handles and levers and little doors through which one stared into its dark cast-iron gut. It sat rusting beneath its canopy, a monument to that moment when the modern world had come to Itibol.

We walked up through the village. The children who played between the huts screamed and ran off when they saw us. Though it was cold enough for our breath to rise in plumes, no one in the village wore anything more than thin rags, and the children went barefoot.

At the top of the village was a tall pole holding aloft a flattened piece of tin on which the initials SPLA had been painted – Southern People's Liberation Army. Beyond was a silent wood. It seemed to be winter up here, and the trees were all bare.

We walked back down through the village to the school. A man appeared in the doorway. He was a small figure, neatly and incongruously dressed in a white shirt, a pair of trousers with a crease and leather shoes. He greeted us in English.

'How do you do,' he said. 'I am the headmaster. My name is Khamis Ali Mogga. People here call me Mogga.'

Mogga was as fine-boned as a child. He had graceful hands and a way of tilting his head to one side when he listened, like a bird. His expression alternated between a shy embarrassment and great earnestness. There was an air of tragedy about him, but he laughed easily and heartily. He sat on the edge of one of the desks and told us the story of his life and the school so eagerly it was as if he had been waiting for ages for someone to come up the track from Gilo on whom he could unburden himself.

188

Mogga was a member of the Kakwa tribe from western Equatoria. Like many southern tribes it is divided by the Sudanese–Ugandan border, and when Mogga was very young his family had gone to live in Uganda to escape the ravages of the Sudanese civil war. For Mogga it had been a fortunate move as the educational facilities in Uganda were far superior to those in Sudan. Eventually he had attended Makerere University in Kampala, which in his day had been the finest university in Africa. He had trained as a teacher.

When Amin fell from power, Mogga's world collapsed. Amin too came from the Kakwa tribe. Like thousands of others who were innocent of Amin's crimes but shared his tribal origins, Mogga was forced to flee to Sudan. He covered the 300 miles on foot in two weeks, keeping to back roads to avoid towns and questions. Over 200,000 people crossed the border into Sudan, like Mogga, as refugees in the wake of Amin's overthrow.

Mogga was shocked by conditions in southern Sudan. He thought longingly of Kampala with its paved streets, its shops and schools and hospitals, its public gardens and fine buildings. Even in Amin's day it had retained something of its former beauty. When he secured the post of teacher at Itibol, and came on the back of a logging truck from Juba, and then up the tortuous track from Katire, he thought he had come to the end of the world.

'I will never forget my first night here,' he said. 'In the darkness. Only a candle for a light. It was bitterly cold. I slept here in the school. The only sounds were drunken shouting from the huts above. I thought really I had come to hell.'

He had lived in Itibol now for five years, and still expressed surprise at the level of ignorance of the local people.

'They grow nothing,' he said. 'only maize, durra and pumpkins. The maize they make into beer. It is their only industry, and the beer is often their only supper. The children are malnourished. Yet look at the country. The soil is fertile. There is plenty of rain. They could grow many vegetables. But they are too ignorant. They know nothing about vegetables, and think only of their beer. I myself grow carrots, cabbage, onions and potatoes. I sent some of my students to pick a few potatoes for me one afternoon. When I went to look for them, I found them in the field eating the potatoes raw. Just like monkeys.'

189

Before the arrival of Mogga the school had existed in name only. Without him, it would soon disintegrate again. His main problem was truancy, not of the students, but of the teachers. The students were remarkably loyal. His school was highly thought of and many of the students walked up from Katire barefoot, a trek of two or three hours in each direction. The teachers were less reliable. Their salaries were always in arrears. When the money did arrive, they would take off to celebrate. Only when the money was all gone would they return.

'They have not been here all week,' Mogga said. 'And now this morning, they sent word with some of the students that they are not coming back until next week.'

He spoke movingly of the old days in Uganda. Life had been so different there. He could think in those days of visiting other parts of the world. His great ambition was to travel to England.

'Now it is not worth thinking of these things. My life has contracted to Itibol. There is no opportunity for improvement here. And I am very much afraid that there is no way out.'

We walked back to Gilo along the track through the forests. The sun was setting into red clouds behind a purple mountain. Birds shrieked from the tree-tops. It grew dark and cold along the track. Raindrops pattered on the leaves above us: the first sound of the Nile.

At the door of the lodge, sheltering beneath the eaves, we found Becky waiting for us.

65

I had not given up the idea of travelling through the Sudd. In Juba we had booked passage on the boat downriver to Kosti. We would return later to Juba and the journey upriver by whatever means available. The manager at the Juba booking office was confident he could smuggle us aboard without permits.

But on our return from Gilo he had disappointing news. The boat coming upriver from Kosti was unable to reach Juba due to the falling river. Passengers would have to travel to Mongalla by truck to meet it, and permits would be checked carefully on the roads. Reluctantly we had to abandon the plan.

Uganda presented similar problems. When we had left England eight months before, reports coming out of Uganda had not been encouraging. The authority of the Obote government was challenged by a number of guerrilla forces. Remnants of Amin's army were said to be terrorizing areas of the north-west, but throughout the country the greatest problem was the government's own soldiers. Ill-paid and ill-disciplined, they preyed upon the local population as a means of supporting themselves.

In Juba however it was clear that travellers were managing to pass through Uganda again. In the market we met a Kenyan truck driver who plied the route between Mombasa and Juba, carrying UN food aid for the Ugandan refugees in Sudan. Dressed in smart clothes, he was a striking contrast to the lorry drivers of southern Sudan in their cast-off mission rags. He looked on the locals as backward and barbaric, beyond redemption, and could not get over the fact that many spoke neither English nor Swahili, only a pidgin Arabic.

For some time he had avoided Uganda, preferring the longer route through northern Kenya directly into Sudan.

'But things have improved,' he said. 'There are still roadblocks and the soldiers who man them are thieves, but there is not the fear for one's own skin.'

He agreed to take us to Nimule, a Sudanese town on the border, where we wanted to stay for a few days before crossing into Uganda.

In the evening in the yard of the hotel Jerry emerged from his room bearing the aroma of coffee and Greek cigarettes.

'So you are leaving us,' he said. 'Everyone leaves Juba but me. They should make me the mayor.'

'We are going to Nimule,' we said.

'Ah, Nimule. Paradise.' He flicked his fly whisk about his ears. The evening was full of midges.

'There is a lodge, I believe, in the game park,' I said.

'Yes. Very beautiful. In the old days we used to travel so much. I was in Uganda many times. Such a beautiful country. You will not believe. Now it is finished, of course. Everywhere is dangerous.

191

Even Juba is dangerous, they say. What can we do?' He shrugged and drew on his long cigarette holder. 'Nothing.'

66

The road to Nimule ran through lightly wooded hills some miles to the east of the Nile. The dry stream-beds which cut down towards the river were full of bleached stones, and the small wooden bridges we crossed made a hollow sound beneath the wheels of the lorry.

We saw no one along the road. Here and there untended fires were burning uncontrollably through the dry grasses. Whole stretches of country were being devoured as we passed and the wind lifted the ash and fluttered it down over us like a soft black rain.

At Opari we stopped for tea. A string of tar-brown huts clung to the roadside. We stood outside one, and a woman brought the glasses of tea out to us. One of our fellow passengers turned out to be the manager of the lodge at the game park at Nimule where we hoped to stay.

Emil was a big man with a flattened face, bruised-looking eyes and a slow, magnificent smile. He carried a black attaché case from which he was never parted. He stood now in the road with the case in one hand and his tea in the other.

'The people here are all refugees from Uganda,' he said. 'Back a little way from the road are huge camps, thousands of people.' He waved his case over our heads towards the east. 'At Magwe they are starving. They have nothing.'

On the lorry again we passed through two resettlement centres set up by the United Nations High Commission for Refugees. Crowds of people milled about the new wooden buildings. Hand-painted signs identified them as schools and workshops and social centres. Beyond them the bush closed in again on the deserted road.

'You are going to a country from which everyone has fled,' Emil said above the noise of the engine.

After a time we gained a high ridge. On either side slopes fell away to flat green plains. Away to the east we could see the

Immatongs, threatened by dark rain clouds. The landscape felt vast and timeless. The marks of man were those which had been there since his first arrival: a few scattered huts dotted across the plain, smoking fires, paths of red earth beaten through the long grasses.

As night fell a high mountain ridge closed towards us from the west. The dark came quickly. High up on the ridge, fires were burning, creeping slowly across the dark slopes. Far ahead of us long fingers of lightning lit up the sky. It grew cold on the lorry, and in the flashes of lightning the trees along the road were grey as ghosts.

We climbed to a high pass and then the road began to drop quickly, twisting downwards in the darkness. Far below we could see a single orange light. Beyond, the sporadic lightning revealed a grey sheen of water: the Nile.

At the bottom of the pass, we got down from the lorry with Emil. When the headlights and the sound of the engine had disappeared up the road the night closed in. Emil, clutching his case, led us up a dirt track. We could see no more than a foot or two in front of us.

'There may be elephants here,' Emil said. 'Just here along the road.' He stopped and listened to the night. We stared into the darkness. 'They come right up to the lodge at night. One must be careful.'

Presently, the orange light which we had seen from the pass reappeared. It was a gas lantern in the window of a low lodge set beneath trees. Beyond it lay the river, a lighter thread of darkness, catching the starlight.

Emil showed us to our room. A host of bizarre insects danced against the screen windows. From the river below we could hear the hippos grunting as they heaved themselves out of the water to graze.

67

The lodge sat on a hill above the Nile at the foot of the high ridge from which we had descended the previous night. Before it lay a vast plain. The hill was the last hill of Sudan. The plain was Uganda.

Away to the south-west lay a range of blue mountains which rose in Zaire on the far shores of Lake Albert. The Nile curved across the plain from the direction of the lake, a wide, serene river in an empty landscape. Beneath our hill it turned through a great U-bend. Downstream the channel narrowed and the current quickened. A couple of miles on lay the Fula Rapids.

Viewed from the lodge Uganda appeared to be an uninhabited country. We could see no villages, and at night no lights or fires were visible in the wide darkness. The river was empty save for the hippos wallowing in the shallows.

We were the only guests in the lodge. No foreigners had visited the park for two years, and only occasionally did Africans come from Juba to stay the night. The morale of the staff, Emil confided to us, was not high. Food was scarce and there was no petrol. The park jeep sat beneath a tree on flattening tyres.

We arrived at Nimule with the wages, which had come from Juba in Emil's black attaché case. They had a purgative effect on the staff, who immediately vanished in the way of the teachers at Itibol. Emil solemnly recited their various excuses to us. He could not bring himself to admit that they were not entirely legitimate.

We were left with the second eleven, a motley crew whose shortcomings kept them out of the permanent staff. They gathered like birds on a large rock near the lodge and drank home-made beer all day in honour of their new temporary positions. From the smoking fires in their midst obsequious and drunken waiters carried forth our meals – inedible mountains of grey rice and bowls of murky soup from whose depths glassy eyed fish heads floated to the surface.

The game wardens were equally uninspiring. In their rag-tag bits of uniform, cradling their ancient rifles, they paraded each morning on a patch of bare earth in front of the park office, a wood hut. They looked like the remnants of a defeated army who hoped the war had moved elsewhere. They were no match for the professional ivory hunters who have decimated the park's elephant population.

In recent years southern Sudan has been the world's leading source of ivory. It has become the currency of personal advancement amongst the army and the police as well as a means for the southern rebels to arm themselves. They trade ivory direct for Kalashnikovs. Well-organized gangs invade places like Nimule where they out-number and outgun the authorities who are powerless to stop them. It is thought that over 10,000 elephants a year are being slaughtered in Sudan for their tusks.

68

Nimule is one of the few parks in Africa where you can still meet the wildlife with only a warden's antiquated rifle to protect you. There are no safari vehicles or glass-topped mini-buses here. There are no roads. When you go to see the animals, you go on foot.

We walked west from the lodge across sloping grasslands, broken by rocks and stunted tamarisk trees, towards the river where the grass shaded from yellow to soft green. Along the bank about a mile from the lodge we came upon a herd of elephants grazing noisily through the river meadows.

With their tough, wrinkled hides and their tusks, they looked primeval, a memory of a distant world of mammoths when simian man had cowered in caves. A bull elephant grasped a young tree with its trunk, uprooting it with self-deprecating casualness. Eleph-ants have the manners appropriate to an ancient breed, restrained and self-assured.

The herd made its way down to the bank and one by one the elephants lowered themselves carefully into the water as if into a too-hot bath. The egrets, who resided on the elephants' backs, alighted and stood about on the bank awaiting their return to dry land. With their trunks the elephants stirred the water and sprayed each other. Even in their sport, they seemed oddly thoughtful.

In the reeds along the bank the guide uncovered a leaky dug-out canoe, half submerged in water. We tipped it out and pushed out into the river. The current was stronger than we had ever seen it, and we were carried a long way downstream before we reached the opposite bank. When we pushed up into the reeds the canoe was just beginning to sink, and we skipped gratefully ashore.

We skirted another herd of elephants and came out along the river again on mud flats which the sun had dried to a hard crumbling shale. Suddenly there was the sound of something breaking the surface of the water and we looked round to see the heads of hippopotami emerging from the river, one by one. They were a herd of about a dozen and they rose from the river spraying water and snorting and bellowing their deep tuba notes.

It was the Greeks who called them hippopotamus. The name means river horse and there is something strikingly equine about them. Riding with their heads and their broad backs just above the surface of the water, they have the same smooth-skinned sensuality. Lolling all day in the river, their lives appear devoted to pleasure. It is reported that the average mating time of a hippopotamus couple is forty-six minutes.

Wallowing in the shallows, their heads resting on each other's backs, they seem such pacific creatures. But bull hippos fight more ferociously and frequently than most other animals. Elderly bulls, no longer able to fight for their territory and too proud to submit, are obliged to leave the herd. They spend their last years in solitary wandering, a cruel fate for such a naturally gregarious animal.

On our way back to the lodge we passed our herd of elephants grazing near the track. We were upwind of them now, and they stopped feeding to scent the air with their trunks. We had agitated them.

Our guide grew nervous, and began to shoo us on to higher ground, waving his rifle at us, as if it was us and not the elephants who were the threat.

'I am shooting if this is getting serious, I am shooting,' he kept saying over and over again. 'These elephants can be dangerous. Many people are getting killed.'

The elephants turned one way and then another. The bulls now came forward to face us. They brought their ears forward in a gesture of alarm and aggression. Their trunks swept the air and they bellowed. The egrets had left them.

But their agitation was as nothing compared to that of our guide.

He had broken into a frightful sweat, and his voice seemed to have risen three registers.

'I am shooting. I am shooting,' he chanted like a kind of mantra. He swept his rifle back and forth as if looking for a target. Melinda and I found ourselves dancing this way and that across the slope trying to keep ourselves out of his line of fire. At our backs the elephants roared and stamped their feet.

'I am shooting. I am shooting,' he trilled.

'Don't shoot. Don't shoot,' we cried, ducking and weaving. Caught between a herd of angry bull elephants and an armed and crazed game warden, it was difficult to know where to turn.

Suddenly the rifle went off. A bullet pinged off a boulder to our left. The game warden, terrified by the shot, dropped the rifle and took to his heels, bounding up the slope towards the lodge like a hare.

We picked up the rifle and followed at a brisk walk, intent on putting as much space as possible between us and the elephants, who eventually turned back towards the river. No doubt they felt a bath was in order after such excitement.

As we came up to the lodge we found our warden being ministered to by the drunken staff on their rock. He lifted his head from a huge bowl of home-made beer and smiled wanly at us.

'Elephants are such jokers,' he said.

69

We soon tired of fish gruel, and walked into town one evening in search of better fare.

Not far from the lodge we passed an abandoned schoolhouse. The tin roofs had been looted and the doors and windows broken. Families had moved into the classrooms. We could see them beneath the blackboards feeding bits of chairs and desks into their fires. They waved cheerily to us as we passed.

Nimule was like a Wild West town. Its one road, a wide thoroughfare of red dirt, ran straight through it. The buildings were all alike, low and tin-roofed with overhanging porches. Most were closed and boarded up. Along the roadside were stalls, lit with candles, where children sold single cigarettes and sweets. At the far end of town a group of Arabs sat on the ground around a gas lantern reading the Koran aloud in the gathering darkness.

We turned back up the wide street, between the candles and the dark buildings, and went into the bar, the only place in town with a generator.

We ordered a beer called Tusker, and asked the barman about Uganda.

'Things seem to be a little better at the moment,' he said. 'There is a new district commissioner at Gulu, and the lorry drivers say he has removed the roadblocks.'

'Stay away from the soldiers,' a man at the bar said. 'The soldiers are vultures. They are all bandits and murderers.'

Behind the bar was an adjoining hotel and an eating room. To reach it we went outside, along a side wall, through a hole in a wire fence and down a dark passage.

The eating room was a small cement box of a room lit by a pink neon light. The generator was just outside one of the curtained doors, and the room acted as a sounding box for it. There were two long tables occupied by hulking young men. We sat down at the end of one of the tables on the only spare chairs. None of the men was eating. No one spoke. The loud thudding of the generator was oppressive.

After a time a young man came through a curtained doorway from a yard where we could see cooking fires.

'What is there to eat?' I asked.

'There is chicken, fish, meat and kebab.'

'Fine. We'll have a plate of chicken and another of fish.'

The men shuffled on their chairs and looked at their hands. They were big muscular men in cast-off mission clothes.

A few minutes later the young man came back through the curtain.

'There is no chicken, or fish,' he said. 'There is no meat either. There are beans.'

'We'll have beans in that case,' I said.

He returned in a moment with a single large bowl of beans and two grubby chapattis. We tried to chat to each other but found our conversation trailing off into whispers. The beans tasted of ash.

After a time a woman came through another curtained door. She was tall and striking, and wore a tribal cloth knotted over one shoulder. Where the cloth parted, it revealed her thigh, naked to the waist. Her knees were grazed. She leant against the wall, smoking a cigarette. When she had finished she threw the stub into a corner and nodded at the man at the end of the other table. He got up and went through the curtain. She followed him, and the men at the table all moved along one place.

70

The borders bequeathed by colonial powers bedevil African politics. Too often they ignore tribal boundaries. Invariably they had more to do with the pattern of European exploration and colonization than with African geo-political realities.

Sudan offers one of the starkest examples of this tendency, combining as it does a desert Arab north with an equatorial African south. British colonial opinion in Sudan did toy with the idea of joining southern Sudan with Uganda, with which it shares so many ethnic and geographical features. But in the end it was decided that it was easier to maintain the colonial entity of Sudan, a decision for which many Sudanese have paid with their lives.

As much as the introduction of Sharia, the present crisis in the south was prompted by Numeri's decision to dissolve the southern regional government and create in its place three smaller forums directly responsible to Khartoum. Its stated purpose was to break Dinka dominance of southern politics, allowing the smaller tribes more say. But its effect was to divide and weaken the southern voice in the northern capital.

Tribal divisions amongst the southern tribes have been a significant feature of this second civil war. The Equatorians – tribes like the Lotuko and the Bari who played a leading role in the first conflict – have largely stood aside. The rebel SPLA is perceived to be a Dinka force.

'John Garang is a Dinka, and the leadership are almost entirely Dinka,' Emil said. 'The other tribes do not trust them.'

Emil had tea with us each afternoon beneath the mango trees overlooking the river. We talked endlessly of the civil war. Before coming to Nimule, Emil had worked in a hotel in Malakal in Upper Nile province. The hotel had closed when much of the province fell into rebel hands.

Whatever his suspicions about other southern tribes, his real animosity was reserved for the northern Arabs. He believed them to be manipulative and hypocritical.

'They think we are savages, and they treat us accordingly.'

Under the pressures of war, relations between northerners and southerners have reached a nadir. The bitterness directed towards the northern Arabs by southerners was a shock to us, for we had always found them charming, considerate and gracious. But war brings out the worst in any society, and the most brutal elements of the Arab north seemed now to dominate the tenor of relations.

The government's decision to rely increasingly on irregular militias to fight the rebels on its behalf has led to a litany of horrors. The militias are supplied with arms and ammunition, but are unpaid. The main recruits are young men impoverished by the famine. They operate independently of the army, and outside any effective form of government control. Their victims are mainly civilians.

By June 1988 chilling reports were emerging from towns like Abyei, 500 miles south-west of Khartoum, near the border of southern Kordofan and Bahr el Ghazal province, effectively the border of northern and southern Sudan. Once a flourishing Dinka cattle-town, it has been devastated by raids from the Missiriyah Arab tribal militia. The Arab merchants and the army have become cattle barons as the starving Dinka, robbed of their land by the Missiriyah, sell off their herds at half the going rate. The streets of the town are crowded with the skeletal figures of women, children and the elderly, most of them near death. Those who have the strength make their way north to work as slaves on Missiriyah farms. In Abyei there are no young Dinka men left. Most have been seized and killed as suspected rebels or collaborators;

those that escape flee to the bush, leaving their families helpless.

It is now widely thought that the catastrophe which has overtaken the Dinka is so great that they are finished as a cultural identity. It is a tragedy of which the outside world is still largely ignorant.

71

One afternoon a man walked up from the town to see me. He wanted my help in overthrowing the Ugandan government.

He was a refugee who had fled the country in 1979 after the fall of Amin, as well he might, for he had been the assistant commissioner of police in Makerere, a post certain to single him out for retribution.

He greeted me as one might greet an old friend encountered by chance in some remote corner of the globe.

'The British,' he declared, 'are our fathers and our brothers. We must never abandon our own blood and kin.'

I must have looked a bit blank.

'The British are the fathers of Uganda, and their children are now requiring their assistance.' He leaned towards me conspiratorially. 'This is why I have made the journey to see you.'

'It is very kind of you to come all this way,' I said.

'Not kind. Not kind at all. But necessary.'

He swelled his chest. 'Your country, Uganda, is in the hands of bandits. It is your duty to help save it.'

'But it is not my country,' I said.

'Oh yes. It is the country created by the British. We were British subjects. Loyal to the Crown. Now we appeal to the British to help us. It is our hour of need.' He seemed to affect an almost Churchillian cadence. I suspected him of conjuring imaginary crowds.

'But the British have no right to meddle in Ugandan affairs,' I said. 'Uganda is an independent country now.'

'It is not independent in the hands of bandits. The British must come back to restore the country. They are our fathers. We are needing their assistance.'

'But what can I do?'

'We are requiring agitators.'

'Agitators?'

He nodded solemnly.

'We are requiring agitators in Britain to whip up support for the independence of Uganda so that when we move, the British will come with us. Where are you living in Britain?'

'London,' I replied.

'Excellent,' he said.

He produced a long letter written on an oily and dog-eared piece of airmail paper. I was to take it to London to publish in newspapers and to show to government ministers. It listed ten points. The first nine rambled at length about the greatness of the British, the ties of loyalty between Uganda and Britain, the British promises of independence, the UN charter, Churchill's steadfastness against Hitler, and the excellence of British education. The last point was entitled 'No Revenge'. It insisted that the exiles had no intention of revenge on Obote and his supporters. It then went on to list, in case revenge proved unavoidable, the names of individuals and of whole tribes who must be eliminated.

72

From the lodge we could watch the weather brewing far across the plain in Uganda. On our last afternoon a tremendous storm arose in the south, and we watched it advance across the plain towards us.

It began as distant patches of rain which gradually consolidated into a grey curtain. As it crept northwards a great shadow went before it. Gradually the plain faded into a murky gloom and disappeared from view.

At the lodge we were still in sunlight, that eerie vivid pre-storm light. The wind was up and a host of birds arose from the hillside to be blown over the grasses like scraps of paper. Dry leaves and blossoms showered down from the trees and scuttled away over the ground, and the doors in the lodge began to bang. The dark veil of rain came on across the plain. Below us the smooth sheen of the river roughened and then we could see the first rain falling on the water.

The light failed, and thunder rolled and echoed from the high ridge behind us. A shutter crashed to the ground.

As the first big drops pattered down on us through the trees, the wind dropped slightly. Then the real rain was upon us. It thundered on the tin roof, and water poured in torrents from the eaves. The trees drooped. A sudden chill came through the screen windows like a breath of winter. Off towards the tukals I could see a man running, bent double, his shirt over his head. We stood in the porch and looked out at the rain. The view was gone. Even the river was hidden by the dark curtains of rain.

In the morning we crossed the border into Uganda.

BOOK III
UGANDA

1

We went to Uganda with three Arabs in a Landrover. They had turned up at the lodge from Juba the night of the storm, planning to travel on to Gulu, a town about sixty miles into Uganda, the next morning. They intended to return to Sudan the same day; Gulu they thought too dangerous a place to spend the night.

The Arabs brought tragic news from Juba. The river-boat on which we had booked passage, the one which had been unable to reach Juba, had been attacked and sunk by rebels on its way north, back to Kosti. Early reports indicated that all passengers were killed. The low river, which had caused such hardship throughout Sudan, had saved our lives.

In the morning we crossed into Uganda with foreboding. There was no border post on the Ugandan side, and the road immediately deteriorated with the most atrocious pot-holes.

The northern flatlands of Uganda were as deserted as they had appeared from the lodge. It was half an hour before we saw the first people. They were soldiers. They waved the car down from the roadside. Their uniforms were so tattered they looked like panto-mime shipwreck victims. As we drew up we saw a ruinous wooden building set back from the road.

Two soldiers leaned through the window and breathed beer into the faces of the Arabs. They wanted a lift. With their heads through the window they looked round the car, and slowly took in the fact that it was full. On the porch of the building stood an officer, neatly dressed and wearing dark glasses. Watching his ragged subordinates importuning us, he began to laugh.

One of the Arabs motioned for the driver to go on. The soldiers held on to the car as we moved off, running along beside it until they fell down in the road in a cloud of dust. Through the rear window we could see their guns propped against a tree and the officer laughing uproariously on the porch.

At Atiak, a desolate place of damaged buildings and abandoned cars, we found the customs post. It was a shell of a building with broken windows and doors hanging from one hinge, staffed by new recruits brought in to end the harassment of travellers. I wondered how long it would be before the old practices reasserted themselves. A shirtless soldier who searched our bags lingered hungrily over my jacket. I was relieved when he put it back. The letter asking for my help in overthrowing the Ugandan government, which I had kept as a souvenir, was sewn into the lining.

Beyond Atiak the country improved. We began to see villages and people. The women wore the marvellous dresses, busutis, that we were to see throughout Uganda – full-length, full-skirted dresses with puff shoulders. They had a curiously Victorian air, but the extravagant patterns and bright colours made them wholly African. The women paraded along the roadside carrying cloth bundles on their heads. Children played beneath trees. The villages and circles of tukals with their smoking fires had a reassuring air of cheerful normality.

The change in the condition of the country reflected our movement from one tribal area into another, and the fate of different tribes in Obote's Uganda. The northern borderlands had been the preserve of those tribes who had ethnic links with Amin. Beyond Atiak we were in the tribal territory of the Acholi, a powerful northern tribe closely related to Milton Obote's own tribe, the Langi, both of whom were prospering in post-Amin Uganda.

2

In the old days everyone spoke warmly of Uganda. It was known as the pearl of Africa. 'Uganda is a fairy tale,' wrote Winston Churchill in 1908, after arriving by train from Kenya. 'You climb up a railway instead of a beanstalk, and at the top there is a wonderful new world.'

At independence in 1962 it seemed to have everything going for it: a good climate, fertile soil, a healthy economy based on coffee and tea exports, a rail network, 1,000 miles of paved roads, and the best university and hospital in Africa, heading education and health systems which were the envy of the Third World.

Milton Obote was Uganda's first Prime Minister. In an attempt at tribal balance the President was Freddie Mutesa, formerly Mutesa II, the Kabaka or King of the Baganda, the most sophisticated and influential of Uganda's tribes. At independence, Idi Amin, a former British army officer, held the rank of colonel in the new army. It was Obote who naïvely saw him as a pliable instrument for his own schemes and promoted him to Chief of Staff.

Obote lost no time in taking all the reins of power into his own hands, eventually suspending the constitution. When the Baganda rose in revolt, he called in Amin who blasted his way into the Kabaka's palace. King Freddie, the last of a royal line which dated back to the sixteenth century, escaped over a garden wall and fled to London where he died, three years later, a penniless alcoholic.

Obote remained in power under an almost continual state of emergency until 1971. His regime was marked by tribalism, corruption and repression. When Amin overthrew him, allegedly with the assistance of the Israeli secret service, the British and American governments were quick to offer him their support. They had grown unhappy, not with the ruthless repression of Obote's government, but with its socialist leanings. In what was to prove an ironic gesture of tribal reconciliation, Amin ordered the body of the Kabaka in London to be returned and buried with his royal ancestors on the hills above Kampala.

Under Amin Uganda quickly slid into bloody anarchy. The economy, weakened by expulsion of the Asians, was further decimated by government neglect and corruption. Inflation reached 1,000 per cent and by the end of Amin's rule the official minimum wage of £20 a month – and few people earned even that – bought only ten loaves of bread. Makerere University was filled with Amin's semi-literate cronies and Mulago Hospital became a disease-infested pit from which few people emerged alive. The roads cracked and fell into pot-holes, schools and hospitals closed for lack of funds, investment dried up. Fear and paranoia gripped the country as torture and massacre became commonplace. It is said that anywhere between 100,000 and 500,000 people were killed or 'disappeared' in the eight years of Amin's dictatorship. The screams which emanated nightly from the headquarters of Amin's secret police in Kampala punctuated a nightmare from which Uganda seemed unable to awake. Bodies were taken by the lorry-load from prisons and army barracks in and around Kampala to be dumped in the Nile.

Late in 1978 Amin attempted to divert attention from his mounting problems by invading the Kagera salient in the north-western corner of Tanzania. The invasion reflected the degree to which Amin had lost any grip on reality; his army, accustomed to torture and plunder, were in no condition for the discipline of war. The Tanzanians, aided by the Uganda National Liberation Army, a coalition of exiles and internal opponents, counterattacked. Amin's army simply melted away, and he and his henchmen fled. Out of the ensuing power struggle, Milton Obote emerged once again as President, confirmed by a rigged election.

But the fall of Amin did nothing to end the nightmare. The horrors continued. Only the characters had changed.

3

After the towns of Sudan, Gulu seemed a substantial place. The buildings were two-storeyed and made, not of adobe, but of brick and mortar with tiled roofs and proper windows. They were laid out in a grid of streets. There were street signs, street lights and in places an attempt at pavements. In the main street was a proper petrol station with a forecourt and pumps. There was a police station with a blue lamp outside and a post office which was a replica of its British counterparts. We found a park with tended flower beds and a tree-lined avenue where men were pruning branches. After the mud lanes and distress of Juba, Gulu seemed the very height of civic order.

But order was a thing of the past. The town had lain in the path of Amin's retreating soldiers who had terrorized and looted the population. The buildings of Gulu were a testimony to their passage. Many were empty and boarded up. Almost every window was broken, and walls were pock-marked with bullet-holes. The petrol station forecourt had been torn up and the pumps smashed. Though years had passed since Amin's fall, nothing seemed to have been repaired or cleared up. The streets were full of cars abandoned by people who had fled north to Sudan in 1979. Stripped down to their rusting frames, they lay about the town like skeletons.

When the Tanzanian forces entered Gulu they were welcomed with garlands and dancing. The Acholi had suffered under Amin long before his looting soldiers had fled through the town. But the victory celebrations were soon cut short by further atrocities which presaged the continuing horrors of post-Amin Uganda. Bands of spear-wielding Acholi warriors appeared in the streets and went through the town in search of people from West Nile province, Amin's tribal homeland. Madi, Lugbara and Kakwa residents, many of whom had lived peacefully in Gulu for years, were hunted down and massacred. Over a hundred innocent people were slaughtered during the course of a single afternoon. The Tanzanians could do nothing to stop it short of opening fire on the whole Acholi population.

4

A ragged man brought us to St Luke's Guest House, a large building on the edge of the town. He had taken a silent but proprietorial interest in us from the moment he saw us get down from the Landrover in the main street. When he left us inside the gate of St Luke's, he gripped my hand and whispered, 'Beware. There is something wrong in the town.'

The ground floor of St Luke's, looted in the 'troubles', had been boarded up and abandoned, but upstairs were five clean and airy rooms furnished with simple cots. The manager, a tall shy man

211

called Jackson, pumped our hands and gave us a pamphlet entitled 'Are you going to Heaven?'

Eight months on the Nile had left us with recurring bouts of intestinal illness, and we thought we would take advantage of the facilities of Gulu to be checked for amoebas.

The hospital was an imposing colonial building behind a screen of birch trees. Inside the gate were the burnt-out shells of two ambulances. From the porch we saw that all the windows along the front of the building were broken.

A nurse took us to a doctor and the doctor sent us to the laboratory. The laboratory was a bare, white-tiled room. We found a technician asleep on a table in a back room.

'You must bring me stool samples,' he said.

We asked him for containers.

'We have no containers here,' he replied, waving a hand around the empty room. 'We have nothing.'

'We have no containers either,' Melinda said.

The man shrugged. 'Wrap your samples in a piece of newspaper. That will be alright.'

We looked at him.

'If we had the kind of stools that could be wrapped in a piece of newspaper', I said, 'we would not be here.'

He seemed to take the point. He disappeared and returned after a time with two thin vials no more than an inch across.

'I am very sorry,' he said, 'it is the best I can do.'

We asked to use the toilets.

'There are no toilets,' he said. 'The toilets were all stolen.'

We went up the hill to the Acholi Inn, part of a government chain of hotels. In the lobby a group of army officers sat drinking whisky. Behind them was a kiosk with loose wires hanging from the wall where the telephone had been torn out. In the toilets, we found the toilet bowls and the sinks intact, but there was no water.

Back at the laboratory, the technician bent over his microscope.

'They took everything,' he said. 'Not the soldiers but the people in the town. They looted the whole hospital. There was no one to stop them. Now they have a hospital with no equipment, no drugs,

212

no supplies. We do not even have toilets. I buried this microscope beneath a tree to save it.'

The results were negative but when we took them back to the doctor he prescribed a course of drugs for amoebic dysentery anyway.

'It is not always advisable', he said solemnly, 'to rely on the results of our laboratory tests.'

The hospital clinic did not have the prescribed drugs but we were able to buy them later on the black market from a car mechanic in the town.

5

We took an early train to Pakwach, a town on the Nile where it emerges from Lake Albert.

It was still dark when I got up. I stood outside on the balcony enjoying the cool of the night. Fields away, roosters were crowing. Voices and soft laughter came from somewhere out of the night, slight intimate sounds filtering down through the dark trees. Beyond the voices, fainter still, I could hear the sound of an organ playing 'Once in Royal David's City', and remembered suddenly that it was only a few weeks to Christmas.

At the station we were seen off, like visiting dignitaries, by a one-legged radio operator. He stood to attention, lopsidedly, outside our carriage window, smiling and nodding, unwilling to leave us until he had seen the train safely away.

There was a ruckus at the last moment. Someone shouted thief. A man ran off across a field and a great crowd set off in pursuit, streaming through a gap in a hedge. Presently they returned driving the culprit before them with sticks. He ran ahead and took refuge in the railway police station, slamming the door behind him. The radio operator tried valiantly to ignore the uproar. He stood facing the train, smiling up at us with a fixed pained smile.

The train was a movable feast. At the stations crowds of vendors descended on the carriages selling peanuts, jars of peanut sauce, toasted corn, finger bananas, sugar cane, boiled eggs, baked matoke and mugs of milky spiced tea. Our fellow passengers enjoyed a continuous banquet, finishing each course just as the train drew into the next station, where they descended on to the platform in waves for more.

We passed gradually from a populated, well-cultivated land to poorer regions. The fields of red earth and the thatched villages gave way to yellow savanna, and the women in their bright busutis to people dressed in rags. Naked children ran after the train through the clouds of dust. We were leaving the land of the Acholi and moving towards the impoverished lands of West Nile province.

The Nile came into view from a low ridge, flowing out of Lake Albert, a broad calm stream. Standing back a little way from the far bank were tall mango trees, their trunks soaking in pools of midday shadow.

6

The Pakwach bridge was guarded by a row of bored soldiers leaning on the rail staring down at their own reflections in the murky water below. They turned to watch the train pass. Just downstream the carcase of an old steamer was moored against the bank. Reeds grew like whiskers through the windows of its wheelhouse. It was the *Lugard* which had run between Pakwach and Nimule before the Albert Nile became one of the most lawless stretches of the river.

Pakwach was a wide dirt road lined with shuttered buildings. We found a petrol station which served food. Two Europeans and an African, sitting at one of the tables, invited us to join them.

The Europeans introduced themselves as Barry and Kurt. The African was Mr Win. Barry was an ex-army sergeant from Skegness, a bluff genial man of simple virtues. Kurt was a schoolmaster from Copenhagen. He was generous, pedantic and long-winded, and had the abrupt movements of a marionette. Mr Win, whom Barry and Kurt introduced as their boss, was a huge bear of a man

214

with wary, intelligent eyes. He smiled a great deal and said little.

Barry and Kurt were in Uganda with a World Bank project to distribute twenty million pounds' worth of educational supplies to schools throughout the country. Mr Win was an official from the Ugandan Ministry of Education who was overseeing the project. They were planning a detour into Murchison Falls National Park and offered us a lift.

7

Murchison Falls National Park is small by African standards, only about half the size of Corsica. It straddles the 'Victoria' Nile which flows between Lake Kyoga and Lake Albert.

We followed a track through high walls of grass which swished along the sides of the car. Eventually it brought us out at Pakuba Lodge, a long modern building of stone and wood. The car park was empty and overgrown with weeds.

We went inside through glass doors to a spacious lobby. It was completely bare, without decoration or furnishing. A door to one side with a sign which read 'Gift Shop' led into a small empty room. The only feature was a huge full-length portrait of Milton Obote which leant against one wall. He stared out at us with lunatic eyes.

We called and our voices echoed up wide stairways. When we turned back a man had materialized beside the reception desk. He was barefoot and wore a pair of ragged shorts held up with a string belt. He gazed at us wide-eyed as if debating whether to stand or run.

'Is there a bar?' Barry asked.

The man pointed silently down the steps to the lounge.

In the bar, the seating areas were divided by low walls. Wild grasses from the savanna had blown in and seeded themselves in the flower pots along the tops of the walls.

We went out on to the terrace which ran the length of the lodge. Immediately beneath it was a swimming pool full of green sludge. Beyond, long slopes of grass led down to the river and the lake. To our right was the main wing of the hotel. The doors were splintered, the windows broken, and bird nests hung from the roofs of the balconies.

Pakuba was one of three luxury hotels which had been built in the park to accommodate tourists. In the 1960s Murchison Falls was one of Africa's most popular game parks. But with Amin, tourism came to an abrupt end and conditions have never been settled enough since for its revival. Nevertheless, a Ministry of Tourism continues to exist, and the park hotels, empty looted palaces, have been kept open for tourists who no longer come.

Back in the lounge bar, ghosts had begun to appear. From doorways and shadows, the staff stood watching us. They all wore ragged T-shirts and shorts as if they were a hotel uniform.

'Is there any beer?' Barry asked.

One of the men stepped cautiously into the room.

'Yes, we are having beer,' he said.

'Can we have five beers?'

The man nodded.

'Is it cold?' Kurt asked.

'Yes, cold,' the man said.

When the bottles of beer arrived Kurt leaned forward to feel them.

'This beer isn't cold,' he said. 'Why did you say it was cold?'

The man stood by the table in his shabby clothes, fidgeting with the opener. When he had come in with the five bottles he had looked so happy.

'Why did you say it was cold when it wasn't?' Kurt was not going to let this opportunity to vent the frustration of a hundred little daily irritations pass him by. He spoke to the man in a voice of patronizing reasonableness. Mr Win looked out of the window at the view.

Kurt waited for his answer. We stood about in embarrassed silence. The man shuffled his feet.

'I thought you wouldn't want it if I said it wasn't cold,' he said at last. He was visibly upset. It was a rare opportunity to serve tourists drinks in the bar, and he hated to see it all going wrong. Barry came forward and waved at the bottles.

'We'll have them anyway. Never mind.'

'I don't want one,' Kurt said.

'Okay. But we'll have ours,' Barry said, looking at us for confirmation.

'There is no electricity,' Barry said when the man had gone. 'They have no way of keeping them cold.'

'I know that,' Kurt snapped, able now with a white man to let the irritation into his voice. 'But then why do they say the beer is cold? Why do they lie?'

'Because the truth is too much of a liability in this country.'

We drank our beer out on the terrace. Below us on the soft meadows along the shore of the lake two bull water-bucks had appeared. They charged, locked horns, then parted, and charged again. From the terrace of the hotel we could not hear the thudding force of the impact. We could not see the panic in the bucks' eyes. Distance robbed the encounter of all its murderous intent and left only a graceful engagement on the lakeshore, a kind of dance, a deceptive ritual to bless the beginnings of the river.

8

We drove on to Paraa.

The sky was vast. Beneath it, the savanna undulated like a great yellow-green sea on which clusters of dark trees and clumps of bush stood becalmed. We saw a herd of water-buffalo crossing a far slope, then water-buck and Ugandan kob. A herd of elephants moved through a dry valley as if in slow motion.

'There used to be so many elephants in this park they didn't know what to do with them,' Barry said. He was an old African hand. 'They were threatening to eat the park out of existence. Now there's only a fraction of them left. There were no wardens in Amin's last years. Only poachers. Then when Amin fell, his army retreated through the park towards Pakwach. They shot every elephant they could get within their sights. Machine-gunned whole herds from the backs of trucks. Everyone wanted their bit of ivory to take into exile.'

Mr Win turned in his seat to enquire what we thought of Uganda. He seemed a decent man and I did not want to deceive him with the usual flattery of the visitor.

'A very beautiful country,' I said. 'But it seems to be in the grip of a nightmare.'

He nodded. 'Yes. It is a nightmare.' He smiled at us over his shoulder. 'But then you do not have to come all the way to Uganda to find nightmares.'

9

Paraa was a small settlement above the only ferry crossing on the Victoria Nile. It contained the park offices, the living quarters of the rangers and wardens, the equipment stores and another luxury hotel, overlooking the river, which had borne the worst of the looting. The whole settlement was overgrown and ruinous.

We stayed in a small bungalow just below the hotel overlooking the river. On the lawn, a few feet from the door, was a huge block of fresh elephant dung.

We showered on the terrace beneath a waterskin then walked down to the riverbank. The evening was honey-coloured. The river was green, and flecked with clumps of white foam which had floated down from Murchison Falls some ten miles upstream. In a still side pool hippos yawned and snorted.

Fishing canoes were coming home with the day's catch, afloat on their own reflections. The waiting crowds hauled the boats ashore, the fish were thrown out on to the grass, and within moments there was all the hubbub of a market.

Waiting in the long grass behind the crowds were about a dozen marabou storks. They were ghastly birds, standing almost three feet high, with bald pink heads, long folds of skin hanging from their bare necks, and small, malevolent eyes. The fishermen threw them the guts of the fish and they shrieked, hopping forward with their ragged wings spread, and squabbled over the pickings.

A little further along the bank we found cruise boats. Two lay in the grass partially dismembered and a third was moored in the water. It was a long narrow craft with a dozen or so seats beneath an awning, and a small wheelhouse and galley in the stern. In the old days the highlight of any visit to the park was a trip upriver in one of these boats to Murchison Falls.

In a garage up the road towards the hotel we found a man washing his shirt in a plastic bowl. Scattered about the greasy floor were jerrycans and bits of engines.

'Are the boats still working?' Barry asked.

The man nodded.

'Is there fuel for a trip up to the Falls?'

'There is,' the man said.

'Where do we book the boat?'

'Here.'

'Can we book the boat for tomorrow morning?'

'Yes.'

His answers all seemed too pat.

'So that's all arranged then,' I said. 'The boat will be ready to take us in the morning.'

'That's fine,' he said.

'What time?' Melinda asked, slyly.

He smiled broadly and spread his soapy hands. 'When you are ready, we are ready.'

10

A full moon rose over the river and the trees around the house cast long shadows across the white lawn. The night was full of animal sounds: hippos grunting on the riverbank, herons calling, hyenas crying and a bull elephant trumpeting somewhere. Once we heard what might have been a lion's roar from up the hill towards the hotel.

On the moonlit river, the endless flotillas of foam glided quickly and smoothly downstream.

We sat up late drinking our way through a case of beer which had emerged from the unlimited supplies in the back of the Land-rover. Mr Win became talkative and amusing, then went to bed early, lumbering away into the dark house. Barry became melancholy and sentimental about Skegness, and finally talked himself to sleep in his chair.

Only Kurt proved tireless, becoming more and more intense behind his thick spectacles. He was obsessed with the horrors of the country, the state of the schools, the lawlessness of the army, the corruption, the bankruptcy, the nightmare of Kampala. The government rarely had the money to pay its own civil servants, he told us. Few of them turned up for work, and those that did were perforce corrupt. Mr Win had not been paid in months, and he was a high-ranking official. When finally, last month, salary cheques were issued, they bounced. Government hotels would not let Mr Win in the door. They knew that his department would never meet the bills.

'The country is in ruins,' Kurt said. 'Only the men with guns have any real influence.'

11

In the morning we found two men preparing the boat, bringing cans of fuel, sweeping the decks and cleaning the seats. A Landrover roared down the hill from the direction of the hotel and two men in dark glasses leapt out and began to issue instructions to the men on the boat. We asked them when it would be ready.

'The boat is not available,' one of the men said.

'But we have booked it to go to the Falls.'

'The boat is being prepared for the Vice-President of the World Bank and his party. No one else will be able to go on the launch. I am very sorry.'

Kurt became indignant and started to protest but Barry silenced him with a bit of army wisdom.

'Soon as they start talking about the Top Brass you might as well shut your mouth.'

We took one of the men aside and explained our position. He was sympathetic and promised to see what he could do. An hour later he turned up at the house to tell us that they had arranged another boat for us.

It was a small open boat, no more than ten feet long, powered by an outboard motor. There were two men aboard, a boatman and a guide. We climbed in and they pushed off. Barry and Kurt and Mr Win stood on the bank waving. In mid-stream, the motor failed and we began to float helplessly downstream, away from the Falls.

12

The river was changing. It was no longer a broad stream turning through vast flat landscapes but had grown narrower between bush and hills. It had become intimate and secretive. It was like the rivers one knew as a child, full of twists and byways and hidden pools. It seemed to be leading us into oddly familiar worlds.

The surface of the water shone like glass. Stands of papyrus and low sandy cliffs and yellow-green meadows hugged the two banks beneath wooded hills. Three giraffes floated across a meadow, their legs hidden by the long grass.

The boatman had eventually brought the engine back to life, but only after we had floated over half a mile downstream. We would have gone further had the current not pitched us on to a bank of reeds. When the engine finally started, the boatman settled on to his seat and smiled uneasily at us. He looked like a man with a guilty secret.

Upriver, crowds of hippos were wallowing in the shallows. A few who had not yet returned to the water from the night's grazing were still wandering in the meadows along the banks. When they spotted us they bellowed and ran to the river, crashing into the water like great boulders.

The boatman brought the boat in close to the herds and as we approached, the hippos submerged in clouds of green bubbles.

221

Inevitably, at that moment, the engine died. While the boatman tried frantically to restart the motor, we gazed at the rising bubbles all about the boat. I knew that hippos could only stay under for about four or five minutes. If one rose beneath us we would capsize as easily as a toy boat in a bath. An angry hippo is a ferocious animal, and I did not like to think of being in the water with one. The minutes which passed while the boatman struggled with the engine were the longest I have ever known. Finally it caught, and we surged out into mid-stream again, just as the massive heads were breaking the surface of the water, roaring with mouths as big as canyons.

We saw our first crocodile on a sandbank. The guide pointed to what looked like a dead branch. Then suddenly it moved, slithering into the water with a wriggling motion. It disappeared so quickly we wondered if we had seen it at all.

But after the first, there were more, basking along the banks in groups of two and three, well-camouflaged against the grass. Usually we did not see them until they stirred, and then only fleetingly, for they moved with the speed of a snake, starting forward for the safety of the water. On the banks they lay with their mouths open to catch flying insects, allowing plovers to pick their teeth unmolested.

Crocodiles are the only survivors of the age of dinosaurs. They first emerged in the Triassic period some 190 million years ago, long before the Ice Ages and the appearance of man, even before the Nile was fully constituted.

But even these great survivors are now threatened. Once they were the lords of the river and were found along its entire length, throughout Egypt and Sudan. Now the reach below the Murchison Falls is the only place that one can be sure to see them. Their valuable skin has betrayed them, and their numbers are diminished by poachers every year. Twenty-five years ago a visitor making the boat trip up to the Falls counted 174 crocodiles along the way. We did not see more than 40.

The Falls had become a distant roar. Balls of foam floated past us in ever greater numbers and at ever greater speed. Finally the roar grew to thunder as we rounded a bend and the Falls came into view. Beyond a wide pool dotted with rocky islets was a green escarpment cut by a steep cleft through which the entire river poured in a torrent of white water. The Falls, less than 20 feet wide, were 30 feet high, swathed in spray and mist and crowned with a small rainbow.

It is the most dramatic moment in the Nile's long course and it is appropriate that it is watched over by crowds of crocodiles on the shores of the pool around its base. They are the river's oldest inhabitants; their distant ancestors had witnessed its birth.

13

Back at Paraa we decided to try the hotel for lunch. Outside in the gravel drive were three new Landrovers with Bank of Uganda emblems on their doors.

In the lobby we found a woman behind a glass counter. The shelves behind her, like the rest of the lobby, were bare, but on the counter she had arranged a few items rescued from some corner of the hotel: two blurred postcards of hippopotami, a map of Uganda printed in 1965 and a clutch of pencils with Murchison Falls National Park printed down their length.

We tried to buy one of the hippopotamus postcards but the woman shook her head. The postcards, the map and the pencils were not for sale. They had been hurriedly assembled for the Vice-President of the World Bank who, it was hoped, would stop briefly at the hotel on his return from the Falls. Everyone was in a state of agitation about his visit.

The drivers of the Landrovers stood nearby smoking foreign cigarettes and eyeing the woman from behind mirrored sunglasses.

We asked her about food. Our interest in the postcards had alarmed her, and she seemed to view us now as a threat to the already fragile plans for the Vice-President's visit.

'There is food,' she said, waving us towards the dining-room with a dismissive gesture.

We went through the empty dining hall and out on to the terrace where we found a single table with a linen cloth.

The woman from the gift shop came hurrying out to us.

'You can't sit there,' she said.

'Where else would you recommend?' I asked, motioning to the empty terrace and the empty dining-room.

'You can't sit there,' she said. There was a note of genuine panic in her voice. 'It is the table for the Vice-President of the World Bank.' Her hands twisted in front of her.

Half an hour later, still fretting about the Vice-President, she brought our food – two bowls of grey cold rice.

The drivers, who in spite of their resemblance to the Tonton Macoutes proved to be pleasant fellows, commiserated with us about the food. They had had to bring everything with them from Kampala, all the food for the Vice-President's picnic on the boat, everything for tea in the hotel should he want it.

'She hasn't even brought us any forks,' I said.

'There aren't any,' the drivers said. 'We brought cutlery, dishes, even that cloth. You are lucky you have bowls.'

14

Sadly for the woman, the Vice-President did not stop at the hotel. Perhaps he was put off by the bats that could be seen suspended from the overhanging porchways outside the ground-floor rooms.

The drivers of the Landrovers had promised to help us with a lift if they could. They were going to Gulu where the Vice-President was due to spend the night. When word came up the hill that the launch was approaching, the three drivers threw their cigarettes aside and sprinted to the vehicles, calling back to us to wait by the roadside. Ten minutes later we heard the Landrovers coming back. They breasted the hill in the manner of a high-speed police convoy. The first two roared past us in a cloud of dust. The third skidded to a stop and a rear door was flung open.

We leapt inside and sped off.

The rear of the third car of the convoy of the Vice-President of the World Bank was full of dried fish and bottles of whisky, on which we now found ourselves precariously perched. The occupants were all officials of the Bank of Uganda and, unlike the Vice-President's immediate party who were being driven to the park's airfield to be flown to Gulu, they were going all the way by road.

The car was a travelling bar, and we became the barmen. Digging beneath the dried fish, we passed a succession of bottles forward.

The front passenger carried on a rambling conversation over his shoulder between draughts of whisky. He was dismissive of the game parks. The country could afford such empty spaces now with a small population. But soon they would need the land for agriculture, for development. He clearly looked forward to this day. It would be a sign of great progress.

He asked what we thought of the National Reconstruction. I replied diplomatically that we had seen too little of the country to comment. He spoke of it with religious fervour. 'The evil days of Amin are over,' he declared. 'Now we can tackle the National Reconstruction and make the country great again. Amin was the Hitler of Africa. Obote is the Churchill of Uganda.'

National Reconstruction, I decided, was a question of perspective. With an important government job in the Bank of Uganda, playing host to the Vice-President of the World Bank, and drinking whisky that someone else had paid for in the front seat of a new Landrover, it must indeed have seemed a great success.

There were no other vehicles on the road, which ran between monotonous banks of bush. In the headlights, we saw only people on foot, trudging along through the dust, women carrying baskets on their heads, men in ragged trousers pushing old bicycles. Blinded momentarily by the headlights, they pressed themselves in against the bush to let the fast car past, before they were swallowed up again by the dust and the darkness.

15

It was late when we reached Gulu. It felt as if we had been away for weeks though it had only been forty-eight hours.

Tired after a long day we decided to treat ourselves to dinner at the Acholi Inn, the only place in town resembling a restaurant. There, in the dining-room, we found the Vice-President of the World Bank. He was the guest of honour at a dinner being given by the Bank of Uganda and various government ministers who had flown up from Kampala. There seemed to be no escaping the man.

We were given a small table in a corner. The dinner was in full swing. The head waiter, a curious looking man with a hairpiece like an Astrakhan hat, was opening bottles of wine with the elaborate gestures of a mime artist. I noticed our man from the Landrover. He had been squeezed in between the Vice-President's wife and a Ugandan woman with an enormous bosom. Someone had put a jacket and tie on him and he sat, slumped slightly to one side, trying desperately to appear sober. He clutched the table and breathed like a fish.

The dinner broke up before we had finished our meal and on his way out the Vice-President paused to speak to us. He looked like a high school quarterback, blond and smiling, still youthful at 40. He shook our hands with the sincerity of a political candidate.

'Been in Uganda long?' he asked.

'Two weeks.'

'Oh, a long time.'

'How are you finding it?' I asked.

'Beautiful country. Great potential. The people are tremendous. Can't do enough for us.' He turned to go, steering his wife towards the door. 'Take it easy now,' he said.

16

The people in the back of the lorry had the glassy-eyed look of animals being transported to market. It was an army lorry and there were four soldiers crowded into the cab. We climbed into the back with about a dozen others who had been waiting, like ourselves, on the roadside for a lift.

We had not gone far when the lorry turned into a side track and drew up by a group of tukals. The people in the back looked nervously over the sides as the soldiers went into one of the huts.

'What are they doing?' I asked the man next to me.

'I think they have gone to drink their breakfast.'

Half an hour later they re-emerged, clutching bottles. One stopped to talk to me.

'Everything alright?' he asked.

'Fine,' I said.

'Are you happy?'

'Yes, very happy.'

'That's good,' he said. 'It's good to be happy.' He spat slowly into the grass, leaning forward to let the spittle drain off his lips, then he walked unsteadily along the length of the lorry and climbed into the cab.

There followed a horrendous journey. We could see the soldiers through a window in the back of the cab. They were drinking bottles of beer and they threw the empties out of the windows, high into the air to smash on the road behind us.

Through the back window we watched the driver tipping his head back to drink, his throat bobbing. Unattended, the lorry was veering off the road. At the last moment one of the other soldiers noticed and reached across to jerk the wheel. We swerved from the edge of a ditch back on to the asphalt. The driver, spluttering beer down his chin, laughed and banged the wheel which he began to jerk back and forth, swinging the big lorry from one side of the road to the other.

There was little traffic. Those vehicles that did appear recognized the army lorry as an object of danger at some distance. Long before we reached them, they had drawn well off the road and stopped their cars.

Presently the driver found a new game. He began to drive at the people walking along the roadside, forcing them to jump to safety across a ditch into the long grass. There was no question that he would have hit them had they not jumped in time. There were a few terrifying near-misses, and once we hit a goat which panicked and hesitated. We heard it squeal, then the sickening thud beneath the wheels.

In our wake, people were picking themselves up out of the long grass, looking for their fallen belongings. Not one of them shook a fist or shouted after the careering lorry. Like our fellow passengers cowering with their bags in the back, they knew that defiance could be fatal.

17

The lorry dropped us off at the junction of the road for Kampala. We had to bang on the roof of the cab to get the attention of the soldiers. The driver laughed, and slammed on the brakes, and the people in the back were thrown forward on to one another.

Karuma Falls lay a short walk down the road. The Nile tumbled over a low shelf of rock, more rapids than falls. From the bridge we looked down into the turbulent waters. Karuma Falls was notorious as a place where bodies were dumped during Amin's regime. It was said that the crocodiles were the only creatures to flourish in the years of terror.

The soldiers who guarded the bridge turned out to be friendly and well-mannered. They helped us find a lift by stopping the first car that came in sight. The driver, who lowered his window nervously, seemed relieved by the innocent request to offer a ride to two harmless foreigners.

Once we were out of sight of the soldiers the driver visibly relaxed. He introduced himself as Paul. He spoke English with a slight American accent.

'I went to college in America,' he explained. 'Did aerospace engineering at UCLA.'

He was a large man of about thirty with fleshy shoulders and a developing paunch. He wore a pair of pressed casual trousers and a blue golfing shirt with a little emblem on the breast pocket. Beside him on the front seat sat a second man. He was small and bony, his clothes had the exhausted look of hand-me-downs. He seemed to be Paul's Man Friday.

The car, a new Peugeot estate, contained all the trappings of the cosmopolitan world: an attaché case, a smart suitcase and a hanging suit carrier, a cooler, thermos bottles, glossy business magazines, and nylon fishing rods and fancy tackle, the equipment of sport not survival. Paul sprawled behind the wheel like an American cab driver. Beside him Man Friday sat very upright, his hands in his lap and his legs straight, with a self-contained African stillness.

The road topped a hill and sunlight glinted on the asphalt far ahead, on the low, dense bushes and the ragged banana groves. Away to the west were the mountains of Zaire rising out of a bed of blue clouds.

'They say this road isn't safe,' Paul said over his shoulder. 'They claim it is so dangerous. Have you seen any problems? I drive this road every week, and never have any problems.'

Man Friday was silent, watching the road ahead.

The sky was darkening. A chill wind blew in at the windows and the car grew cold. The rain came suddenly, sweeping over the road in long gusts, dancing on the tarmac which looked white now through the streaming windows. Away ahead the road shone like a river.

The storm passed as suddenly as it had come. The sky lifted and the sun revealed a new world of dense colour. The air had been washed clear, and the road, still gleaming from the rain, was now striped with the long shadows of eucalyptus trees which bordered the red and green fields.

In this post-deluge landscape, the engine of the car began to miss. It coughed and spluttered until finally the car stalled on the brow of a hill. We got out, and examined the engine. Eventually we got it to start and drove on. But after four or five miles it coughed and stalled again. We went on like this for some time, stalling, starting and stalling again.

'It's the fuel,' Paul said. 'The petrol we bought in Kigumba. It came out of jerrycans. I should know never to buy fuel out of jerrycans. There is always dirt in it.'

The car became progressively worse. Paul and Man Friday grew agitated. We were still a long way from Kampala and night was coming on. It had grown cold and the road was empty. Standing on the roadside with the bonnet up, the landscape appeared vast and alien and comfortless. There seemed to be nowhere to turn for help.

We were rescued by two Europeans in an old Volkswagen. They

229

were Swiss, and taught in a training college near Kampala. They dug an enormous tool kit out of their back seat and within minutes had taken the carburettor apart. Then they drained the tank and gave us a can of clean petrol.

'How far are you going?' they asked us when they had finished.

'Kampala,' I said.

They were wiping their hands on rags. 'This road isn't safe at night. I wouldn't advise going to Kampala.'

'We are with this man,' I said. 'He lives in Kampala.'

'Be careful then. Four Europeans were shot on this road earlier this year.'

18

The Luwero triangle is one of those tragic places, like Dachau and Dresden and My Lai and Hiroshima, whose name will always be linked with the horrors which occurred there. It is an area of some 4,500 square kilometres to the north of Kampala, the heartland of the Baganda tribe, where guerrilla forces based their campaigns against the Obote government. In response Obote's army was let loose on the area and its civilian population.

Early in 1983 a free-fire zone was created by rounding up civilians, as many as 140,000 people, and putting them into concentration camps, known as resettlement centres. Conditions inside the camps were appalling. There were no medical facilities, water sources were quickly polluted, and the inhabitants had to forage for food and fuel, aware that they could be shot if they were found outside the perimeter fence.

The Ugandan army, notoriously ill-disciplined, unpaid and invariably drunk, spent much of their time terrorizing the inhabitants of the camps. Abduction, rape, torture and murder were commonplace. In one incident members of the youth wing of the UPC, Obote's political party, swept through a camp at Kikyusa with pangas, axes and knives slaughtering everyone in sight. At least 200 people were killed in this particular incident.

The camps were inhabited by women, children and old men. The young men, viewed as potential rebels, were taken to prisons in Kampala, or killed. In the week of the Kikyusa massacre, eighty men were slaughtered in the army barracks in Bomba, and fifty more corpses were dumped from an army lorry at Masulita. The men held in detention centres were systematically tortured. They were beaten repeatedly with hammers, iron bars and barbed wire. Their genitals were burnt with strips of plastic, and their testicles were crushed with cattle-gelding instruments.

Early in 1984 the concentration camps were closed down. The inhabitants were ordered out and their makeshift huts were put to the torch. But the closure of the camps did not end the horrors. Most of the former inmates had nowhere to go. Their villages had been ransacked by the army and their crops destroyed. Many fled the area. The ones who remained lived like wild animals, hiding from the army in the swamps and forests by day, foraging for food by night. Stories of atrocities became Luwero's gossip. Every week in the shells of burnt-out villages, in roadside ditches, in forest clearings, more and more bodies were found, mangled and invariably decapitated.

19

As we drove we saw nothing out of the dark windows but our own imperfect reflections. The wheels battered in and out of pot-holes, and the night's chill crept through the car.

In the headlights a roadblock appeared, a long pole between two barrels. Beyond it we could see army lorries parked at the roadside. Paul drew up before the pole, switched off the engine and the headlights, and then turned on the interior lights. We sat in the car, illuminated like exhibits, unable to see anything in the darkness around us. This was the form. They wanted to see you, without being seen themselves.

But we could feel them around the car, something restive and menacing in the darkness, the sound of breathing. Then suddenly we could see them, and we were not sure if they had stepped forward or if our eyes had merely adjusted. About a dozen soldiers were around the car, all cradling guns which were pointed casually at us. One of the soldiers came to Paul's window, his rifle scraping along the door panel.

He leaned into the car. He was chewing something and his lips were wet. He said nothing.

Unprompted, Paul explained where we were going and why we were on the road after dark. The soldier chewed, and looked at us one by one. The sour smell of sweat came into the car.

'You have something for me?' he said at last.

Paul dug in his breast pocket and handed him some money. The soldier straightened up slowly and motioned with his rifle for us to pass. The pole lifted and we drove off.

Ten miles further on we came to a second roadblock, and waited again like sitting ducks in the lighted car. Again a soldier eventually materialized at Paul's side of the car, his paunch filling the window. He asked for identification and disappeared with our passports into the darkness. We waited. Frogs were croaking, and we could see figures with guns crossing to and fro on the road in front of the car.

We waited a quarter of an hour before the soldier returned.

'Where did you pick up this girl?' he asked me, indicating Melinda.

'You mean my wife?' I asked. It did not seem the moment to discuss the respective merits of marriage and co-habitation.

'Your names are not the same.' He held up the passports.

'We are newly-weds,' I said. 'We have come to Uganda for our honeymoon.'

He threw the passports through the window and jerked his rifle for us to pass.

Near the outskirts of Kampala we came to a third roadblock. Again we sat with the interior lights on. In the silence I heard a thudding sound, and then the sound of someone groaning.

Suddenly a voice barked out of the darkness, 'Get out of the car.'

We climbed out.

'Go round to the front,' the voice shouted.

We made our way round to the front of the car.

The groans were subsiding into a pained whimpering.

232

Out of the corner of my eye I saw a soldier by the side of the car. He leaned in through the open window and switched the headlights on. Blinded in the glare, we waited for long, tense minutes. When the voice shouted again, it made us all jump.

'Who are you? What are your names?'

A soldier had appeared on the periphery of the light. Behind him we could see the ghostly figures of other soldiers. All of them had their rifles trained on us.

Paul gave his name, slowly and clearly. Then Man Friday gave his name. We were about to give ours when the soldier lowered his rifle and stepped forward into the light. He greeted Paul in a quiet voice and they shook hands. They stood talking for a moment in the language of their tribe. Their names had revealed that they were Acholi. It had been the right tribe.

Walking back to the car, my legs felt weightless. In the half-moment before the engine started I could hear the groaning man. He seemed to be pleading with someone, 'no, no, no, no', a pained, muffled voice buried somewhere in the darkness.

20

Kampala that first night looked like a city which had suffered a bombardment. The streets were full of pot-holes as deep as bomb craters. The few streetlights which worked illuminated ruin: peeling and cracked walls, windows broken or boarded up, the carcases of burnt-out cars, vacant lots overgrown with weeds and rubbish.

Paul manoeuvred the car gently in and out of the pot-holes. We crept along wide shattered boulevards. We passed roadblocks whose soldiers were acting as pimps for huddled groups of women in tight dresses. We passed the university, a large area of darkness. Eventually we stopped in an empty street in front of a tall, dark building.

'I think there is a hotel here,' Paul said, peering up at the building.

I got out with Man Friday. The doors and windows of the building were festooned with bars, padlocks and chains. Above one of the doors was a sign: *Rooms*. We knocked.

After a long wait we heard footsteps and then a voice through the door.

'A foreigner is looking for lodgings,' Man Friday said.

There was the sound of bolts. The door opened to reveal a man in his undershirt. We followed him upstairs into a small lobby. There were doors on all four sides, and two corridors lit by dim bare bulbs led away towards the rear of the building. Doors were ajar and we could see beds of rumpled sheets. Someone was shouting drunkenly. The place reeked of faulty plumbing.

The man in the undershirt had disappeared and Man Friday and I sat on two wooden chairs in the lobby and waited. A woman wearing only a towel knotted about her waist appeared in the doorway of one of the rooms. Her breasts were heavy with long, dark nipples. Across one shoulder she had a large weal.

'Foreigner,' she said.

'Hello,' I said.

'You like me?'

'Yes. I'm very pleased to meet you.'

'You come to see me.'

'No, I don't think so.'

She lit a cigarette and blew smoke into the lobby.

'I like you,' she said. 'You come see me. I do very good fucking.' She lifted one of her breasts and stroked the nipple and smiled at me. Two of her front teeth were missing.

Man Friday, sitting primly on the edge of his seat, was suffering. He tried to ignore the woman by staring at the wall ahead of him. He looked exhausted. It had been a long day.

After a time a man came up one of the corridors. The woman in the towel went into her room and closed the door.

'What do you want?' the man asked.

'He is wanting lodgings for himself and his wife,' Man Friday said desperately. 'If you haven't anything, we are proceeding.'

The man began to laugh. Man Friday got up and hurried down the stairs.

Outside we found two soldiers peering at our bags in the back of the car. We got in and Paul drove off leaving the soldiers in the empty street.

'It may be difficult to find anywhere at this time of night,' Paul said at last. 'I would be happy to welcome you at my home.'

21

After dinner Paul went straight to bed and we sat talking with his wife in the living-room. Her name was Laverne. Though they had lived in the house, which was in a wealthy suburb, for four years, their presence seemed temporary. The furniture was lined up around the walls, as if no one could decide where it should go. On the bare walls were two framed degree certificates, his in aerospace engineering and hers in English literature.

She was a West Indian, from Jamaica, and Paul had seemed a terribly romantic figure to her on campus in Los Angeles, a real African. She had been disappointed when they had married in a registry office, rather than in a traditional ceremony in Africa.

In America they had both been foreigners, and it had helped to make them closer. Now here in Uganda, even as Paul's wife, she found she was still a *muzungo*, a foreigner. Her friends were other expatriates.

We went to bed about midnight. Laverne sat on in the living-room watching a video, a Western. Through our door we could hear the pop-pop-pop of the film's gunfire.

In the morning from the bedroom window we could see Lake Victoria.

22

When Speke, searching for the source of the Nile in 1862, arrived at Rubaga, one of the seven hills of what is now Kampala, he found the royal court a place of casual violence. Concubines, courtiers and pages were executed daily at the Kabaka's whim, often for offences as slight as a breach of etiquette. At night Speke's sleep was regularly interrupted by the screams of women being dragged to their death through the palace gardens.

Into this tyranny Speke saw fit to introduce the gun, a weapon hitherto unknown in Buganda. He presented a carbine pistol to the Kabaka who immediately sent a page outside to try it out on someone.

Sleep in our time in Kampala was disturbed not by screams but by gunfire. It was hardly noticed by the inhabitants. In the morning the harvest of bodies was discovered by early-morning shoppers and commuters making their way through the pot-holed streets.

We found Kurt in an office in the Department of Education. The department was housed in Crested Towers, a high-rise which had been one of Kampala's show-pieces. Unmaintained, the building was literally falling apart. The lifts no longer worked and the Minister of Education, arriving each morning in his chauffeur-driven limousine, was obliged to walk up eighteen flights of stairs to his suite of offices.

Kurt and Barry were in a despondent mood. They had arrived back from their tour of the country to find that their entire shipment of school supplies had been stolen from a warehouse where it was waiting for customs clearance. It was almost certainly an inside job. Everyone was corrupt, Kurt said. They had no choice. They had to eat.

Kampala by daylight was even more ruinous than it appeared by night. Half the city seemed to be boarded up. Even those buildings which still functioned appeared derelict. Everywhere windows were broken. Piles of rubbish festered in alleyways and broken pipes fed ponds of black water. The city stank of decay. Twenty years ago it was the most beautiful city in Africa.

Over this ruin Milton Obote looked down from the wall of every shop and office, while his soldiers prowled the streets looking for a living. It was nearly Christmas, and in the streets around Nakasero market, muzak Christmas carols blared from the shops. The refrain 'glad tidings of comfort and joy' became inextricably linked with nervous crowds, shattered shops, heavily armed soldiers in their dark glasses and the sweet mingling smell of petrol and rubbish.

Up on Kampala Road government ministers in black Mercedes roared past, as fast as the pot-holes allowed, flanked by motorcycle outriders and Landrovers full of soldiers armed with machine guns and rocket launchers. Beyond, on the rooftops of the notorious Nile Mansions, the headquarters of the secret police, marabou storks unfolded their wings like requiem banners. At day's end the bats of Wandegeya left their gum trees and, streaming through the dusk, swirled over the gardens near the city centre.

The civic gardens were tiny anomalous oases in this shabby city. There were only a few of them, north of the Kampala Road, places like Jubilee Park, but they were surprisingly well-tended. The grass was mown and rolled, and the hedges trimmed. There were bushes of oleander and poinsettia and blue ipomoea. At dusk, with bats filling the air, the gardens were scented by frangipani.

In the ruins of Kampala the gardens were like a miracle, reminiscent of St Paul's in the Blitz, standing up unscathed amongst the surrounding rubble. I never saw the gardener but I longed to meet him. Such was my fascination with him that I found myself conjuring him from the shrubbery.

I pictured an elderly gentleman who had held the post since colonial times through all the vicissitudes of the new nation. In the breakdown of government bureaucracy, I suspected he had been lost, and no one in officialdom now even knew he or his post existed. I imagined him coming to work through the gunfire of street battles and coups, digging in manure while governments toppled. I pictured him trimming his hedges while municipal lorries went past collecting corpses. I saw him pausing in his work to listen to the bulbul chattering in the border shrubs, hardly hearing the loudspeakers announcing a new President. Among the moon flowers and the ginger lilies he seemed to have found some form of immunity. I could never decide if it was the product of innocence or wisdom.

23

But the real story of Kampala lay with things unseen and unheard. In army barracks and detention centres in and around the capital, torture and murder were routine. In the pot-holed streets, filled with the blare of electronic Christmas carols, one knew nothing of these things. The people who had witnessed them were either dead or too frightened to speak.

One of the most notorious of Uganda's 'prisons' was Makindye military barracks in Kampala. On arrival at the barracks prisoners were first held in an area known as the 'quarter guard' where conditions were so crowded that they had to sleep in a squatting position one behind the other. Here they were routinely beaten with iron bars, cable, pieces of wood into which nails had been driven, rifle butts and machetes. Many died as a result of these preliminary beatings.

Those that survived were sent on to an area of the barracks known as the 'go-down', a long, windowless concrete building with a corrugated iron roof. It housed over a hundred prisoners at a time.

Prisoners in the 'go-down' were given food and water infrequently, perhaps twice a week. The food consisted of a watery bean stew which was poured into prisoners' cupped hands and was invariably too hot to hold, or a maize porridge, riddled with maggots, which was thrown on to the floor amidst the dirt and excreta. The prisoners' thirst was so great that they often drank each other's urine. The only latrine was an oil drum which was emptied about once a month. There was no bedding and the floor was invariably wet.

Besides the routine beatings, the prisoners were tortured. Their genitals were mutilated, hot irons were applied to their stomachs, burning tyres were suspended above them so that the hot rubber would drip on to their faces. The women were repeatedly raped.

It is not known how many people suffered thus as political prisoners under the Obote regime, but informed sources believe the number to run into the thousands if not tens of thousands. Many fled the country. Obote's reign of terror resulted in over a quarter of a million refugees.

24

The debate about the source of the Nile which in some form or another had been going on for well over 2,500 years, reached its climax in 1862 when Speke breasted a hill some fifty miles to the east of Kampala and looked down on a large river pouring out of Lake Victoria. His claim to have solved the riddle of the Nile's source was thought somewhat premature, for the hostility of the local tribes prevented him from following the river. But Speke's intuition about what he had seen was soon confirmed when more thorough explorations by Baker and Gordon revealed that Speke's river was indeed the Nile. Today the town of Jinja stands on the shore of the lake where the Nile begins its long journey.

We went to Jinja in a shared taxi which smelt of sweat and tobacco. There were seven other passengers, a driver and a mountain of baggage which bulged out of the rear doors. At the roadblocks the driver handed his bribes through the window without even stopping. The bribes were included in the fare.

The road to Jinja, bathed in sunlight, ran through a green country of deep grass, banana groves, dense hillsides of tea and tropical forests. We crossed the Nile, a couple of miles from its source, on a bridge above the Owen Falls Dam which supplies electricity for much of East Africa. Above the dam the river was a smooth, thick sheet of water. Below, rapids foamed in a steep gorge.

We came into the town along a boulevard lined with genteel boarding houses. We got down in a greasy square of buses and taxis and walked through the town to the Ripon Falls Hotel, a splendid white timbered colonial establishment which overlooked the lake.

The horrors of Uganda's recent history seemed to have entirely passed Jinja by. There were no broken windows or boarded-up buildings or burnt-out cars. It seemed an innocent provincial place of dusty tree-lined streets where children played on grassy hills and women chatted on street corners. It reminded me of nothing so much as the small town in Canada where I had grown up: the grid of spacious streets, the houses set back behind big yards, the smell of cut grass, the big shade trees, the banging of screened doors, a certain quality of the afternoon light. The feeling of my own childhood came upon me so suddenly and unexpectedly in this remote place that I found myself momentarily tearful.

A path led up to the long veranda of the Ripon Falls Hotel between beds of red and yellow dahlias. In the lobby, the face of

Milton Obote and the stuffed head of a water-buck, mounted side by side, stared glassily down at us. The hotel was a delightful place of wooden panelling and wide wooden floorboards. There was a bar with a window seat and the air of a country pub. Between the mirrors and the framed prints you could see the circular mark on the wall where a dart-board had been. A wide staircase with a polished banister led to the upper floor. Our room was along the front of the hotel with a balcony that overlooked the garden. Beyond the hedge and the road, strewn with fallen blossoms, one looked down a green slope to the fishermen's huts on the shores of the lake. Inevitably, we were the only guests.

We had tea in the garden. A waiter came out and spread a white cloth on one of the tables in the shade of a huge acacia tree. The afternoon rang with the high constant note of insects.

After tea we set off to discover the source of the Nile.

25

We followed the road between white-trunked palm trees, past the golf-course, green and immaculate against the blue of the lake. We cut down over a rocky hill and into the waist-high grass beyond. We followed a track down a steep slope and up the other side to a flat-topped hill where we found ourselves looking down on the first reach of the river. It flowed out of the lake between grassy banks, a solid mass of green water, already more than 300 yards wide.

Before the building of the Owen Falls Dam, a couple of miles downstream, the Nile had emerged from the lake rather less quietly, dropping over low falls in a white torrent. Speke had named them the Ripon Falls after a future Viceroy of India who had been helpful in raising funds for his expedition. The dam, which was completed in 1954, has raised the level of the river enough to submerge the falls beneath a smooth sheet of water.

Two long islets of grass lay moored in the first few yards of the river. White egrets stood in lines along the banks, lifting their feet out of the water as if they were cold. Out across the river, kingfishers broke its surface of light.

We followed a path down to a short stone pier on the bank. At the end of the pier was an outcrop of rock which supported a large tree. From all over the river cormorants were arriving to roost in its branches. Their large webbed feet were ridiculously ill-suited to perching in trees, and they looked like a troupe of clowns floundering on the branches in outsize shoes.

On the slopes above us was a public garden of bougainvillaea and purple hibiscus. There was a monument to Speke who had first laid eyes on the river's source from the heights of the opposite shore.

We sat on the pier and watched the river sliding past, starting its long journey towards Nimule and Juba, Dongola and Abri, Luxor and Minya, all the way to Cairo and Rashid. The river linked all the places we had visited and all the people we had met, just as it linked the past with the future. This enviable continuity was a kind of reassurance, a promise, against all the disappointment and distress which crowded its banks.

The wind chased ruffled patches across its surface. A flock of Egyptian geese flew downriver. Their calls were like laughter. On the far bank a drum was beating. It was late and the sun raked down across the hillsides of grass and cast a swath of silver light across the beginning of the river.

Had we expected something wild and romantic we would have been disappointed. The source of the river, a place so remote that for centuries it was the subject of conjecture, was now entirely tame. You could drive here from Nairobi without ever leaving asphalt roads. Your only adventure would be the unpredictable roadblocks. It was the river's final irony that you could reach its source in a family sedan. We had come 4,000 miles to find a suburban garden.

I thought of a poem by C.P. Cavafy, that I had read in Alexandria:

> Ithaca gave you your fair voyage.
> Without her you would not have ventured on the way,
> but she has no more to give you.
> And if you find Ithaca a poor place, she has not mocked you.
> You have become so wise, so full of experience,
> that you should understand by now what these Ithacas mean.

241

At Rashid the river had seemed the purveyor of adventure, a stimulus and a catalyst. Now it had become only a refuge. And one was thankful for it. In the horrors of Uganda, the river was a kind of balm. I understood now that that was all one could hope for.

We walked over the hill and back to the hotel. In the evening we went down to the shores of the lake where the fishermen in their thatched huts were grilling Nile perch over beds of charcoal. They tasted deliciously of the river. In the quick darkness chill breaths of wind came off the lake and the stars shone beneath the water like phosphorus. Above us the yellow windows of the hotel were splintered by the branches of the acacia trees, and the white trunks of the palm trees were ghostly along the road.

The next morning we took a shared taxi back to Kampala. On the outskirts of the city we saw a man shot against a tree. He sat down heavily, his back to the trunk, his head slumped forward.

26

In the second century AD the geographer Ptolemy, who worked at Alexandria, ventured the opinion that the Nile sources lay in high mountains somewhere in the middle of Africa. He called them the Mountains of the Moon. The streams of these mountains, he said, fed two lakes which were the river's reservoirs.

When Europeans finally traced the sources of the White Nile almost 2,000 years later they found that Ptolemy had been right all along. The lakes were Lake Albert and Lake Victoria, from which the Nile emerges, fully fledged. The mountain streams which feed the lakes lie in the Mountains of the Moon, the Ruwenzoris. We booked a first-class sleeper to Kasese, which lies at the foot of the mountains near the border with Zaire.

The burgundy-coloured carriages waiting at the platform in Kampala station had been built in Britain in the 1940s. The compartments, fitted with wood and brass, had seats like deep sofas. Everything – the porcelain sink, the reading lamps with their tasselled shades, the folding writing tables, the old ceiling fans – was in perfect working order. Like Jinja, the train had miraculously escaped the depredations of Uganda's recent history.

The train ran through the rich cultivation of western Uganda. The sunlight was warm at the train windows and the settlements of wattle-and-daub shacks had a feeling of ease. A man slept beneath a tree, a line of women passed in their elegant busutis, children waved from the dust.

When we looked again we were passing through dense forest. Here and there fields of cassava and settlements of tukals and wood-smoke and red lanes broke the endless tangled succession of trees. Women carried pails of water up green paths from streams some-where below in the forest shadow. At the open window we listened to the falling liquid notes of the forest birds, and to the woodpeckers knocking. In the cuttings, with the sun low, the train ran through the cool shadows of the trees.

I poured us two tumblers of whisky. After the distress and ruin of Uganda, the train was reminiscent of another time, another Nile.

'Does Rashid seem like nine months ago?' I asked Melinda.

She shook her head. This was a game we had played all along the Nile. We would look at our diaries to see where we had been a week ago, two weeks ago, a month ago. It always amazed us. A week seemed ages ago, a month another lifetime.

'Rashid is so long ago it seems like a dream,' Melinda said.

The train wheels clattered. I felt a wave of sadness like nostalgia. It was journey's end.

'Do you remember passing the tomb at Rashid,' I asked. 'And the boatman's saying?'

' "The wind blows and the boat goes, and we have no power to stay," ' Melinda said.

The evening was blue and smoky. The sound of frogs came in at the window, sounding oddly like tinkling bells. As night fell the land was entirely black but the sky was a vivid metallic blue pricked with the first stars. When the full night came it was moonless and the sky brimmed with cold stars. We sat for a long time with our noses at the open window, enjoying the smells of the night. When the insect life became too assertive, we put up the screen and went to dinner.

243

27

Kasese was a sleepy town beneath the mountains. In the early morning men rode by on their bicycles trailing long, thin shadows. The streets were wide and white, the air smelt of eucalyptus, and the town was full of establishments with names like Saad Hotel, Happy Valley Restaurant, Paradise Bar and Moonlight Lodgings.

We found a room at the Moonlight Lodgings. The ground floor was a restaurant. Upstairs our room had blue-washed walls, two sturdy cots and a carpet of reed matting. It overlooked a yard partitioned by lines of pink sheets where the food for the restaurant was cooked in huge black pots over charcoal braziers. Beyond the yard one looked over the tin and tile roofs of Kasese to the Mountains of the Moon.

We had breakfast in the restaurant, a large room with windows overlooking the street. In Kasese they had a curious way of serving tea. You were given a large mug of steaming milk, an empty cup and saucer, and a bowl of tea leaves. You put the tea leaves in a small sieve and poured the hot milk through it into the cup, then left the sieve sitting in the cup until your tea had achieved the desired strength. We had had many strange permutations of tea along the Nile, but this was the most delicious I had ever drunk. With hot *mandazis*, freshly baked ginger buns, breakfast in the Moonlight Lodgings was paradise.

After breakfast I sat on the steps waiting for Melinda. A fellow resident joined me.

'How is it?' he asked as he sat down.

'Fine.'

'Where are you coming from?'

'England.'

'Ah.' There was a long pause, then he asked, 'How is the religion spreading in your area?'

'The usual way, I guess. Word of mouth.'

After a long silence he tried again in a different voice, like an actor taking on a different character. 'How is the religion spreading in your area?'

'The churches are getting smaller,' I said.

He considered this. As he considered he nodded his head, bouncing his chin up from the bottom of each nod like a rubber ball. In an effort to put a stop to this mannerism I repeated myself.

'Every year the churches are growing smaller. Not like here, I believe. Your churches are growing larger.'

'They are expanding.' He made a gesture with his hands.

'Yes,' I said. 'In England they are contracting.' I made the gesture with my hands.

He raised his eyebrows suddenly. 'So,' he said, 'you are supporting the Russians.'

'No.'

He found the contradiction confusing. We sat in silence for a time. Then he leaned towards me and whispered. 'I am a Latter-Day Saint.'

This sounded dangerous. I made my excuses and went to look for Melinda.

28

Early one morning we went to the Equator, which lies a few miles to the south of Kasese, in an old Peugeot taxi with fourteen other people. One person sat on my lap and another on my feet. The driver appeared to have someone between him and his door. Four people lay in a pile in the back in the narrow space between the baggage and the roof.

As we left the town the whole assembly of passengers began to swathe their faces in scarves. It looked for a moment as if we had fallen among a party of thieves. Then we hit a stretch of unpaved road and the car filled with clouds of choking dust.

The Equator was marked by a white line across the road and two upright concrete circles, emblazoned with the word Equator. We uncoiled ourselves from the Peugeot and got down. Masked and bemused faces stared at us from the rear window as the car sped away.

Below the road through a stand of dry scrub was a crater lake, as round as a liquid globe. I had hoped for a swim but the water was foul. Around the shore were animal droppings: elephant, some sort of antelope and what might have been lion. But the animals never appeared. The only sound was the dry bushes tapping in the wind. The sun, directly overhead, stood in an unfathomable sky. Round the horizon were tall, blue mountains. We were alone at the centre of the world.

29

The Ruwenzori Mountains rise behind Kasese to blue and fantastic heights, their heads buried in cloud. We left the town early one morning to walk into the foothills.

On our way out of town we stopped at the office of the District Commissioner to enquire if we required permits. The DC proved a friendly fellow and he gave us an official letter of such rare and admirable directness that I append it here as a model for administrators everywhere. Our names and passport numbers appeared at the top, followed by:

> They are British. They are tourists. They are visiting the district of the Ruwenzoris. They have our kind Permission.

His signature and official stamp completed the missive.

The African name 'ruwenzori', a Lunyoro word, means 'place of rain'. Wind currents from opposite sides of the continent, from the Atlantic and the Indian Oceans, clash above its peaks and form an almost permanent bank of clouds. It rains in the Ruwenzoris almost one day in three, seventy-five inches a year, making it one of the wettest places in the world. This rain is the true beginning of the Nile.

We followed the road to Kilembe, a copper-mining town in the first foothills, along the valley of the Nyamwamba river. As the road turned with the narrowing valley it revealed new vistas of higher and higher peaks in the mountains ahead. They were gaunt, brooding heights with rainclouds trailing from their shoulders.

Beyond the town the road crossed the river on a narrow bridge.

It was a mountain stream now, green and white, coursing down a steep slope over fat boulders. The water was ice-cold. It had come straight from the glaciers in the clouds above us. It was not easy to relate this quick, pure stream, one of many which feed Lake Victoria and Lake Albert, to the broad, majestic river of Middle Egypt, just as it was difficult to remember, in these rain-fed uplands, how crucial this water was to become to the lives of millions.

We came at last to a high shoulder from where we looked down into the first of the mountain valleys. We had the sense of having crossed an invisible boundary. The valley before us was like a miniature country, a land set apart, remote and complete, which could only be reached on foot. There were no roads here, only paths. It seemed a fairytale land with a silver river and smooth water meadows and fields pitched high up on steep slopes at impossible angles and thatched cottages with smoking chimneys and cotton-soft woods in the hollows of the hillsides. In the clear, still air we could hear the river chuckling amongst its boulders. High up beyond the steepest fields, we could see a clearing in the forests, an alpine meadow where reed-bucks were strolling, as undisturbed as unicorns. Beyond, blue mountain peaks soared into a heaven of silver and pewter clouds.

We sat for an hour gazing down at the valley watching the cloud shadows sail across the sunlit meadows. A trio of women were climbing a far slope, carrying water from the stream to a tiny homestead set high up on a narrow ridge. Sometimes we lost them, then they reappeared, slightly higher on the slope, three bright flecks of colour against the layered green of the hillside.

The valley, as fine and as spacious as a dream kingdom, was the end of our journey and the beginning of the river. It seemed both familiar and fabulous. The wind, singing through the elephant grass, carried a sweet smell which I recognized but could not place, some nostalgic smell with a hint of bread and smoke and over-ripe fruit, which had me searching in vain through my own childhood.

The High Ruwenzoris, bound in their swaddling clouds, were an astonishing place. Botanical expeditions return from their highest reaches with stories of the strange phenomenon of gigantism. They report seeing heather which grows to forty feet in height, mighty forests of bamboo, groundsels and lobelia as tall as a man. Whole

247

forests are draped in veils of yellow lichen and here and there the gloom between the trees is lightened by carpets of crimson moss. Beyond the tree-line this colour and excess is succeeded by a monochrome emptiness. Dark lakes lie in a landscape of black rock and sudden precipices. Higher still lie the glaciers, the Nile's cold fountains, a still and innocent world of snow.

It was time for us to go home. The day was late and long shadows were creeping across the hillsides. The three women were finally emerging on their ridge and children ran down a slope from the huts to meet them. Their voices came across the valley with the clear, pure sound of bells.

30

We got a ride from Kilembe back to Kasese with the Bishop of Fort Portal who was travelling in a white pick-up. He was a plump man with shiny white robes, a red skull-cap, and an elaborate cross round his neck. His cheeks glowed.

The Bishop sat in the cab with his driver, and we sat in the back with a huge fish which had been filleted and laid on a bed of banana leaves. It was a gift from one of his flock, and must have been three feet long.

The Bishop let us off in front of the Moonlight Lodgings. We went to his window to thank him, and he asked us where we were from.

'Ah, London,' he said wistfully. 'I was in London many years ago. A wonderful city.'

He shook hands with us through the open window, holding them for a moment and patting them. His palms were fleshy and warm.

'Goodbye then. Goodbye,' he said.

The pick-up started. He waved through the window, slightly turned in his seat.

'Goodbye,' he called. 'And give my greetings to everyone in London.'